The Legacies of Jean-Luc
Godard

Film and Media Studies Series

Film studies is the critical exploration of cinematic texts as art and entertainment, as well as the industries that produce them and the audiences that consume them. Although a medium barely one hundred years old, film is already transformed through the emergence of new media forms. Media studies is an interdisciplinary field that considers the nature and effects of mass media upon individuals and society and analyzes media content and representations. Despite changing modes of consumption—especially the proliferation of individuated viewing technologies—film has retained its cultural dominance into the 21st century, and it is this transformative moment that the WLU Press Film and Media Studies series addresses.

Our Film and Media Studies series includes topics such as identity, gender, sexuality, class, race, visuality, space, music, new media, aesthetics, genre, youth culture, popular culture, consumer culture, regional/national cinemas, film policy, film theory, and film history.

Wilfrid Laurier University Press invites submissions. For further information, please contact the Series editors, all of whom are in the Department of English and Film Studies at Wilfrid Laurier University:

Dr. Philippa Gates, email: pgates@wlu.ca
Dr. Russell Kilbourn, email: rkilbourn@wlu.ca
Dr. Ute Lischke, email: ulischke@wlu.ca
Department of English and Film Studies
Wilfrid Laurier University
75 University Avenue West
Waterloo, ON N2L 3C5
Canada
Phone: 519-884-0710
Fax: 519-884-8307

The Legacies of Jean-Luc
Godard

Douglas Morrey,
Christina Stojanova,
and Nicole Côté,
editors

WILFRID LAURIER
UNIVERSITY PRESS

This book has been published with the help of a grant from the Canadian Federation for the Humanities and Social Sciences, through the Awards to Scholarly Publications Program, using funds provided by the Social Sciences and Humanities Research Council of Canada. Wilfrid Laurier University Press acknowledges the financial support of the Government of Canada through the Canada Book Fund for our publishing activities.

Inspiring Lives.

Library and Archives Canada Cataloguing in Publication

The legacies of Jean-Luc Godard / Douglas Morrey, Christina Stojanova, and Nicole Côté, editors.

(Film and media studies series)
Includes bibliographical references and index
Issued in print and electronic formats
ISBN 978-1-55458-920-3 (bound).—ISBN 978-1-55458-922-7 (epub).—
ISBN 978-1-55458-921-0 (pdf)

1. Godard, Jean-Luc, 1930– —Criticism and interpretation. I. Morrey, Douglas, editor of compilation II. Stojanova, Christina, editor of compilation III. Côté, Nicole, 1957–, editor of compilation IV. Series: Film and media studies series

PN1998.3.G63L45 2014   791.4302'33092   C2013-903860-4   C2013-903861-2

Cover design by Blakeley Words+Pictures. Front-cover image by Ian Wallace, *Enlarged Inkjet Study for Le Mépris VI*, 119 x 89 cm. Courtesy of the artist and Catriona Jeffries Gallery, Vancouver and Yvon Lambert, Paris. Text design by Carol Magee.

This book is printed on FSC recycled paper and is certified Ecologo. It is made from 100% post-consumer fibre, processed chlorine free, and manufactured using biogas energy.

Printed in Canada

RECYCLED
Paper made from
recycled material
FSC   FSC® C103567

Contents

Contents

Illustrations

FIGURES

TABLES

Foreword

Douglas Morrey

Jean-Luc Godard has received considerable public attention in the past few years for a number of reasons: the widely publicized release of Godard's new feature film, *Film socialisme* (2010), which makes him one of the very few remaining New Wave directors still active (following the recent deaths of both Claude Chabrol and Eric Rohmer); Godard's 80th birthday and his proposed Academy Award for Lifetime Achievement, both of which have received much press attention; the recent publication of significant biographical studies in both English and French—Richard Brody's *Everything Is Cinema: The Working Life of Jean-Luc Godard* (Metropolitan Books, 2008) and Antoine de Baecque's *Godard: Biographie* (Grasset, 2010)—both of which have given rise to polemics around the author due to accusations of anti-Semitism and even pedophilia levelled against him by his biographers. In this context, a new volume of essays devoted to Godard's work is timely.

The editors are of course aware that few filmmakers have received so much commentary or been the object of so many scholarly books over the years as Godard. In particular, there was a flurry of publications on the director around the turn of the millennium, led by Michael Temple and James Williams's *The Cinema Alone: Essays on the Work of Jean-Luc Godard 1985–2000* (Amsterdam University Press, 2000), which sought to take account of *Histoire(s) du cinéma* and review Godard's career in the light of his significant but, at the time, little-seen late work. However, in the years since *Éloge de l'amour* (2001), scholarly publications analyzing Godard's oeuvre have been fewer in number, the most significant being the aforementioned biographies and two studies providing precise documentary details on Godard's working methods: *Jean-Luc Godard Documents* (ed. Brenez et al., Centre Pompidou, 2006) and Alain Bergala's *Godard au travail: Les années 60* (Cahiers du cinéma, 2006).

In this context, we believe a new volume assessing Godard's career and his diverse cultural legacies will be welcomed. Godard is both a director of universal significance, whose films (especially the early works) are regularly taught in undergraduate film programs, as well as a figure of specialist scholarly attention whose entire output is scrutinized in considerable depth. Our volume contains material to appeal both to a non-specialist audience—with discussions of canonical films like *Vivre sa vie* (1962) and *Alphaville* (1965) and treatment of themes popular within university cinema studies programs (e.g., film philosophy, cinema, and ethics)—and also to academic specialists on Godard—with chapters on recent works including *Dans le noir du temps* (2002) and *Voyage(s) en utopie* (2006), interventions in long-running academic debates (e.g., Godard, the Holocaust, and anti-Semitism), and treatment of rarely discussed areas of Godard's work (e.g., choreographed movement).

Acknowledgements

We are grateful to Dr. Sheila Petty, Dean of the Faculty of Fine Arts (University of Regina), for her unwavering help and encouragement; to Dr. Christine Ramsay, the former Head of the Department of Media Production and Studies (U of R), for her invaluable financial and moral support; and to Dr. Garry Sherbert, former Acting Director of the Humanities and Research Institute (U of R), for the grant towards the publishing of this book. We also wish to thank the participants in the SonImage international conference at the University of Regina (September 16–18, 2010), out of which this volume emerged, and particularly our co-organizers—Jeannie Mah, Dr. Philippe Mather, Professors Charlie Fox and Rachelle Viader-Knowles, as well as Dr. Béla Szabados—for initiating the conference and working with Christina and Nicole through its very successful end. And last, but not least, we would like to acknowledge the support of Wilfrid Laurier University Press, and especially of Lisa Quinn, its Acquisitions Editor.

Douglas Morrey
Christina Stojanova
Nicole Côté

August 2013

Introduction

Nicole Côté

Few filmmakers have had such pervasive and lasting influence, across artistic and intellectual fields, as Jean-Luc Godard. With a career in cinema spanning over fifty years and a hundred or more distinct works in numerous media, Godard has had an impact that cannot be overestimated, not only on the evolution of cinema worldwide, but on creative fields as diverse as television, video art, gallery installation, philosophy, music, literature, and dance. This collection marks an initial attempt to map the range of Godard's legacy across these different fields. It arises from the international conference "Sonimage: The Legacies of Jean-Luc Godard," held September 16–18, 2010, at the University of Regina (Canada), in honour of Godard's 80th birthday, and features fourteen essays, selected from the most original papers presented, that together delineate the impressive scope of Godard's interdisciplinary influence on philosophy, society, culture, and the arts through film.

The *Legacies of Jean-Luc Godard* takes a close look at how Godard opens the gates of possible pasts and futures with the breadth of his imagination, spanning the social and the personal, the emotional and the conceptual, as reflected in various works in the arts and humanities influenced by him. Indeed, Godard's cinema is just as invested in the past as it is in the future, the two being searched as earnestly as the present. Paul Ricoeur, in his article "Ideology and Utopia as Cultural Imagination," helps us understand Godard's concerns with this widened present, as he brings together ideology and utopia within a single conceptual frame, where ideology preserves a human order that could otherwise be smashed by historical forces, and where utopia, with its vision of alternative societies, works as the most formidable critique of what is. Since ideology works towards social integration, and utopia, towards social subversion, both must be kept in a state of tension to produce a stable yet progressive society, says Ricoeur.[1] Godard has indeed been preoccupied with both forces, documenting throughout his career the precarious maintenance of certain rituals (the repeatable): work, love, daily life. His recurrent interest lies in the recent past as history—that is, the shaping of the world through events brought about by various circumstances—as well as in utopic impulses taking over culture as tradition and helping it progress. However, several authors in this anthology consider Godard's representation of history as cyclical in its eventuality, a paradoxical and quasi-fatalistic stance that would link history, events driven mainly by utopic impulses, to ideology as understood by Ricoeur. Hence, perhaps, the conjuring function of cinema, its capacity not only to witness history in an ever-renewed attempt to memorialize various representations of it, but also to invent what could have been, what could still be: utopia.

Godard has been interested in utopias throughout his career, from *Alphaville* (1965) to his more recent exhibition *Voyage(s) en utopie* (2006). As Christina Stojanova and André Habib rightfully note, the overt/covert utopic impulse foregrounds the messianic inspiration in Godard's oeuvre. Utopia, a "nowhere" from which to take a good look at reality, actually denaturalizes it, thus opening the realm of the possible.[2] In his *Archaeologies of the Future: The Desire Called Utopia and Other Science Fictions*, Fredric Jameson notes the denaturalizing function of utopia: "utopian form is itself a representational meditation on radical difference, radical otherness. The fundamental dynamics of any Utopian politics will therefore lie in the dialectic of identity and difference."[3] Indeed, a definition of difference being *that which is not considered part of the self*—and therefore has not yet been included in identity, identity necessarily entailing an exclusionary logic—the artistic vision could widen identity, since it allows a glimpse of "oneself as another." An art as rife with utopic impulses as Godard's condenses the possibilities of experiencing otherness, renewing art, and seeking a more inclusive universal. Godard's cinema invites a revisiting of reality that enlarges it by the same token, offering new models of perception with its paradigmatic ("parametric," say Long and Lapointe) linking of images, as is perhaps most obvious in *Histoire(s) du cinéma* (1988–98).

One could say that Godard has steadily been working at enlarging the realm of cinema's identity, making of it the (post)modern genre par excellence of reflection, despite his aversion to technology's encroachment on our minds and to Hollywood's commodification of cinema and recent history. Were we to consider only the rich and varied contributions that shape this book, we could already envision Godard's utopian legacy: by ever widening the realm of cinema, by formally and representationally annexing new, uncharted territories, Godard has freed our imagination, hostage to traditional boundaries between cinema and other arts, between documentary and fiction films, between Hollywood and art films, between the intellectual and the worker or actor, between the masculine and the feminine, the conceptual and the emotional, the political and the cultural, the utterable and unutterable, and therefore redefined what can be considered memory/history. With the variety of his films—a telling example of inclusionary logic—Godard has contributed more to the archiving of the real—both material and immaterial heritage—than any other filmmaker. Yet even here, he lets the viewer do the final collage—as in his *Histoire(s)*, *Je vous salue, Marie* (1985), *Passion* (1982), or in his *Voyage(s) en utopie* exhibition—considering that creative freedom means agency, and that all humans share an associative, symbolic logic.

***

The book is divided into four parts that examine various aspects of Godard's legacy. **Part I, Godardian Legacy in Film, Music, and Dance,** considers both horizontal (influence on contemporaries) and vertical (influence on a younger generation of artists) meanings of "legacy." Douglas Morrey and John Carnahan see this legacy as Godard's substantial inspiration of other artists, be it of a younger generation of filmmakers—as Morrey discusses ("Jean-Luc Godard, Christophe Honoré, and the Legacy of the New Wave in French Cinema")—or of his contemporaries, as John Carnahan suggests with dance ("Jean-Luc Godard and Contemporary Dance: The Judson Dance Theater Runs Across *Breathless*"), and Jürg Stenzl, with music ("Jean-Luc Godard: *Dans le noir du temps* (2002)—The 'Filming' of a Musical Form").

Part II, Godardian Politics of Representation: Memory/History, focuses on two aspects of the temporal politics of representation in Jean-Luc Godard's cinema: the contemporary as future archive, and the past as recreated through representations, both creating a repository with its attendant ethical issues of what is included and what is left out. Michel Cadé defends Godard's representation of contemporary factory work as well as its political implications ("The Representation of Factory Work in the Films of Jean-Luc Godard: Reaching the Impossible Shore"); Junji Hori examines the representation of the Shoah as Godard would ideally have it, as opposed to Spielberg's actual representation of it ("Godard, Spielberg, the *Muselmann*, and the Concentration Camps"); Russell Kilbourn ("'The Obligations of Memory': Godard's Underworld Journeys") and Céline Scemama ("Jean-Luc Godard's *Histoire(s) du cinéma*: Assembling History through Montage") examine Godard's answers to the co-opting of memory and historical inheritance in Hollywoodian cinema, particularly in his work since the 1990s.

Part III, Godardian Legacy in Philosophy, takes another look at the two-way dialogue between Godard's films and twentieth-century philosophy, examining not only the legacy of philosophy to Godard's films—hence, Christina Stojanova's association of Godard's complex relationship with technology to the later work of Wittgenstein ("Jean-Luc Godard and Ludwig Wittgenstein in New Contexts") and David Sterritt's heterodox interpretation of Deleuze and Guattari's concepts ("Godard, Schizoanalysis, and the Immaculate Conception of the Frame")—but also Godard's idio-syncratic legacy to philosophy, either through the filmmaker's changing representation of reflexivity and ontological depth, as in Glen Norton's discussion of inwardness ("The 'Hidden Fire' of Inwardness: Cavell, Godard, and Modernism") or through his ambivalent representation of philosophers in his films, as in Tyson Stewart's illustration ("The Romance of the Intellectual in Godard: A Love–Hate Relationship").

Part IV, Formalist Legacies: Narratives and Exhibitions, considers hitherto under-researched formalist leitmotifs and crossovers between Godard's formalist strategies in his films and in his exhibitions, showing both the legacies Godard inherited and those he bequeathed. Julien Lapointe discusses Godard's parametric construction in *Passion* ("Principles of Parametric Construction in Jean-Luc Godard's *Passion*"); Timothy Long applies this parametric construction to Ian Wallace's pictorial composi-tions, heavily influenced by two of Godard's early films ("'A Place of Active Judgment': Parametric Narration in the Work of Jean-Luc Godard and Ian Wallace"); and André Habib shows, through Godard's "failed" Pompidou exhibition, *Voyage(s) en Utopie, JLG, 1946-2006* ("Godard's Utopia(s) or the Performance of Failure"), the filmmaker's preoccupation with the failure of cinema to represent history, this failure being the very condition of the creative proliferation found in his exhibition.

***

Turning now to the individual chapters in this collection, we come first to the essay "Jean-Luc Godard, Christophe Honoré, and the Legacy of the New Wave in French Cinema." In it, Morrey remarks that, even though the media did not miss the Godardian lineage in Christophe Honoré's films, Honoré quickly moved beyond this heritage. While the ongoing success of New Wave cinema is attributable to its emotional truth, Honoré's films, according to R. Dyer's definition of pastiche quoted in his essay, allow "the possibility of inhabiting [their] feelings with a simultaneous awareness of their historical constructedness." Morrey suggests then that what differen-tiates Honoré's films from his New Wave models is "the seriousness of [their] emotional terrain." By contrast, in Godard's films, "emotions … most often appear as ideas rather than as states believably attributable to credible characters" because of their fragmentation (see p. 10). Another anchor of emotional truthfulness in Honoré's films, Morrey suggests, might have to do with his families, which are "the object of complicated, ambivalent sentiments," whereas Godard's characters do not seem to belong to any families (p. 11). Morrey interestingly suggests that while Godard uses intertextuality at large, including works of art, as arguments of authority to inject emotions into his films—as if emotions were a dangerous territory to tread—in Honoré's *Dans Paris*, intertexts "are coloured with the emotion already generated by the film" (p. 12). Morrey concludes that if Honoré can be considered "the most worthy inheritor of Godard and the New Wave currently working in French cinema ... it is because his stylistic games and self-regarding cleverness (also present in Godard) are embedded in an emotional maturity that was too often missing from the work of Godard and his peers" (p. 13).

In the second essay, "Jean-Luc Godard: *Dans le noir du temps* (2002)— The 'Filming' of a Musical Form," Jürg Stenzl notes that the structuring of *Dans le noir du temps*, Godard and Anne-Marie Miéville's concluding contribution to the omnibus film *Ten Minutes Older: The Cello*, "reveals surprising parallels to the way composers work" (p. 17). Literally, the short film uses the ten final minutes of the omnibus film as the ten hypothetical final minutes of the world, each appearing with a title. What strikes Stenzl is that different though these minutes are, they have a highly unified, circularly evolving musical basis provided by Estonian composer Arvo Pärt (*Spiegel im Spiegel* [1978]). According to Stenzl, the music reflects the structure of Godard's film in its two features, since the slow addition to a nucleus creates the impression of an "imperceptibly evolving circular motion," achieved only "through octave transposition," the musical material being voluntarily limited. Stenzl adds that this "'global processuality' ... entails a continuous *spatialization* of the sound," thereby maintaining the visual dynamism of the film (pp. 20–21). "Motionlessness and evolution," Stenzl argues, played a central role in Godard's late work (p. 21), and the film's correspondences between images and sound are "rooted in a cyclical structure" (p. 24). Since Godard and Miéville, in *Dans le noir du temps*, allow music and film to contrapuntally reflect one another, their particular contribution lies in reversing the traditional respective roles of image and music that the cinematic tradition granted.

John Carnahan defines his essay, "Jean-Luc Godard and Contemporary Dance: The Judson Dance Theater Runs Across *Breathless*" (Chapter 3), as an experiment in translating "a vocabulary for figure movement on film from the language of dance and performance art" (p. 37). Following his discovery of the striking autonomy of movements in Godard's films, Carnahan sees Godard "as a choreographer and maker of performance events" (p. 37). Specifically, Carnahan concentrates on the inter-influences of Godard and the Judson Dance Theater, both Godard and the Judson choreographers, Carnahan argues, being "students of gesture as reproduced and analyzed by film" (p. 37). Carnahan studies the new approach to movement of Yvonne Rainer's 1966 composition *Trio A* before briefly broaching her *Terrain*. *Trio A* is remarkable for its absence of pauses between the movement phrases, and it is precisely the flowing of images, which allows the same movement from one shot to another, however different, that Godard said helped him link discontinuous jump-cuts in *Breathless*. More generally, contends Carnahan, "the compositional priority Godard has given to movement 'ever since *Breathless*' makes the quality of movement in a shot at least as important as its narrative relation to other shots" (p. 42). Arguably, then, Godard's cinematic images of flowing human movements constitute a legacy to dance in general, and to the Judson Dance Theater in particular.

In Part II, Chapter 4, "The Representation of Factory Work in the Films of Jean-Luc Godard: Reaching the Impossible Shore," Michel Cadé discusses Godard's paradoxical relationship with the representation of factory work on screen. In his view, Godard, the filmmaker who, even before 1968, was most strongly committed to the far left, "did not see fit to give factory work a predominant place in his works" (p. 53). Cadé sees two reasons for Godard's avoidance of a direct stance on this type of labour: first, that being foreign to the labour process, Godard did not want to use a veristic approach to represent it; second, that the labour's *mise en scène* soon appeared dated to him. In opposition to Marin Karmitz, Godard did not use factory workers, but famous actors (Yves Montand, Jane Fonda), in order to make representation palpable, as he humbly recognized having no direct experience of labour. Some of the scenes, says Cadé, had been "just as effective as the verism of Karmitz in displaying the almost military environment created by the scientific organization of work" (p. 56). While the motions of work are of utmost interest to Godard, their reproduction through *mise en scène* appears unfeasible to him; thus he uses the informal style of the television or video medium to ask, outside of their workplace, an unemployed welder, a farmer, a young woman, to go through the motions of their work. Through the reconstruction of their daily gestures, Godard feels he can overcome the barrier between his subjects and himself. He refuses "both verism and artifice" because of his unfamiliarity with factory work, a position that Cadé hails as honest and considers a Godardian legacy (p. 60).

Concerning the representation of the past in Godard's films, Junji Hori discusses in "Godard, Spielberg, the *Muselmann*, and the Concentration Camps" Godard's ambivalent relationship to the younger Steven Spielberg and his depiction of the Shoah. According to Hori, Godard's repeated criticism against Spielberg could be a "defence mechanism" (p. 68), since *Schindler's List* "usurped some of Godard's ideas as to how to represent concentration camps," a leitmotif in *Histoire(s) du cinéma* (p. 69). It was, says Hori, the daily routine at the concentration camps that fascinated Godard, illustrating the "banality of evil." This fascination allowed him to avoid resorting to obscene images, which were against his ethics of representation (p. 69). Hori discusses at length Godard's persistent interest in the term *Muselmann* (Muslim, a camp jargon term used for desperate, dying Jewish prisoners by other Jewish prisoners). The term went from reflecting, in the 1970s, Godard's pro-Palestinian, anti-Zionist position— foreshadowing the Israeli–Palestinian conflict, said Godard—to being an emblem of history's cycles, pointing to "a primal scene of repetitive calamities that Muslims have suffered in Lebanon, in Algeria, or in Sarajevo, albeit in completely different historical situations." The term echoes Godard's "idiosyncratic historical imagination," which "highlights the *repetitive* aspects of historical events," says Hori (pp. 74–75). He considers Godard's historiographic method a most valuable legacy in our particularist times, as it is not based on identity politics.

In "'The Obligations of Memory': Godard's Underworld Journeys," Russell Kilbourn focuses on some of the issues Hori discussed, particularly the unacknowledged legacy that Godard and Spielberg received from one another. Whereas Hori posits that Godard resents Spielberg's success in depicting the concentration camps, Kilbourn unravels the various Godardian strands leading to the making of *Schindler's List*. Since *Éloge de l'amour* (2001), according to Kilbourn, "frames a response in terms of Spielberg's (re-)construction of the past out of historical or mnemic appropriation," Kilbourn zooms in on this film, but not without first having traced a quick genealogy of its influences and themes through Godard's own *Alphaville* and Jean Cocteau's *Orphée* (1950). In *Éloge de l'amour*, argues Kilbourn, not only is love "almost entirely couched in the past tense, inextricable from mourning, guilt, and regret," but the representation of memory "finds a highly evocative, complex cinematic form" which is pitted against "a classical Hollywood cinema predicated on ... manufactured desires and identifications" (p. 82). Godard is preoccupied here with Spielberg's co-opting of memory through simplification, by the same token presenting it as unmediated, thus commodifying it, erasing the issue of representation. As Kilbourn explains: "What Spielberg (and post-classical Hollywood) obscures, and Godard repeatedly lays bare, is that eyewitness testimony of past events is always already subject to, indeed constituted by, pre-existing structures: the genres, clichés, and tropes of memory, dominated by variations on the flashback" (p. 84). Here, says Kilbourn,

"Godard's ongoing critique of the commodification of the image" touches "the cultural amnesia at the heart of late capitalist modernity" (p. 84). Thus is brought about the paradox at the heart of the image in a film like *Éloge de l'amour*: "if the image is to save us, first we must save the image." However, Kilbourn is also quick to point out, despite the film's pervasive melancholia, the filmmaker's resistance to "unreflective nostalgia and the melodramatic trappings of contemporary Hollywood narrative," keeping in mind "cinema's general status as pre-eminent prosthetic memory for the twentieth century" (p. 85).

In "Jean-Luc Godard's *Histoire(s) du cinéma* Brings the Dead Back to the Screen," Céline Scemama discusses Godard's "monumental" *Histoire(s) du cinéma*, and threads the same Godardian motifs of a co-opted Hollywoodian cinema, a legacy that the filmmaker rejects, suggesting his own in its wake. Indeed, Godard's postmodernist stance in *Histoire(s) du cinéma* offers a harsh critique of cinema as a consumable commodity. The four-hour film, opening "the way to the final period in Godard's works" (p. 99), is a montage of images borrowed not only from cinema but from other arts, as well as from various discourses about culture that predate the production, organized by Godard's sombre voice-over commentary. According to Scemama, "the work as a whole creates an apocalyptic effect," while being indescribably beautiful (p. 99). "The shot itself as a unit of cinema [has lost] its contours.... This history finds neither unity, nor harmony, nor completion" (p. 100). Godard's vision of history is bleak, says Scemama, because memory will necessarily fail its duty to witness all, especially the war traumas. But also, she writes, "no beyond can heal the wounds of humanity," and there is no resurrection, even for Christ, except in images (p. 103). Quoting Alan Wright, Scemama argues that this impossible cinematic representation hints at a Lacanian "absence that haunts ... the traumatic kernel of the Real," which Godard associates with the concentration camps (p. 104). Thus Godard recognizes the impossible task of doing justice to reality, yet comes forward as the humble guardian of the "museum of the real" (p. 107).

Part III opens with Christina Stojanova's chapter, "Jean-Luc Godard and Ludwig Wittgenstein in New Contexts," where she examines twentieth-century philosophy's legacy to Godard, especially that of Ludwig Wittgenstein. Stojanova brings to the fore another side of the filmmaker's paradoxes: his manifest interest in the latest technology, yet his serious concerns with the very real dangers brought on by its unchecked invasion. Stojanova reads Godard's ambiguous attitude towards technology in light of Wittgenstein, who recognized the movement of progress toward complexification, but sought clarity and simplicity in any structure. Considering

Godard's and Wittgenstein's respective searches to redesign their fields with the available tools, whether conceptual or technological, Stojanova looks at Godard's *Alphaville* in light of two of Wittgenstein's most quoted propositions.

For Godard, says Stojanova, "the ultimately 'unutterable ... contained in what has been uttered,' is the impossible love, whose various dimensions Godard has been exploring since the early 1980s" (p. 134). Stojanova associates Godard's endeavours with those of the late Wittgenstein, who preferred language games to logic and philosophy. Indeed, language games produce "the kind of emotional understanding that consists in seeing connections," replacing the old images with new ones, replete with possibilities (p. 134). Godard's preoccupation, says Stojanova, perhaps especially in his monumental *Histoire(s) du cinéma*, has been with making connections through montage. If "history breaks down into images, not stories," as Walter Benjamin is quoted as saying, the most efficient tool in this deconstruction of history is montage, which Godard considers "cinema's unique contribution to the history of art," a "new form of critical thought" (p. 135). "The montage in *Histoire(s)*," contends Stojanova, "uncannily evokes Wittgenstein's language games," as "words, released from the metaphysical constraints and launched into new contexts of 'ordinary' and 'private' languages, evoke the images of *Histoire(s)*, emancipated from the narrative hierarchies of cinematic storytelling," creating the "unutterable" and the "imponderable" through poetry (pp. 135–36).

In Chapter 9, "Godard, Schizoanalysis, and the Immaculate Conception of the Frame," the two-way legacy between Godard's cinema and twentieth-century philosophy is again given emphasis. Here, David Sterritt examines Gilles Deleuze and Félix Guattari's concept of schizoanalysis in order to frame his own study of Godard's *Je vous salue, Marie*. Sterritt's interest in Godard's film lies in its "complex blend of narrative drama, theological speculation, Catholic iconography, and Protestant music" (p. 144). These particularities of style reflect Deleuze and Guattari's deterritorialization, according to Sterritt, who sees similarities with "the film's painterly impulses" reaffirming the power of images, as Renaissance Catholicism did (p. 150). Sterritt maintains that "God has long been an alter ego for Godard, who imagines himself a 'distant as well as omniscient and omnipotent creator'; hence the special vitality of light in his aesthetic ... a symbol of ... the divine" (p. 150).

Concerning montage, Sterritt considers *Je vous salue, Marie* perhaps "Godard's most far-reaching essay in the irrational cut," as the constant edits, added to the blurring of foreground and background, destabilize the primary narrative, which is itself so intercut with subplots that viewers have difficulty following the narrative. With these devices Godard "turns narrative thrust," says Sterritt, "into a rhizomatic assemblage of ontological conundrums" (p. 151).

Glen Norton's essay, "The 'Hidden Fire' of Inwardness: Cavell, Godard, and Modernism," highlights Godard's singular legacy to philosophy. In it, he discusses "Godard's modernist skepticism regarding the cinematic depiction of inwardness" in the early 1960s (p. 157). Norton argues against Stanley Cavell's idea that Godard's work after *Breathless* lacks inwardness—"inwardness" connoting the depth of a person. Starting with Cavell's idea that cinema's natural relationship with cinematic inwardness is its capacity to present characters as personified types, *À bout de souffle* (1960) would be, according to Cavell, Godard's masterpiece, since the later films qualify as "debased modernism" due to their male protagonist's lack of inwardness. However, using *Vivre sa vie* (1962), Norton argues instead "that Godard's early cinema consistently examines the modernist conditions under which an acknowledgement of inwardness is cinematically possible" (p. 157). Norton is here drawing upon what Cavell, borrowing from Baudelaire, labels "hidden fire"—defining the type of character who has a capacity to embody inwardness as a certain self-assuredness, "a seemingly unlimited capacity for self-knowledge" (p. 159).

Yet, to Norton, Godard does not assert inwardness; he rather explores its conditions of possibility. In fact Norton sees a change from *Breathless* to *Vivre sa vie*, where the female protagonist, Nana, does not embody the "'cool' self-awareness" (p. 164) of *Breathless*' male protagonist, but represents the self's isolation from society. This brings into high relief the way "conceptual thinking impedes the depiction of cinematic inwardness" (p. 166). Hence, when Nana asks philosopher Brice Parain, "What do you think of love?" his answer to her spiritual question reduces love "to the mechanics of the body," says Norton (p. 166).

In "The Romance of the Intellectual in Godard: A Love–Hate Relationship," Tyson Stewart offers another take on Godard's ongoing relationship with philosophy through cameo integrations of real philosophers in his early fiction films. The social role of the intellectual runs through Godard's entire oeuvre, according to Stewart, with the intellectual also standing in for his nation or community. By having the philosophers debate with the actors, Godard pits the thinkers against the actors, often men and women of action, says Stewart, and thus opens up the circulation of knowledge. However, the actors often come off as more "revolutionary" than the real-life intellectuals when they are asked to respond spontaneously to the ideas under discussion, whereas the (male) intellectuals remain within the boundaries of their role. Stewart thus reminds us that there is always an intellectual stance underlying the construction of character, the Godardian cameos of intellectuals denying the possibility of living outside representation. Nonetheless, the brief cameo sequences of intellectuals in Godard show them as disposable. Indeed, with knowledge's increased commodification, intellectual discourse is compressed, reduced, fragmented. Godard's films, then, "attempt to chart the decline of intellectualism in the West," contends Stewart (p. 170).

Julien Lapointe, in "Principles of Parametric Construction in Jean-Luc Godard's *Passion*," is the first author in Part IV to consider formalist leitmotifs in Godard's films and their genealogy. Lapointe frames these motifs as "parametric narration," a problematic aesthetic mode in that it is not attached to any "national tradition, mode of production, or historical era" (p. 185). David Bordwell defines the parametric narrative films as those in which the "stylistic system creates patterns distinct from the demands of the ... [plot]" (p. 185). Studying the parametric construction of Godard's 1982 feature film *Passion*, Lapointe seeks to understand the film from another point of view than that of plot, since the handling of the sound and image tracks calls attention to the form, interfering with the spectator's grasp of the story. Lapointe argues that "patterning of various kinds, such as those detailed in *Passion*, will provide a semblance of stability to an otherwise chaotic flux of sounds, images, facts, and figures" (p. 193). As Lapointe gauges the impact of Godard's forays into parametric cinema, it being "something of a minority practice," he reminds us that some of the most recognized modernist filmmakers have delved into it. As well, we might discover other Godard films that use the parametric mode, since "it is no secret that Godard's films have long been redolent in stylistic constructions that seek to challenge the viewer's comprehension" (p. 194).

Timothy Long's chapter, "'A Place of Active Judgment': Parametric Narration in the Work of Jean-Luc Godard and Ian Wallace," deals with Godard's formal influence on Ian Wallace, a member of the Vancouver School of photo-based art who has been particularly influenced by *Masculin féminin* (1966) and *Le Mépris* (1963). Both artist and filmmaker, according to Long, use "parametric" devices to break the frames of painting and cinema respectively, in order to create for the viewer "a place of active judgment." Wallace considers that the two early fiction films as well as the 1985 video *Soft and Hard* "situate the question of judgment in relation to the cinematic and social construction of gender binaries" (p. 197).

Wallace's *Masculin/Féminin* series shows a range of parametric strategies inherited from Godard. Long highlights the kinship between them, as both hover between representation and abstraction, and as Wallace brings together "the representational conventions of photography with the formal experimentation of the modernist avant-garde" (pp. 208–9). Interested in the semantics of parametric narration—"what is produced by [a] parametric approach beyond a novel aesthetic form?" (p. 209)—Long finds behind Wallace's combination of monochrome abstraction and photography, "a pictorial 'ground zero,' replete with the utopian possibilities of transcendence." Wallace, just like Godard, pushes the boundaries of the possible in his art, which Long interprets as "the relationship of the content to the frame and of the frame to the audience" (p. 209), the frame being "essential for producing presence" through an exclusionary logic separating the image from its context. Godard's framing of cinema takes place on a number of levels, one of which is the "*mise en abyme* of characters attending a film" (p. 210). In both the cases of Godard and Wallace, "the reconciling frame of cinema is shown to be a house divided, an ineffective mediator between the sexes," which nevertheless "opens the frame to multiple points of view" (p. 210).

In the final essay, "Godard's Utopia(s) or the Performance of Failure," André Habib presents Godard's Pompidou exhibition *Voyage(s) en utopie, JLG, 1946-2006, À la recherche d'un théorème perdu* and bears witness to Godard's continued legacy in art, a legacy so wide it includes the done, the undone, and the yet-to-be-done. Indeed, this project, leading to a "fantastically dense and complex self-reflexive exhibition ... every version of the exhibit seem[ing] to coexist in this inchoate state of flux between promise and ruin" (p. 224), explores the state of the world through images. Godard and his assistants "created a combinatory vertigo that encapsulated the different stages of the project," which "the mesmerized visitor" was asked to piece together as one is asked to make temporary sense of history (p. 228).

Despite the utter failure of critical reception, Habib, along with others, considers this performance "a masterpiece of wit and intelligence, in the line of *Histoire(s) du cinéma*" (pp. 224–25). Interestingly, Habib ties this "performance of failure" to the mode of utopia prevalent in most of Godard's projects, from the late 1960s onwards, through a dialectical motion. This motion, at the root of Godard's creativity, according to Habib, can be read as a metaphor of his *Histoire(s) du cinéma*. Habib therefore considers the necessity of the tragic failure pole, since only the memory of failure allows for changes, these changes being first envisioned through utopia. Habib summarizes by contending that the Godardian archive is replete with unfinished projects, Godard's failures merging with cinema's failure. This negativity, says Habib, "becomes the condition of possibility of new work," (p. 225) and thus leaves Godard's legacies yet to be inventoried.

NOTES

My thanks to Christina Stojanova for her remarks on the first draft of the Introduction, and to Douglas Morrey for his remarks on the last.

1 Paul Ricoeur, "Ideology and Utopia as Cultural Imagination," in *Being Human in a Technological Age*, ed. Donald M. Borchert and David Stewart (Columbus: Ohio State University Press, 1979).
2 Ricoeur, "Ideology and Utopia as Cultural Imagination."
3 Frederic Jameson, *Archaeologies of the Future: The Desire Called Utopia and Other Science Fictions* (London: Verso, 2007), xii.

BIBLIOGRAPHY

Jameson, Frederic. *Archaeologies of the Future: The Desire Called Utopia and Other Science Fictions*. London: Verso, 2007.
Ricoeur, Paul. "Ideology and Utopia as Cultural Imagination." In *Being Human in a Technological Age*, edited by Donald M. Borchert and David Stewart, 112–21. Columbus: Ohio State University Press, 1979.

Part I
Godardian Legacy in Film, Music, and Dance

1

Jean-Luc Godard, Christophe Honoré, and the Legacy of the New Wave in French Cinema

Douglas Morrey

THE FILMS OF Christophe Honoré perhaps provide the most obvious example of the influence of Jean-Luc Godard and the New Wave in contemporary French cinema—at least in his most internationally successful films *Dans Paris* (2006) and *Les Chansons d'amour* (2007). Unsurprisingly, film critics in France were not slow to draw comparisons to the New Wave: *Libération* called *Dans Paris* "a manifesto for modern cinema" that was "in the direct lineage of the New Wave."[1] *Les Inrockuptibles* suggested the film could be seen as "a catalogue of everything we think we know about the New Wave."[2] Reviews of the film were littered with references to directors and films from the New Wave and the post–New Wave of the 1970s: Godard, François Truffaut, Jacques Demy, Jean Eustache, *Le Mépris* (1963), *Jules et Jim* (1962), *Bande à part* (1964), Truffaut's Antoine Doinel series, Pialat's *Nous ne vieillirons pas ensemble* (1972). But the general consensus seemed to be that Honoré had absorbed and internalized the influence of the New Wave the better to move beyond it. *Libération* suggested the film constituted "an affectionate loan rather than a bashful quotation";[3] *Le Journal du dimanche* asserted that Honoré accepted the influence of the New Wave in order to transgress its limits and move beyond it;[4] *Les Inrockuptibles* intimated that, compared to French filmmakers of the 1980s, Honoré was sufficiently distanced from the New Wave no longer to be intimidated by it, and that he was instead able to adapt its principles to his own ends;[5] *Le Figaro*, meanwhile, saw Honoré as "appropriating and reinventing" the codes of the New Wave.[6] Commentators noted that Honoré followed the New Wave model by working very quickly: *Dans Paris* was written, produced, shot, and edited all within six months, and, only six months later, the follow-up *Les Chansons d'amour* was released. This rhythm of work, which Honoré has subsequently kept up (*La Belle Personne* [2008], made for television, was bashed out in a hiatus in the filming of *Non ma fille tu n'iras pas danser* [2009], partly as a timely response to a public remark by Nicolas Sarkozy denigrating *La Princesse de Clèves*), has not been seen in French cinema since the early years of Godard, Truffaut, and Claude Chabrol, and it demonstrates, aside from a willingness to improvise projects based on available materials and funds, something of the contagious joy of filming that makes the New Wave so enduringly likeable.[7] In addition, like Godard and the other canonical New Wave directors, Honoré first wrote criticism for *Cahiers du cinéma*, in which he attacked what he saw as the rather stale social realism of contemporary French filmmaking, and he has railed, in interview, against the return of a certain "tradition of quality," which, as we know, was precisely what the original New Wave positioned itself against.[8]

Dans Paris is a film that wears its New Wave, and especially its Godardian, influences on its sleeve, and this is clear from the very start. Within the first five minutes, we witness the following markers of influence from the Nouvelle Vague:

- the film presents strikingly large and bold credits comparable, for instance, to the title card for *À bout de souffle* (1960), itself often thought to be a reference to *Citizen Kane* (1941);
- but it is notable, too, that Honoré uses red, white, and blue in the credit for Marie-France Pisier, herself an actress associated with New Wave directors (Truffaut's *Antoine et Colette* [1962], Jacques Rivette's *Céline et Julie vont en bateau* [1974]), and we might compare Godard's use of coloured credits in, for example, *Une femme est une femme* (1961) and *Pierrot le fou* (1965);
- it opens with a cool jazz soundtrack comparable to Miles Davis's score for *L'Ascenseur pour l'échafaud* (1958) or Martial Solal's score for *À bout de souffle*, itself reminiscent in places of John Coltrane;
- the dusky (or possibly dawn) views of Paris streets that open the film quickly suggest that the city will itself be a kind of character in the fiction (if this were not already clear from the title);
- in the spirit of the New Wave, there is, in these opening minutes, the deliberate inclusion of amateurish camerawork—a shaky zoom on Louis Garrel and Romain Duris;[9]
- the introduction to the narrative proper starts with a shot of three young people in a bed together, recalling Jean Eustache's *La Maman et la putain* (1973) (at this stage we do not yet know that Jonathan and Paul [Garrel and Duris] are brothers);
- the film continues with Louis Garrel/Jonathan's direct address or "apostrophe" to the spectator, from the balcony in front of the Eiffel Tower;
- with this gesture, a character effectively hijacks the fiction (Jonathan admits that this story isn't really about him, yet, by becoming its

narrator, he makes it as much about him); there is a long tradition of relatively minor characters taking over screen time in New Wave films and Godard's in particular;

- Jonathan then delivers a very casual exposition of what this film will be about (for instance vaguely situating the subsequent scene in the "potato-shaped *département*"): traditional concerns for establishing verisimilitude are abandoned in favour of an approach that seeks to move directly to the emotional core of a scene; in the same way, the status of Paul and Anna's (Joana Preiss) relationship is established in a handful of gestures and looks).

Of all these examples, it is perhaps Garrel's direct address to the camera that bespeaks the greatest degree of audacity on the director's part. Not that it is especially unusual for characters to address the camera in the cinema these days; on the contrary, precisely to appropriate a technique that has become so mundane, and to do so in front of the Eiffel Tower, the most iconic image of all French cinema, implies a willingness to tackle head-on the most tired clichés of the medium with a swaggering confidence in the director's capacity to rehabilitate them. The sense that Honoré is arrogantly measuring himself against the greats of French cinema persists when *Dans Paris*'s first major sequence is a sixteen-minute presentation of the messy breakdown of a couple's relationship, a scene that models itself unmistakeably on those lengthy evocations of domestic disputes that Godard invented in the 1960s.[10] Numerous characteristics of this sequence in *Dans Paris* are reminiscent of Godard's sixties films, most especially *Le Mépris*:

- the elaboration of domestic space facilitated by having characters address each other from different rooms;
- the use of sex not as a spontaneous gesture of affection and desire, but as a tactical weapon intended to wound the partner;
- sudden and awkward changes of tone within the sequence (as when Paul tries to lighten the mood by hitting Anna with a pillow, only to annoy her further);
- a tendency for characters to announce what the other is thinking, in an attempt to second-guess each other;
- a mixture of colloquial language and non-naturalistic, stylized dialogue (as in Anna's "Je cherche les raisons de ton inélégance" ["I am trying to find reasons for your inelegance"]);
- a very deliberately designed colour scheme (in *Dans Paris*, autumnal; in Godard, primary colours);
- the unannounced introduction of flashbacks to happier times (and the particular flashback in *Dans Paris*, in which Paul and Anna skip

and dance together through a wood, is a fairly direct quotation of *Pierrot le fou*);

- characters in various states of undress;
- a quick montage signalling the decline of the couple, shown through failed communication (arguments), absent communication (Paul lying in front of the car that Anna is driving), and non-verbal communication (dancing, etc.);
- use of (diegetic) music and dancing both to set or reflect mood and as a prop for the argument;
- quotations from books, placed diegetically in the scene (in *Dans Paris*, Paul reads from the poetry of Richard Brautigan);
- "jump-cuts" (*faux raccords*) in space, on dialogue, and in emotion (e.g., from an argument to the sudden suggestion of conceiving a baby together).

In its opening quarter-hour, in other words, *Dans Paris* fairly clearly presents itself as a pastiche of a New Wave movie, in the sense implied by Richard Dyer's no-nonsense definition: "pastiche is a kind of imitation that you are meant to know is an imitation."[11] But, as Dyer further points out, "pastiche deforms the style of its referent: it selects, accentuates, exaggerates, concentrates."[12] And it is perhaps this concentration of New Wave traits and motifs that makes the opening of *Dans Paris* less than entirely successful, rendering it on the contrary rather grating for some viewers. One key difference between Godard's interior scenes and Honoré's sequence is that, by taking place more or less in real time, Godard's domestic moments in *Le Mépris*, *A bout de souffle*, etc., opened up a sense of spaciousness within the narrative and balanced out his generic plots with more leisurely pacing. Honoré's sequence, on the other hand, edits together at least three different episodes indoors and three more outdoors, cutting quite rapidly between them in a way that some reviewers found irritating and confusing: the critic for *Le Point*, for example, called the first fifteen minutes of the film "unbearable," almost enough to make the spectator walk out.[13] There is perhaps a sense, then, in this opening sequence of *Dans Paris*, that Honoré is conspicuously paying his dues and this cluttered, slightly hysterical domestic scene appears rather forced as a result. It is as though Honoré needs to get this somewhat awkward homage out of the way—in the process nailing his New Wave colours to the mast—before moving on to the film proper.

Dans Paris is thus painstakingly self-aware; but what Richard Dyer's original interpretation of pastiche points out is that pastiche "demonstrates that self-consciousness and emotional expression can co-exist," thereby "allowing us to contemplate the possibility of feeling historically."[14] In other words, what pastiche gives to a film is "the possibility of inhabiting its feelings with a simultaneous awareness of their historical constructedness."[15] To put this yet another way, pastiche "recognises its own difference from past forms while acknowledging their emotional truth."[16] This strikes me as crucially important when considering the influence of the New Wave because, as Naomi Greene has recently pointed out, one of the key factors determining both the popular success of the Nouvelle Vague and its subsequent undiminished appeal for several generations of spectators is precisely its emotional truth.[17] Greene cites Truffaut, who argues that, because the young filmmakers of the New Wave could not afford the technical sophistication to match the "icy perfection" of the established cinema, they were obliged to find a variety of ad hoc solutions to the filming of their scenes, which had the added benefit of conveying "the truth of the streets." As Truffaut puts it, "one reaches a profound truth by a superficial one and sophisticated cinema had lost even superficial truth."[18]

In other words, the emotional truth of the New Wave might be seen as a fortuitous outgrowth from the enforced spontaneity of its conditions of production. As Truffaut insists, it was this spontaneous aspect to the direction of New Wave films that touched spectators at the time.[19] *Dans Paris* seeks to appropriate this spontaneity through the seemingly arbitrary, unmotivated detours of its narrative (or, at least, whose motivation only becomes clear in retrospect). Thus, just when we are thoroughly involved in Paul and Anna's story, the narrative returns to Paris and informs us that this is not, in fact, what the film is about. We have spent some sixteen minutes in the company of this beautiful, affluent couple observing their sexual games, their hysterical arguments, and Paul's suicide attempt, before this narrative ground is taken out from under our feet and revealed as nothing but a prologue to the real story. And, crucially, the material with which Paul and Anna's relationship is replaced appears, by comparison, banal to the point of abjection: thus we have Jonathan with his bad breath on the sofa bed; his dad (Guy Marchand) with his dressing gown, his Italian game shows, and his chicken soup; and Paul with a big beard, impassive as a statue, sitting on the toilet. But this, too, belongs to the domain of the New Wave: if not the new narrative material per se, at least the audacity with which Honoré sets up the elements of a story only to take a sudden and disorienting change of direction (Truffaut did something similar in *Tirez sur le pianiste* [1961]). Subsequently, then, the "plot" of *Dans Paris* is organised around Jonathan's apparently spontaneous wager that he can get to the Bon Marché in under half an hour and, again, this willingness to weave a narrative out the flimsiest of pretexts is another important New Wave trait. The meaninglessness of the wager itself is demonstrated by the fact that Jonathan actually takes over seven hours to make his journey, since he stops to engage with the people that he meets along the way, again apparently spontaneously (clearly this spontaneity is only apparent, since everything that happens in the film is scripted in advance; however, in terms of the narrative logic it is spontaneous because these encounters do not occur in response to any setting of goals or deliberate action on the part of Jonathan). As critics remarked, it would be easy to get the impression that nothing really happens in *Dans Paris*, yet it is, as *Le Journal du Dimanche* put it, one of those films that manages to say a lot without apparently telling a story ("un de ces films qui ne racontent rien, mais qui pourtant disent beaucoup").[20] As a result, *Dans Paris* wears its narrative ambitions lightly and this lightness (*légèreté*) is another of the New Wave's most likeable traits. Honoré, in interview, has suggested that this lightness of touch cannot be faked, but is instead a state of mind, and results from the pleasure taken in the process of filming itself.[21]

But how, exactly, is lightness of touch, or this impression of spontaneity conveyed? I suggest it has something to do with the curious sense of narrative space developed in *Dans Paris*, which, once again, is reminiscent of New Wave films. Consider for instance the short sequence in which Jonathan and Alice (Alice Butaud) play around in the streets of Paris. The sense of space is confused here, partly because we see a series of what are almost tableaux without clear indications of their spatio-temporal relationship (although we also see the recognizable landmark of the Invalides), but also because the voice-over dialogue, in which Jonathan seems to be trying to persuade Alice to have sex in a public place, is further detached from the images, taking place in some other, unseen space. The peculiarly ludic sense of space and time established here is a little reminiscent of the on-street games and theatrical tableaux performed by Jean-Paul Belmondo and Anna Karina in Godard's *Une femme est une femme*. What this approach to filmmaking does, I want to suggest, is at once to contract and to dilate space and time. It contracts because, in the example from *Dans Paris*, presumably several hours are condensed into a handful of shots (Jonathan spends most of the afternoon with Alice); but it dilates by creating this rather uncertain space and time, set apart somewhat from the logic of the narrative, which, since it contributes little in terms of story information, serves mostly as a showcase for *acting*. In *Dans Paris*, this is also related to Jonathan's function as narrator, since as such he is occasionally able to step outside the space and time of the narrative proper, for instance when he protests that he didn't slam the door on leaving the apartment, or when he calls to his mother from the balcony, despite the fact that he wasn't present when she visited. As Jean-Michel Frodon has commented, the direct address at the beginning of the film sets up an intermediary space in which Jonathan/Louis Garrel circulates at once as character and as actor.[22]

The French New Wave introduced a couple of important innovations regarding the use of actors in cinema. First, there was a cinephile's attention paid to an actor's previous incarnations, and a willingness to reference earlier roles, either implicitly or explicitly, in the creation of a new character. Honoré works in this tradition by his casting of Marie-France Pisier and Guy Marchand, both actors with important New Wave and post–New Wave pedigrees, in the roles of Jonathan and Paul's mother and father. But the other great novelty of New Wave acting was a voluntary move away from naturalistic performance to embrace instead a playfulness in the acting register that could incorporate clowning and grandstanding alongside more interiorized and "serious" performance. The undisputed master of this mode was Jean-Pierre Léaud, who is also Louis Garrel's acknowledged role model. In interview, Garrel has referred to Léaud as his "absolute master" and spoken knowledgeably about the New Wave actor's use of space (Léaud, he notes, has a curious way of constantly seeming to exit the frame, whereas most actors are always trying to enter it).[23] He also suggests that the tempo of Léaud's acting has something of the complex, unpredictable or improvised quality of jazz.[24] It is, surely, the energy and ebullience of Garrel's acting that succeeds in turning Jonathan into a likeable character (in much the same way that, for instance, Michel Poiccard, the petty hoodlum of À bout de souffle, is rendered charming by Jean-Paul Belmondo's performance). Jonathan, after all, is a selfish, childish, and unreliable character; his father remarks on his bad breath and Alice confirms that he is dirty and smelly; he sleeps with three different women in one day without the slightest scruple, and his attitude toward relationships is further demonstrated by the fact that he owes Alice €3000, a debt that he dismisses with little more than an irritated shrug. Yet such an apparently odious personality becomes adorable thanks to the verve and lightness of touch with which Garrel incarnates it. And, more to the point, the impression of spontaneity that the film carefully cultivates in its style and its actors becomes, at the level of the diegesis, an important value attached to the characters. I mean to say that it is Jonathan's spontaneity that makes him a likeable character: if he takes what he wants (in sexual terms at least) without thought of the consequences, he also gives his affection spontaneously: perhaps Jonathan's finest redeeming moment is when, without hesitation, he climbs, fully clothed, into the bath in order to empathize with and comfort his traumatized and post-suicidal brother. And the same quality is valued in other characters, as when Paul spontaneously sympathizes with Alice, evoking for her sake the story of his dead sister, Claire, which he has not discussed with any of his family members.

Clearly, then, Honoré wears his influences on his sleeve; the marks of Godard and the New Wave are emblazoned everywhere in this film. But, if there were nothing to *Dans Paris* other than the "funny and tender homage to the French New Wave" announced by the DVD box, it would never rise above the level of a sycophantic tribute. What sets Honoré's film apart from its New Wave models, I want to suggest, or at least from Godard specifically, is the seriousness of its emotional terrain—the depression that paralyzes Paul after his break-up with Anna—and this interest in difficult adult emotions is something that Honoré has pursued in subsequent films, exploring the effects of grief in *Les Chansons d'amour* and the fallout from divorce in *Non ma fille tu n'iras pas danser*. It is a common criticism of Godard that, for all the high seriousness of his films, he often fails to get to grips with the emotional reality of his characters. The persistent fragmenting of all aspects of his films (dialogue, images, bodies, narratives) and the coolly clinical gaze of the camera (which, far from being instigated by the "structuralist" works of the late sixties, can be traced back at least as far as *Le Petit Soldat* [1961]) mean that emotions in Godard's films most often appear as ideas rather than as states attributable to credible characters. As Manny Farber complained, Godard dissociates everything: "talk from character, actor from character, action from situation, and photography from scene."[25] How, then, does Honoré succeed in instilling his film with real emotion even while playing with much of the trickery and ironic self-reference that Godard also favours? It is, I would argue, largely as a result of the performances he encourages from his actors. Romain Duris plays Paul as effectively collapsed in upon himself, hidden behind his beard, moving with agonizing slowness, struggling even to lift his eyes to his interlocutor. He gives an impression of unlimited weariness, as though barely able to hold his body upright, as indeed his constant return to the horizontal demonstrates over the course of the film. Louis Garrel, by contrast, is altogether hyperactive, and anecdotal evidence would suggest that, for some viewers, his restless, overexcited turn as Jonathan is the hardest aspect of *Dans Paris* to swallow. It is true that, in his admiration for Jean-Pierre Léaud, Garrel risks aping his predecessor's tendency toward exaggerated theatricality which, beyond the naturalistic innocence of *Les Quatre cents coups* (1959), often rendered Léaud's performances enjoyable but rather unbelievable. But it is important to grasp a certain counterpoint in the acting and characterization of *Dans Paris* that opposes Jonathan's openness and spontaneity to Paul's enclosure within himself and inability to communicate, Jonathan's continuous patter and the sheer rapidity of his speech with Paul's mumbled monosyllables and thousand-yard stares. It is, I suggest, the seriousness of the subject matter that allows Honoré to anchor Garrel's performance and exert a degree of control over the actor's natural ebullience. His performance is, after all, nuanced enough to show Jonathan following his brother with concerned eyes, even as he clowns around under the shower.

For the relationship between these two brothers turns out to be at the heart of Honoré's film. This is clear from the close-up two-shot of the two brothers, articulated around a warm bedside lamp, in which the stakes of the film's narrative wager are laid: as already mentioned, Jonathan bets Paul that he can make it from the apartment to the Bon Marché store in under half an hour and, if he pulls it off, Paul must emerge from his torpor to go and join him. In other words, Jonathan's picaresque trajectory across the city is not as playfully aimless as it may appear, but instead signifies the younger brother's desire to entice his beloved sibling out of his catastrophic depression. Not only that, but Jonathan's casual sleeping around during the course of his wander does not simply demonstrate his vanity, egotism, and irresponsibility, as all the characters within the fiction insist, but is also his own defensive way of dealing with his fears for Paul's safety by seeking displaced comfort. As Jonathan himself admits at the end of the narrative, if he finds solace in the arms of a third woman it is because he is terrified that Paul, not answering his phone, may have killed himself: when he asks to kiss the girl (Annabelle Hettmann) in front of the department store windows, declaring it "a matter of life and death," he isn't joking. What separates Christophe Honoré's films perhaps most clearly from those of Jean-Luc Godard is, therefore, their focus on the family. As François Truffaut memorably said, no one, in any of Godard's first dozen movies, appears to have a family: no one discusses where they are from, or so much as mentions their parents or their childhood.[26] And if Godard is an extreme case, he is hardly exceptional: where families exist, in the French New Wave, they do so mainly in a form that stifles and constrains, present in the narrative only in order to be left behind. In Honoré's cinema, on the other hand—and perhaps we might relate this fact to his earlier career as a children's author—families are the object of complicated, ambivalent sentiments as they usually are in real life, at once infuriating hindrances and deeply necessary support structures regarded with profound affection. If it sounds far-fetched to say that Jonathan's womanizing in *Dans Paris* is accomplished, in a sense, "for" his brother, that is to overlook the logic of family communication that pertains elsewhere in the film. For Paul's depressive mutism is only the most visible manifestation of a generalized inarticulacy that reigns in the apartment: in the first scene between Jonathan and his father, the two get on each other's nerves in comical fashion, but the real stake of the scene is the concern of both for Paul, which each struggles for formulate, and their encounter becomes more poignant in retrospect, when we know that Jonathan has learned of his brother's suicide attempt during the night. The family's unarticulated sadness is deepened by the phantom presence of Claire, the sister of Paul and Jonathan, who committed suicide at seventeen, having been haunted by an inexplicable sorrow throughout her life. When Paul raises the issue with his father, the latter appears at first uncomfortable and then defensive; and when he later broaches it with his ex-wife, she changes the subject.

When Paul finally does talk about Claire, it is to a stranger, Jonathan's girlfriend Alice, who has come to the apartment to wait for him. The scene demonstrates the importance of outsiders in releasing the pressure and altering the perspective that can take hold within an unhealthy family atmosphere. But it also sets up the two key final sequences of the film, two of Honoré's most audacious conceits, again borrowing heavily from the New Wave. First, there is the sequence in which Paul and Anna sing a duet to each other over the telephone, a scene which is credible as an expression of overpowering emotion precisely because we have watched Paul holding his feelings in all day. The awkwardness of this scene is similarly prepared by the abundant evidence of emotional inarticulacy provided by the film, given that neither Romain Duris nor Joanna Preiss seems entirely confident of their singing voices and therefore the duet emerges only hesitantly. The film's last important scene occurs when Jonathan finally returns home and, in Paul's room, asks his older brother to read to him from a children's book. What begins as a sort of joke, with Paul reading quickly and in a rather sarcastic tone, gradually becomes more moving, through the tight framing in extreme close-ups on the pages of the book and the faces of the brothers, and in Paul's increasingly soft and slow reading. Without overemphasizing his point, Honoré allows the children's narrative to stand as a metonymic representation of the film's story, since it teaches of the importance of trying to empathize with other people's fears. Now, appealing to another text entirely at a crucial juncture of the film is, as we know, a technique common in the films of Jean-Luc Godard. Admittedly Godard almost never uses the full text of another work, preferring fragmentary quotations. However, this insertion of Grégoire Solotareff's *Loulou* into *Dans Paris* is comparable to Godard's use of whole pop songs in some of his films (Aznavour's "Tu te laisses aller" in *Une femme est une femme* and Ferrat's "Ma môme" in *Vivre sa vie* [1962]), a device already borrowed by Honoré in the scene in which Paul mumbles along to Kim Wilde's "Cambodia" alone in his room. What I want to suggest, however, in conclusion, is that Godard often seeks to import emotion wholesale into his films through the quotation of other artworks (as he would frequently do, later, with Beethoven, or the ECM musicians), whereas in *Dans Paris* the intertexts are coloured with the emotion already generated by the film.

"Cambodia" is not in itself a particularly moving record, but it becomes so through the spectacle of Paul's tentative desire to break out of his lethargy, his distant gaze suggesting a bittersweet communion with a younger self. Similarly, the reading of *Loulou* touches us because it makes visible the fraternal affection that the film has gradually built up through its narrative detours and its nuanced performances. If Christophe Honoré is the most worthy inheritor of Godard and the New Wave currently working in French cinema, in my contention it is because his stylistic games and self-regarding cleverness are embedded in an emotional maturity that was too often missing from the work of Godard and his peers.

NOTES

1 Philippe Azoury and Gérard Lefort, "Quinzaine des réalisateurs," *Libération*, May 26, 2006.
2 Christophe Honoré, interview by Jean-Baptiste Morain, *Les Inrockuptibles*, October 3, 2006.
3 Azoury and Lefort, "Quinzaine des réalisateurs."
4 Carlos Gomez, "Mon frère, ce héros," *Le Journal du dimanche*, October 1, 2006.
5 Honoré, interview by Morain.
6 Emmanuèle Frois, "Christophe Honoré très Nouvelle Vague," *Le Figaro*, October 4, 2006.
7 Jean-Michel Frodon, "Jo et Paul vont en bateau," *Cahiers du cinéma* 616 (October 2006): 25.
8 See Isabelle Regnier, "Christophe Honoré: 'Je n'accorde aucune importance au scénario,'" *Le Monde*, May 23, 2007.
9 Honoré states that this shot is taken from a series of tests effected in order to check light conditions a fortnight prior to the start of shooting proper. He notes that, while Garrel is simply himself in this shot, Duris is already inhabiting his character. See Cyril Neyrat, "Ces deux comédiens composent une photo de famille du cinéma français," *Cahiers du cinéma* 616 (October 2006): 27.
10 Jean-Pierre Esquenazi has suggested that Godard invented a new type of scene combining elements of the "scène de ménage," or slightly farcical domestic dispute traditional in French cinema, and the love scene drawn from American comedies. *Godard et la société française des années 1960* (Paris: Armand Colin, 2004), 84.
11 Richard Dyer, *Pastiche* (London: Routledge, 2007), 1.
12 Ibid., 56.
13 François-Guillaume Lorrain, "*Dans Paris*," *Le Point*, September 28, 2006. The view was shared by *La Tribune Desfossés*, October 4, 2006, and *Le Nouvel Obervateur*, October 5, 2006.
14 Dyer, *Pastiche*, 4.
15 Ibid., 130.
16 Ibid., 81.
17 Naomi Greene, *The French New Wave: A New Look* (London: Wallflower, 2007), 9.
18 François Truffaut, quoted in Greene, *French New Wave*, 9.
19 Anne Gillain, ed., *Le Cinéma selon François Truffaut* (Paris: Flammarion, 1988), 45.

20 Gomez, "Mon frère, ce héros."
21 Christophe Honoré, interview by Dominique Widemann, *L'Humanité*, October 4, 2006.
22 Frodon, "Jo et Paul vont en bateau," 24.
23 Isabelle Regnier, "Les acteurs peuvent être des singes carnivores," *Le Monde*, May 27, 2006.
24 Neyrat, "Ces deux comédiens," 27.
25 Manny Farber, *Negative Space: Manny Farber on the Movies* (London: Studio Vista, 1971), 262.
26 François Truffaut, cited in Antoine de Baecque, *Godard: Biographie* (Paris: Grasset, 2010), 673–74.

BIBLIOGRAPHY

Azoury, Philippe, and Gérard Lefort. "Quinzaine des réalisateurs." *Libération*, May 26, 2006.

De Baecque, Antoine. *Godard: Biographie*. Paris: Grasset, 2010.

Dyer, Richard. *Pastiche*. London: Routledge, 2007.

Esquenazi, Jean-Pierre. *Godard et la société française des années 1960*. Paris: Armand Colin, 2004.

Farber, Manny. *Negative Space: Manny Farber on the Movies*. London: Studio Vista, 1971.

Frodon, Jean-Michel. "Jo et Paul vont en bateau." *Cahiers du cinéma* 616 (2006): 24–26.

Frois, Emmanuèle. "Christophe Honoré très Nouvelle Vague." *Le Figaro*, October 4, 2006.

Gillain, Anne, ed. *Le Cinéma selon François Truffaut*. Paris: Flammarion, 1988.

Gomez, Carlos. "Mon frère, ce héros." *Le Journal du dimanche*, October 1, 2006.

Greene, Naomi. *The French New Wave: A New Look*. London: Wallflower, 2007.

Honoré, Christophe. Interview by Dominique Widemann. *L'Humanité*, October 4, 2006.

———. Interview by Jean-Baptiste Morain. *Les Inrockuptibles*, October 3, 2006.

Lorrain, François-Guillaume. "*Dans Paris*." *Le Point*, September 28, 2006.

Neyrat, Cyril. "Ces deux comédiens composent une photo de famille du cinéma français." *Cahiers du cinéma* 616 (2006): 26–27.

Regnier, Isabelle. "Christophe Honoré: 'Je n'accorde aucune importance au scenario.'" *Le Monde*, May 23, 2007.

———. "Les acteurs peuvent être des singes carnivores." *Le Monde*, May 27, 2006.

2

Jean-Luc Godard: *Dans le noir du temps* (2002)— The "Filming" of a Musical Form

Jürg Stenzl

THE ONLY PROJECTS in which Jean-Luc Godard made primary or even exclusive use of a single pre-existing work of music (or a movement from such a work) as a film score are his four film-essays *Lettre à Freddy Buache* (1982), *De l'origine du XXIᵉ siècle* (2000), *Liberté et patrie* and *Dans le noir du temps* (both 2002).

Dans le noir du temps was Godard and Anne-Marie Miéville's concluding contribution to the omnibus film *Ten Minutes Older: The Cello*. In many respects it seems at once like a backward glance at, and a further projection of, his *Histoire(s) du cinéma*, being what might be called a "four-years-older view" of the monumental *Histoire(s)*. In the same film Godard and Miéville also incorporated several quotations from *The Old Place*, an essay created for the Museum of Modern Art in 1998, the same year that *Histoire(s)* was completed.[1]

"*Tout de même, tu m'avoueras que tout cela est bien triste*" ("All the same, you have to admit that it is all very sad"). Thus the question of human happiness in *De l'origine du XXIᵉ siècle* (2000). The answer: "*Mais, mon cher, le bonheur n'est pas gai*" ("But my dear man, happiness is not merry"). Anne-Marie Miéville had wanted a slightly more upbeat ending for *Dans le noir du temps*, something like "the last minutes of hypocrisy." Then came September 11. Godard added: "We weren't capable of doing it. It was Bin Laden's fault."[2]

AN "OMNIBUS FILM" AFTER HERZ FRANK

Wim Wenders's central idea for the two omnibus films *Ten Minutes Older: The Trumpet* and *Ten Minutes Older: The Cello* was to combine several (seven and eight, respectively) ten-minute episodes by fifteen different directors. The point of departure was *Par desmit minutem vecaks*, the extraordinary documentary film of 1978 by the Latvian filmmaker Herz Frank (b. 1926), which was released worldwide as Frank's masterpiece with the English title *Ten Minutes Older* and received many awards. Within the space of ten minutes all that can be seen are the faces of children rapturously watching a sort of marionette play between Good and Evil. The observer, however, sees and hears nothing of the story being performed, but only the faces and reactions of the children, whose intense expressions and gestures seem to tell a multitude of further stories. The film was accompanied by specially composed music by Ludgards Gedravicus and Jirji Pauer (with solo clarinet, solo flute, and a small instrumental ensemble), who perhaps relate another story or stories—audible *Histoire(s)* …

At first the producers Nicholas McClintock, Nigel Thomas, and Ulrich Felsberg approached seven film directors with the temporal theme of "ten minutes." Then Aki Kaurismäki, Victor Erice, Werner Herzog, Jim Jarmusch, Wim Wenders, Spike Lee, and Chen Kaige created *Ten Minutes Older: The Trumpet*, each independently of the others. Their contributions were linked with music composed by Paul Englishby for the trumpeter Hugh Masekela. The producers found the result so convincing that in the same year, 2002, they invited another eight well-known directors—

Table 2.1 *Godard's "Final Minutes" and "Final Vision"*

		1'26"
LES DERNIÈRES MINUTES	**THE FINAL MINUTES**	
de la jeunesse	of youth (1)	0'49"
du courage	of courage (2)	0'32"
de la pensée	of thought (3)	0'16"
de la mémoire	of memory (4)	1'23"
de l'amour	of love (5)0'31"	
du silence	of silence (6)	1'11"
de l'histoire	of history (7)	1'10"
de la peur	of fear (8)	1'09"
de l'éternel	of the eternal (9)	0'43"
du cinéma	of cinema (10)	0'40"
DERNIÈRE VISION	**FINAL VISION**	
soir	evening	
dit-il	he says	0'45"
dit-elle	she says	
disent-ils	they say	
		———
		10'35"

Bernardo Bertolucci, Mike Figgis, Jiří Menzel, István Szabó, Claire Denis, Volker Schlöndorff, Michael Radford, and Jean-Luc Godard—to create an analogous film entitled *Ten Minutes Older: The Cello*. In the second film it was the cellist Claudia Bohórquez who played Englishby's connecting pieces of music.

The double film is dedicated, of course, to Herz Frank, as well as his young, early deceased Riga colleague Juris Podnieks and a founding father of French documentary film, Chris Marker, the director of *La Jetée* (1962) and *Sans soleil* (1983), which takes its title from Modest Mussorgsky's famous song cycle *Sunless*.

Godard's contribution is the only one in either film that dispenses with actors. Instead, like *Histoire(s) du cinéma*, it is made up largely of images, film excerpts, and textual quotations. Still, Godard takes the title quite literally: his short film, which also brings the entire project to a close with regard to content, takes the "ten minutes" in the sense of ten "final minutes," each labelled with a corresponding title card. At the end, as a sort of epilogue, is a "Final Vision" (*Dernière Vision*) (see Table 2.1).

VISUAL TIME AND ACOUSTICAL TIME

Godard's manner of structuring the predefined total duration of ten minutes is remarkable and reveals surprising parallels to the way composers work. The Swiss composer Klaus Huber once remarked, following the premiere of a work by Karlheinz Stockhausen that had occasioned puzzlement and discomfort (a reaction Huber shared), "Granted, but it is obvious that Stockhausen is a master of musical time. Never does a caesura or an event come 'too soon' or 'too late.'"[3] (Not surprisingly, the remark applies equally well to Huber's own music.) Given the temporal nature of film as an art form, it would have been logical to partition the total duration into ten approximately one-minute segments for the ten "chapters" of *Dans le noir du temps*. But Godard's mastery of cinematic time is not orientated on a ticking clock: the average length of each of the "ten minutes" (excluding the prologue and epilogue) amounts to some 50 seconds, with the roughly equally long Chapters 6 to 8 (*silence*, *histoire* and *peur*) forming a temporal midpoint. To view this as a grouping of the twelve segments is, I feel, pure speculation, because the *cinematic temporal structure*, with Prologue (the first one-and-a-half minutes), Minutes 1–10 and Final Vision (45"), amounting to a total of 10'35", is artfully combined with a *musical temporal structure*. In *Dans le noir du temps*, as so often in Godard's films, it is instructive to *watch* the film *without sound* and to *listen* to it *without pictures*. This has indeed actually happened in the case of *Nouvelle Vague* and the whole of *Histoire(s) du cinéma*, whose soundtracks have been released on CD by ECM—which brings us to the music that Godard used in this film.

THE MUSIC IN *DANS LE NOIR DU TEMPS*

As different as these ten "final minutes" may be in their duration and contents, they have a highly unified, continuous, slowly revolving musical basis from a composer who, like Herz Frank, hails from the Baltic countries: *Peegel peeglis*, better known by its German title *Spiegel im Spiegel* ("Mirror in the mirror," 1978), by the Estonian composer Arvo Pärt (b. 1935). For his film, as befits an omnibus film subtitled *The Cello*, Godard chose the version for cello and piano, which, according to the composer's specifications, lasts nine to ten minutes. Purely mathematically, the 126 bars of *Spiegel im Spiegel*, written in 6/4 metre, last 9'27" if played at the prescribed unchanging tempo of a quarter note = ca. 80. Yet the ECM recording Godard used, performed by Dietmar Schwalke and Alexander Malter, is considerably shorter at 8'57", averaging a quarter note = 84.[4]

Even those who cannot read music and do not play the piano will be able to recognize, on the first of the score's seven pages, what the ear readily comprehends (see Fig. 2.1). The right hand of the piano plays evenly pulsating quarter notes in an undulating motion that continues without interruption to the end of bar 126. Each of the first three bars contains two identical three-note broken chords consisting of the pitches c^2–f^2–a^2. In bar 2 the left hand plays an octave F in the lowest register of the instrument, as happens again in bars 6 and 10. This *three-bar group*, enclosed in a box and marked with an X in our music example, occurs unchanged 18 times from the opening to the final six bars of the piece, and thus in 54 of the total of 126 bars. Indeed, it occurs no fewer than four times in our music example. At the fourth occurrence, however, the left hand no longer plays a low octave F in the middle of the three bars, but a very high octave C.

Very low and very high pitches of this sort also occur in the second halves of bars not included in the boxed three-bar groups: the high c's in bars 4, 12, and 15, and the high f^3 in bars 8 and 18. They sound like bell strokes; indeed, Pärt himself has called this compositional device his tintinnabular or "bell style." The bell tones, whether high or low, are added to the first layer, the "undulating" quarter note motion. Arrows in the music example indicate when the same pitches are found both in the undulating broken chords and in the "bell notes." This is not the case in bars 4 (c^3), 8 (f^3), or 18 (f^3), but very much so in bars 10, 12, 15, and 17.

Initially one bar (mm. 4 and 8) is interpolated between the identical three-note groups marked X, then two bars (mm. 12–13 and 17–18), each time with new chordal material. These bars are labelled A, B, C, and D in our example. The number of "interpolated pitches/bars" increases incrementally to eight. As early as bars 12–13 (with initial pitches a^1 and bb^1) and 17–18 (with initial pitches e^2 and d^2) it becomes clear that the new pitches

Fig. 2.1 *Arvo Pärt's* Spiegel im Spiegel, *mm. 1–18. (Universal Edition, Vienna [1978])*

in bars 12–13 move upwards (a^1– bb^1) while those in bars 17–18 move downwards (e^2–d^2), and thus in the very "mirror relation" mentioned in the work's title, *Spiegel im Spiegel*. When three pitches are later interpolated after the X groups in bars 22–24 and 28–30, the first three (*b–a–g*) again move downward and the following three (*d–e–f*) move upward, and so forth, until the entire octave scale (ascending from *G* to *g* and descending from d to D) is introduced in bars 102–109 and 113–120. Thereafter the piece comes to an end with a final (duplicate) occurrence of the three-bar group X, again unchanged.

The isolated bars A to E interpolated between the X groups, as well as the bars F to H that follow, are defined by their initial pitches, that is, the bottom pitches of their broken chords (bb^1 in A, d^2 in B, a^1 in C, e^2 in D). Half of these chords are tonally consonant in the conventional sense of the term, while the other half are dissonant (and thus analogous to the "bell notes" added to the undulating motion). Equally analogous are the intervallic differences between the chords themselves: 4–6 in X (c), 5–2 in A and B (d), 3–4 in C (c), and 4–3 in D (c). In other words, half are consonant (c) while the other half are dissonant (d).

Finally, in addition to the undulating and tintinnabular levels, there is a third level, namely, that of the solo instrument, in this case the cello. It is firmly connected with the undulating motion for the full length of the piece, since it also sustains the highest pitch in the broken chord during the entire bar (or during the entire three-bar group). In our example these pitches are enclosed in boxes and connected by reference lines. In other words, the cello does not play a "melody" in dotted whole notes, but rather ascending (or ascending-scalar) segments, beginning with isolated pitches (mm. 4 and 8) and extending to f–g, c^1–bb, and so forth.

Thus, the very first page of the score reveals that Pärt, as has been characteristic of "minimal music" in the United States since the early 1960s, composed what Steve Reich calls "music as process"—a process that is precisely defined by rules set down by the composer, and that evolves rigorously from its beginning to its logical destination.[5] The music consists of very precisely subdivided and expanding units of time.

Two basic features of *Spiegel im Spiegel* are fundamental to Godard's film. The first is the internal unity of the evolving process, that is, the additive expansion of the nucleus heard in its opening bars and restarted at every recurrence of the three-bar group X. It creates the impression of a successively and imperceptibly evolving circular motion, a motion rooted to the spot. The second is that the extremely limited musical material is constantly changing, namely through octave transpositions in high and low registers. The constant expansion, beginning with the fundamental c^2 of three-note group X and proceeding upward and downward into the upper and lower octave, respectively, opens up a successively expanding tonal space that only comes to an end shortly before the conclusion, following the descending eight-note scale (mm. 113–120), by returning to its starting point, the (duplicated) X group. At the same time, this "global processuality" of *Spiegel im Spiegel*—a circular movement in situ—entails a continuous *spatialization* of the sound, thereby preventing the visual dynamism of the film from conflicting with musical staticity. The progress from the first to the last of the *"dernières minutes"* plus epilogue in the visual temporal structure stands in opposition to a musical temporal structure that differs in kind: "motionlessness and evolution" in image and sound alike, a combination that has played a central role in Godard's late work. The key prerequisite for this sort of combination of image and sound is the highly developed feeling for music in Jean-Luc Godard, the musician.

COUNTERPOINT OF IMAGE AND SOUND

To illustrate this combination of image and sound, it is useful first to examine the film's dramatic structure. There is one thing that *Dans le noir du temps*, unlike, say, Godard's *Armide* (1987), definitely does not set out to do: to *interpret* a work of music in and with the resources inherent to cinema. At the same time, there is not the slightest doubt that Pärt's music does not, in this short film, fill the role of conventional "film music" by replicating the pictures. The processual autonomy of the music vis-à-vis the autonomy of the extremely contrasting images of the "ten minutes" constitutes the film's true *invention* in the sense of Johann Sebastian Bach's *Two-Part Inventions*—in that the music and the images contrapuntally interact.

The "score" of the film (reproduced in the Appendix [Table 2.3]) assigns labels to the "ten minutes," primarily references to textual quotations and excerpts from Godard's own films. An attempt was made to transcribe both the diegetic and the voice-over texts as accurately as possible.[6] (The time markings are taken from the DVD, beginning at Chapter 9.)

The music does not begin until shortly before the end of a sort of prologue (84'26" ff.) in which the question of the darkness of the times (the *"noir du temps"* of the title) is posed and an answer is provided by the old man, the film director Vicky (this is a quotation from Godard's *For Ever Mozart* [1996]). The activating word is *"étoiles"* (stars). From then on *Spiegel im Spiegel* is heard without interruption, albeit with two telling fade-outs. The first comes at the end of Minute 4 (*"mémoire,"* mm. 48 ff., 87'33–43") with the images of corpses being dragged from a concentration camp, images that Godard has quoted several times elsewhere. Pärt's music again becomes audible at the sung opening of Minute 5 (*"amour"*), *"Dites moi quand il est temps de partir, l'heure de mourir"* ("Tell me when it is time to leave, time to die," mm. 50 ff., 87'43"). It fades out a second time at the end of Minute 7 (*"histoire"*) at the final repetition of King Lear's words "She's gone forever!" (m. 89, 89'57"), with the appearance of a harrowing image of a dead woman lying on the shore of Lake Geneva and a back-lit rear view of Lear (from Godard's *King Lear* [1987]). Music becomes inaudible at

21

"Death," or, as in Minute 2 ("*peur*"), it is rendered inaudible by the cries of the victims and the noise of war. Precisely this inaudibility or drowning out of music makes it clear that here, too, music, though it has been statically revolving throughout almost the entire film, is related to the overall film virtually as an autonomous element of the plot. It withdraws for a brief moment into the inaudible.

When a single element—the three-bar group we have marked "X"—recurs 18 times at ever-increasing intervals, as in *Spiegel im Spiegel*, the question arises, as in the use of Ravel's *Boléro* in *Lettre à Freddy Buache*, regarding how the sectional articulation of the film into "Prologue—Minutes 1 to 10—Epilogue: *Dernière Vision*" relates to the musical structure with its own internal "process." How were the formal design of the music and the sectional articulation of the film coordinated, and how are they related to the Final Vision, in whose middle the musical "process" of Pärt's *Spiegel im Spiegel* comes to an end (93'00")?

Table 2.2 illustrates the interaction between picture and music. The left half summarizes the series of X groups and interpolated bars, each bar represented by a dot (•), together with the corresponding bar numbers. The right half lists the openings of the ten "final minutes." These openings are also indicated in the first column with a vertical stroke (|) to make visible the co-ordination between the musical and pictorial structures.

To begin with, this table shows that Godard's approach is anything but schematic. It is by no means the case that the ten "final minutes" invariably change at analogous positions, such as the beginning of an X group or the end of the interpolated bars. Minute 1 begins at bar 4, Minute 2 at bar 17 (both are found in our music example). The beginning of Minute 4 (m. 44), on the other hand, is different but comparable, occurring just before the ninth statement of X in bars 45–47. But then only Minute 8 (in m. 92) begins on the first bar following an X group (the 15th occurrence). Minute 3 begins at bar 24, one bar before the sixth occurrence of X. All the other beginnings (Minutes 6, 7, 9, and 10) enter in the ever-longer sections between the X groups. Minute 5 begins in the (inaudible!) bar 50 while the music has been faded out.

But here we notice a point in common that can hardly be accidental. Minutes 6, 7, 9, and 10 invariably begin at the second bar *after* a repeat of an X group, and thus at the very moment in which the cello starts its scalar motion from the first to the second pitch, proceeding at first to five pitches and then (twice) to eight. One might say that, following the silent opening of Minute 5, each of the remaining "minutes," even Minute 8 (which already begins in the first bar after X rather than waiting for the second bar), opens with those sections of the music that, unlike the motionlessness

Table 2.2 *Interrelation of Pärt's* Spiegel im Spiegel *and Godard's* Dans le noir du temps

Arvo Pärt, *Spiegel im Spiegel*			Jean-Luc Godard, *Dans le noir du temps*		
Music	*No. of bars*	*mm.*	*Picture*		
X |•ᵃ	3 + 1	1–4	1–3		Prologue–End (84′25″)
			m. 4	1st m. after X	1. Youth
X •	3 + 1	5–8			
X ••	3 + 2	9–13			
X |••	3 + 2	14–18	m. 17	1st m. after X	2. Courage
X •• |•	3 + 3	19–24	m. 24	3rd m. of X	3. Thought
X •••	3 + 3	25–30			
X ••••	3 + 4	31–37			
X •• |••	3 + 4	38–44	m. 44	3rd m. after X	4. Memory
X •• |•••	3 + 5	45–52	[m. 50	3rd m. after X]ᵇ	5. Love
X • |••••	3 + 5	53–60	m. 57	2nd m. after X	6. Silence
X ••••••	3 + 6	61–69			
X • |•••••	3 + 6	70–78	m. 74	2nd m. after X	7. History
X •••••••	3 + 7	79–88			
X |•••••••	3 + 7	89–98	m. 92	1st m. after X	8. Fear
X • |••••••••	3 + 8	99–109	m. 103	2nd m. after X	9. The Eternal
X • |••••••••	3 + 8	110–120	m. 114	2nd m. after X	10. Cinema
X	3	121–123			
X	3	124–126	m. 125		*Final vision*
			m. 126 (end)		"evening he says …"

a A vertical stroke (|) marks the beginning of the "final minute" indicated in the right-most column, and, as stated in the text, each dot (•) stands for one bar.
b Mm. 48–52 are faded out.

of X, contain *motion* or *change* (given that the motion is strictly scalar, the term "development" would be an exaggeration), even when this "motion" inevitably returns to the motionlessness of the X group.

This becomes especially clear when we compare the abrupt contrast in the *Dernière Vision* at the end of the film with the ten one-minute sections. Minute 10 ends with the penultimate X group of bars 121–123; the *Dernière Vision* begins in mid-measure during the final recurrence of X, the penultimate bar of *Spiegel im Spiegel*, with the repeat of the title card "SOIR DIT-IL." The corresponding title card that follows, "SOIR DIT-ELLE," is left without music. But then completely different music begins—mighty organ sounds that have nothing in common with the piano piece except that both were composed by Arvo Pärt: his organ piece *Trivium* of 1976, accompanied by the third title card, "SOIR DISENT-ILS" ("evening they say"). Just as the tintinnabula of *Spiegel im Spiegel* turn into the roaring of the organ, the image too now changes fundamentally: if a flickering candle in a cave was seen at the opening of the Final Vision, we now see richly coloured images of orientalesque masks, apparently part of a ritual whose intensive reds brighten the nocturnal darkness at the end of the film.

These correspondences between "motionlessness" and "motion," between the structure of the music and the sectional articulation of the images, may perhaps seem like an over-interpretation, or even an "analytical construct." However, no analysis of a work of art can *prove* its findings. In the case of *Dans le noir du temps*, there can be no question that Godard's musico-pictorial montage is based on a masterly handling of time and motion within time—a mastery both cinematic and musical in nature. It is the same sort of "temporal mastery" that Klaus Huber emphasized in Karlheinz Stockhausen. The correspondences between the pictorial quotations for the ten "final minutes" and the structural divisions of the music used in the film are all rooted in a cyclical structure. The music appears ahistorical, but in Minute 4, "*Les dernières minutes de la mémoire*," it falls silent, faced with the "ineradicable" ("*L'Imprescriptible*") of the concentration camp images. It is restored to audibility at "*Les denières minutes de l'amour*" to coincide with the singing of Anne-Marie Miéville's chanson "*Dites moi quand il est temps de partir, l'heure de mourir.*" It is precisely by falling silent, and by returning to audibility, that music is able to generate the deep impact of this moment.

Spiegel im Spiegel comes to an end after the repeated "SOIR DIT-IL" at the beginning of the Final Vision, following a quotation from Chapter 2B (4'35", CS 4'12")[7] of the *Histoire(s)*: Anna Magnani's fall in Rossellini's *Roma, città aperta* (1945), Shirley MacLaine's death as Ginny Moorehead in Vincente Minnelli's *Some Came Running* (1958).[8] But then the music is heard afresh in a completely different guise. The Final Vision is not an end, but an opening into a new and different world, a world with mighty sounds—and without words …

After the last of the ten "final minutes," Jean-Luc Godard's backward glance at the "darkness of the times"—at his *Histoire(s) du cinéma* (stories of the failure of an entire century) and at the origin of the 21st century (*De l'origine du XXIe siècle*)—ends in a *"Dernière Vision"* with the surely utopian possibility of a new and completely different era. We need only think of the final bars of *Abschied* in Gustav Mahler's *Das Lied von der Erde*. What follows upon an ending of this sort is a question for the future, and thus a question for all who have passed through *Dans le noir de temps*—with eyes *and* ears equally open.

Translated from the German original by J. Bradford Robinson

Appendix

(Table 2.3)

TEN MINUTES OLDER: THE CELLO (GB/F 2002), Nr. 8 (CD # 9):

Jean-Luc Godard: *Dans le noir du temps*

83'10"	[waves]			
83'27–56"	Signature JLG			
83'58"	**DANS LE NOIR DU TEMPS**			
		JLG, *For Ever Mozart* (1996) [text, 39 ff.] [23'59"–24'27"]	Pourquoi fait-il noir la nuit, Monsieur Vicky? Peut-être qu'autrefois l'univers avait encore votre âge et que le ciel resplendissait de lumière, et puis que le monde a vielli il s'éloigne, et quand je regarde le ciel entre deux étoiles	Why is the night dark, Monsieur Vicky? Perhaps because the universe was once as young as you are and heaven glowed in the light. As the world got older, heaven drew away from the world. When I look at the sky between two stars,
84'26"	**Start of music: Arvo Pärt, *Spiegel im Spiegel***			
			je ne peux donc voir que ce qui a disparu.	I see only what has disappeared.
84'36"	BLACKOUT			
84'36"	[1.] **LES MINUTES DERNIÈRES**			
84'40"	**DE LA JEUNESSE**			

84'43"		JLG, *Made in USA* (1966) [57'39–47" and 75'05–27"]	Si je te parle du temps, c'est qu'il n'est pas encore, si je te parle d'un lieu, c'est qu'il a disparu.	If I talk to you about time, it is because it hasn't come; if I talk to you about a place, it is because it has vanished;
84'55"			Si je te parle du temps, c'est qu'il n'est déjà plus. [Queneau, *L'Explication des métaphores*] Si tu devais mourir, tu préfères qu'on te prévienne ou que la mort arrive tout à coup? Tout à coup! Maman! Si je te parle d'un homme, il sera bientôt mort.	if I talk to you about time, it is because it is no longer. If you had to die, would you rather be warned or should it come suddenly? Suddenly. Mama! If I talk to you about a man, he will soon be dead.
85'26"	BLACKOUT			
85'28"	**[2.] LES DERNIÈRES MINUTES DU COURAGE**	ibid., [89'29"– 33"]	Oh Paula, tu m'as dérobé ma jeunesse.	O, Paula, you've stolen my youth.
85'36"	BLACKOUT			
85'39"		JLG, *De l'origine du XXIᵉ siècle* (2000) [3'18"]		
85'46"	BLACKOUT			

(continued next page)

85'48"		[3'22"]	[Vietnamese woman, soldier]	
85'51"		[2'58"]	[Hanged women]	
85'59"	BLACKOUT			

86'00"	**[3.] LES**			
	DERNIÈRES			
	MINUTES			
86'03"	**DE LA**			
	PENSÉE			
86'06"		[stairway/ garbage bags]		
86'12"		JLG, *For Ever Mozart* (1996), [text, 37], [21'57"–22'17"]	[AMM]: Je pense, donc je suis. Le jeu du "je suis." Il n'est plus le même que le "je" de "je pense." Pourquoi?	"I think, therefore I am." The game of "I am." It's no longer the same as the "I" in "I think." Why?
		[22'41–56"]	Le sentiment que j'ai de l'existence n'est pas encore un "moi."	The sense I have of existence is not yet an "I."
86'38"		[table/books, JLG]	C'est un sentiment irréfléchi, il y est en moi, mais sans "moi."	It's an unreflective sense; it's inside me, but without an "I."
86'47"			JLG: Oh, on ne peut rien dire de rien.	JLG: But nothing can be said about nothing.
			C'est pourquoi [il faut] voir mythes ou nombre de livres. Tous les corps, ensemble, et tous les esprits et toutes leurs productions ne valent pas le moindre mouve- ment de charité.	That's why we [have to] look at myths or countless books. All bodies together, and all minds together, and all their products, are not worth the least charitable impulse.

			Cela est d'un ordre infiniment plus élevé. [Pascal, *Pensées*]	This is of an order infinitely more exalted. [Pascal, *Pensées*]
87'07"	BLACKOUT			
		[garbage truck]	[Cela fait partie de l'infini.]	It forms part of the infinite.
87'14"	BLACKOUT			
87'16"	**[4.] LES DERNIÈRES MINUTES DE LA MÉMOIRE**			
87'23"		[concentration camp, corpses]		
87'31"	L'IMPRE-SCRIPTIBLE			
87'33"	**Music** interrupted until 87'43"			
87'34"		[concentration camp, corpses]		
87'39"	BLACKOUT			
87'39"	**[5.] LES DERNIÈRES MINUTES**			
87'43"	**DE L'AMOUR**		[Chanté:] 'Dites moi quand il est temps de partir, l'heure de mourir' Chanson de Anne-Marie Miéville)— Eh bien oui, tu es jeune, tu es dans ta beauté et dans ta force.	[Sung:] "Tell me when it's time to go, time to die." [Song by Anne-Marie Miéville]— You're young, you're beautiful and strong.
87'49"		[woman's head]		

(continued next page)

			Essaye donc. Moi, je vais mourir. Adieu, adieu. Je ne veux pas te quitter, je ne veux pas te reprendre, je ne veux rien, rien, rien. J'ai les genoux par terre et mes reins brisés. Ne me parle de rien.	So try! I shall die. Farewell, farewell. I don't want to leave you, I don't want you back. I want nothing. I'm down on my knees, my back is broken, I don't want to hear anything.
			Tu m'avais blessée et offensée, et je te l'avait dit aussi. Nous ne nous aimons plus, nous ne nous sommes pas aimés … [lettre de G. Sand à Musset, 1835]	You've hurt and insulted me, and I told you so. We don't love each another anymore, we've never loved each other … [Letter from G. Sand to Musset, 1835]
88'11"		BLACKOUT		

88'11"	[6.] LES DERNIÈRES MINUTES DU SILENCE			
88'20"	BLACKOUT			
88'23"		JLG, *Le Petit soldat* (1960)	C'est à qui que vous téléphoniez? Quel numéro vous aviez?	Who did you phone? What number did you have?
		[55'29" & 35"]	Qui et quel numéro?	Who and what number?
88'39"	BLACKOUT			
88'47"	BLACKOUT			

88'48"		Qui et quel numéro? C'est à qui que vous téléphoniez?	Who and what number? Who did you phone?
89'00"	BLACKOUT		
89'04"		Quel numéro? Qui et quel numéro?	What number? Who and what number?
89'17"	BLACKOUT		

89'19"	**[7.] LES DERNIÈRES MINUTES DE L'HISTOIRE**		
89'26"	BLACKOUT		
89'27"			And in me too the wave rises.
89'30"		JLG, *King Lear* (1987) [84'33"]	It swells; it arches its back. I am aware [once more] of a smart desire, something rising beneath me like the proud horse whose rider first spurs and then pulls back. Against you I will fling myself unvanquished
89'54"	BLACKOUT		and unyielding,
89'57"			O Death! [V. Woolf, *The Waves*] She's gone forever! [2x] I know when one is dead, and when one lives. [2x]

(continued next page)

31

				[She's dead as earth.] Lend me a looking-glass. [Shakespeare, *King Lear*, V/iii]
90'28"	BLACKOUT			

90'30"	**[8.] LES DERNIÈRES MINUTES DE LA PEUR**			
90'38"		JLG, De *l'origine du XXIe siècle* (2000) [13'25"]		
90'41"	BLACKOUT			
90'41"		[battle scene]	[…]	
90'53"	BLACKOUT		bien, et après? Venez avec moi. […]	good, and afterwards? Come with me.
90'55"		JLG, *The Old Place* (1999) [12'05"]	Prince Andrej répondait lui-même: "Je ne sais pas ce qui vient après. Je ne veux et je ne peux le savoir, mais si c'est cela que je veux, si je veux la gloire, si je veux être célèbre, si je veux être aimé des hommes … je ne suis pourtant pas coupable de le désirer, de ne désirer que cela." [Tolstoi, *Guerre et paix]*	Prince Andrew answered himself: "I don't know what will happen and I don't want to know, and can't, but if I want this—want glory, and to be known to men, want to be loved by them—it is not my fault that I want it and want nothing but that and live only for that." [Tolstoy, *War and Peace*]

91'19"	**[9.]**	**LES DERNIÈRES MINUTES DE L'ÉTERNEL**		
91'27"			P.P. Pasolini: *Il vangelo secondo Matteo* (1964) = JLG, *The Old Place* [28'29"]	
91'43"		BLACKOUT		
91'45"			[idem., Christ on the Cross]	
91'52"		BLACKOUT		
91'54"		VIVRE SA VIE	JLG, *Vivre sa vie* (1962)	
92'00"			[15'57"–16'06"]	Anna Karina
92'02"		BLACKOUT		
92'03"	**[10.]**	**LES DERNIÈRES MINUTES DU CINÉMA**		
92'12"			JLG, *The Old Place* (1999) [38'02"–39'11"]	Flickering screen (masquerade), from 92'29–41"
92'33"				double-exposed with child's head from S. Eisenstein, *Ivan the Terrible* (1945–46)
92'42"		BLACKOUT		
92'42"		**DERNIÈRE VISION**		
92'46"		BLACKOUT		

(continued next page)

33

92'48"	**DERNIÈRE** **VISION** **SOIR DIT-IL**		evening he says
92'51"		cave, candle	
92'59"	**SOIR** **DIT-IL**		evening he says
93'00"	**END OF MUSIC Arvo Pärt,** *Spiegel im Spiegel*		
93'01"	**SOIR** **DIT-ELLE**		evening he says
93'03"	**MUSIC Arvo Pärt,** *Trivium* **for organ**	[JLG, *Histoire(s)*, 2B, 4'12"]	
93'03"	**SOIR** **DISENT-ILS**		evening he says
93'05"		oriental masks[a]	
93'27–33"	BLACKOUT		

a It was only after the completion of this essay that André Habib (Montréal) drew my attention to Godard's film *Les Enfants jouent à la Russie* (1993), where similar masks can be seen beginning at 15'25", likewise accompanied by Arvo Pärt's organ work *Trivium*.

NOTES

1   These two films should be augmented with *De l'origine du XXIe siècle* (2000), commissioned by the Cannes Festival for its own anniversary, and *Liberté et patrie*, created for Switzerland's Expo 2002. All four were made available by the ECM publication of 2006 and are discussed in Chapter 6 of Jürg Stenzl's *Jean-Luc Godard—musicien* (2010).

2   Richard Brody, *Everything Is Cinema: The Working Life of Jean-Luc Godard* (New York: Metropolitan Books, 2008), 614.

3   The work in question was Stockhausen's *Kathinkas Gesang als Luzifers Requiem* for flute and six percussionists, premiered at Donaueschingen on October 16, 1983. It forms the second scene of *Samstag aus Licht*, work 52 (1983).

4   As the durations reproduced on CDs include the pause at the beginning of the next track, the duration of ECM 449 958-2 (Munich, 1999) is actually 9'15". Besides the version for cello and piano, the CD contains two different performances by Vladimir Spivakov and Sergey Bezrodny, the first lasting 10'19" (quarter note = 72–76), the

second 9'37" (quarter note = 76–80). The first is thus much slower than the specified metronome mark, the second (on average) slightly less so. Both versions have the same gentle *accelerando* of four metronome steps per minute. The sheet music is available from Universal Edition, Vienna, with the cello version bearing the catalogue number UE 30336 (© 1978, 1996, final rev. version 2004). *Spiegel im Spiegel* is dedicated to the violinist Vladimir Spivakov. The first version (1978) was written for violin and piano; later versions are for piano with oboe, clarinet, viola, double bass, or French horn.

5   For the origins of minimal music and its processual nature, see Klaus Ebbeke, "Minimal Music," *Schweizerische Musikzeitung/Revue musicale suisse* 122 (1982): 140–47.

6   The almost unattainable model for this approach is the "score" of the entire *Histoire(s) du cinéma* presented in Céline Scemama: *La "partition" des "Histoire(s) du cinéma de Jean-Luc Godard"* (Paris: Centre National de l'Image, 2006), http://cri-image.univ-paris1.fr/accueil.html, with source references for films, texts, and music.

7   The first time indication relates to the DVD of the Gaumont edition, the second to Céline Scemama's "score" of *Histoire(s) du cinéma* (see note 6).

8   Both are connected with Pärt's *Trivium* in Chapter 2B of *Histoire(s)*.

BIBLIOGRAPHY

Brody, Richard. *Everything Is Cinema: The Working Life of Jean-Luc Godard*. New York: Metropolitan Books, 2008.

Ebbeke, Klaus. "Minimal Music." *Schweizerische Musikzeitung/Revue musicale Suisse* 122 (1982): 140–47.

Scémama, Céline. *La "partition" des "Histoire(s) du cinéma de Jean-Luc Godard."* Paris: Centre National de l'Image, 2006. http://cri-image.univ-paris1.fr/accueil.html.

Stenzl, Jürg. *Jean-Luc Godard—musicien*. Munich: Text + Kritik, 2010.

3

Jean-Luc Godard and Contemporary Dance: The Judson Dance Theater Runs Across *Breathless*

John Carnahan

PHRASES

THE FOLLOWING ESSAY is an experiment in interdisciplinary criticism, towards importing a vocabulary for figure movement on film from the language of dance and performance art. It is inspired by a desire to describe the striking autonomy and clarity of figure movement in Jean-Luc Godard's films, a quality that seems to me as much a signature of Godard's direction as his aphoristic dialogue and essayistic narratives. The reader is asked to see Godard as a choreographer and maker of performance events, parallel in era, and often parallel in theory and practice, to contemporary choreographers like Merce Cunningham.

Specifically, I will use instances of admitted and likely influence that link Godard to the Judson Dance Theater—an influential *nouvelle vague* of 1960s dance that included Carolee Schneeman, Trisha Brown, Simone Forti, Deborah Hay, Steve Paxton, and Lucinda Childs, among others—as an occasion to point out sympathies between Godard's movement direction and contemporary choreography. A broader concern of this essay is to suggest the influence of the film medium on contemporary thinking about movement in general. The common ground between Jean-Luc Godard and the Judson choreographers, I would argue, is that they are both students of gesture as reproduced and analyzed by film. This convergence of interests is strongly demonstrated by the Judson group's citation of Godard in Yvonne Rainer's *Terrain* (1963). But before turning to the sourcing of the Judson choreographer Yvonne Rainer's 1963 *Terrain* from Godard's 1960 film *Breathless*, I would like to begin by considering the cinematic qualities of Rainer's more famous (and more easily viewed, on the internet) 1966 composition, *Trio A*. In this now-classic composition, dance subtly and literally incorporates cinema—an aesthetic that was heralded, three years earlier, by Rainer's sourcing of movement from Godard's *Breathless*.

Trio A is a sequence of movements to be performed in a continuous motion, which usually requires about four and a half minutes. The dancer must avoid repetition, eye contact, and above all, shows of effort, as opposed to what Rainer calls (her emphasis) the *actual* effort needed for the movement. Her distinction can be explained as follows: if I point out something to you on the Champs-Élysées, as your friend, my body enacts a muscular cycle to raise, sustain, and then release my arm; but if I point out something on stage, as a dancer, I will belabour the marshalling, sustaining, and ceasing of effort in order to *portray* that I am pointing. Dancers call this cycle of effort and/or of display a "phrase." If you see someone evidently phrasing, and then evidently repeating the phrase, he or she must be dancing, as opposed to merely moving.

Trio A is merely moving. This quality of movement was also called "ordinary" or "task-based" by Rainer and her colleagues in the Judson Dance Theater. *Trio A* seeks the "ordinary" by suppressing phrasing and repetition. As Rainer writes,

> One of the most singular elements in [*Trio A*] is that there are no pauses between phrases ... the end of each phrase merges immediately into the beginning of the next with no observable accent.... What is seen is a control that seems geared to the *actual* time it takes the *actual* weight of the body to go through the prescribed motions.... Endurance comes into play very much with its necessity for conserving (actual) energy (like the long-distance runner). The irony here is in the reversal of a kind of illusionism: I have exposed a type of effort where it has been traditionally concealed and concealed phrasing where it has been traditionally displayed.[1]

In *Being Watched: Yvonne Rainer and the 1960s*, Carrie Lambert-Beatty suggests that the showy phrasing and "heroic" postures the Judson dancers questioned may have been partly an artifact of dance's documentation by still images. Snapshots of artists like Vaslav Nijinsky or Martha Graham in mid-motion show how dance is supposed to look, so dancers try to produce, and their audiences try to find, what Rainer calls "moments of registration." Although *Trio A*'s "phraseless continuum of movement"[2] also looks gesticulating and blurry in photographs, in a viewing of Sally Banes's "antispectacular" film document, "in which a stationary camera frames a bare space where Rainer performs at a deliberate pace and with quiet concentration, *Trio A* chugs along like a well-running, if slightly quirky machine.... A danced summation of 1960s aesthetics, it beats on, funky but determined clockwork."[3] The Judson Dance Theater's low-key, "task-based" serialism is usually explained as "anti-theatrical," but perhaps it is also, in two senses of the phrase, pro-filmic.

For if the traditional dancer anticipates commemoration in a still image, the *Trio A* dancer seems to want to be filmed. Or to be a film. When Rainer returned to choreography with 1999's *Trio A Pressured*, she made her performers enact the sequence backwards. As Lambert-Beatty explains, dancing "in retrograde" is a "choreographic exercise in which the dancer reverses both the sequence of movements and the motions themselves ... like a film rewinding."[4] The fact that "rewinding" phrases has become a standard exercise, and sometimes a mode of performance, is a powerful sign of film's role in the imagination of contemporary dancers. Or rather contemporary dance is a powerful sign of film's role in the human imagination of movement.

Physical versus visual phrasing, clock-like continuity of action, effort sufficient to a real task versus feigned effort, and cinema as a school of movement—the concerns that Lambert-Beatty detects behind *Trio A*—are also, I would suggest, germane to a consideration of Jean-Luc Godard's *Breathless* from the perspective of choreography—and specifically, the sequence that Rainer and the Judson Dance Theater restaged in *Terrain*: the closing scene in which Jean-Paul Belmondo, as a petty crook who has been shot in the back by the police, staggers down a long, long street to his death.

In the distance with his back to us, Belmondo weaves down to the end of the street in a nearly minute-long following shot relieved only by a reverse angle insert of Jean Seberg running after him. The elements of suspense in this scene are the clearly demarcated length of the "stage," the startled, real-life foot and car traffic, past which runs Belmondo pressing his hand on the imaginary wound in his back; Belmondo's impossible task of running as fast as he can while pretending to die; his pace and stamina, and the camera operator's effort to track him without resorting to an edit. Belmondo alone can end the shot, by his decision to fall in the crosswalk where the side street meets the busy Boulevard Raspail. Then, after his ragged, attenuated *cinéma-vérité* run, the camera and the shoes of the cops and the skirt of his double-crossing girlfriend close in on the space around his supine body with a precise timing.

"I have made only one discovery in cinema," Godard told *Cahiers du cinéma* in 1967:

> I discovered this technique in *Breathless*, and have applied it system-
> atically ever since ... to move smoothly from one shot to another,
> when each shot has a different pace or movement, or even, which is

more difficult, to make an effective transition from a moving shot to a still shot ... you simply have to pick up movement on the same level at which it ended in the preceding shot [*reprendre le mouvement au stade où on l'a laissé dans l'image d'avant*]. In this way you can link one shot with any other shot; you can move from a car to a bicycle, or from a crocodile to an apple, for example.[5]

How is Godard's "discovery ... in *Breathless*" different from the "classical construction" he had explored as a critic, which also uses movement? The distinction seems to be that one starts with movement to build up a composition rather than starting with the composition and finding movements to illustrate it. As in choreography, movement is the material; a development or stage [*stade*] of movement is the unit, and the visual plane is the frame. Godard emphasizes to *Cahiers* that he means "editing in strict relation to what appears on film ... rather than cutting based on a change in ideas, as Rossellini does at the beginning of *India*, which is another problem altogether."[6] In the long conversation in Patricia's (Jean Seberg) hotel room, following the actors' movements *as a measure* differs in a subtle way from the classical tendency to cut up movements *as a means* to teleport across space and provide a curtain for changes of perspective: "If [alternatively] one adheres to formal editing practice," Godard tells *Cahiers*, "cuts must be restricted to moments when the person or thing in movement is hidden by another, or crosses another. Otherwise, there is a slight shock."[7] There are fewer shocks, less choppiness, when one soloist steps forward to replace another in a dance. Coincidentally, "picking up the movement" (equivalent to Godard's *reprendre le mouvement*) is part of the informal, descriptive vocabulary of dance in English. I have often heard a choreographer ask a dancer to "pick up the movement from where so-and-so left it."

Movement flows on, despite changes in background, despite even a change of figures. This is the continuity that permits *Breathless*'s famously "discontinuous" jump-cuts: for example, the three jumps at the hour-and-five-minute mark, as first Seberg, then a cop, then Belmondo, cross the same shop window from left to right—three solos, rather than a trio within one shot—three jump-cuts that barely register as separate but for the changing foot traffic in the background. Six years later, in *Made in U.S.A.*, this "pickup" transition, usually aided by a sound bridge, is, as Godard says, systematic: at 49 minutes a male actor rises away from a restaurant table toward screen right, cut to Anna Karina departing from a different table, in the same stage of the movement (unfolding, starting to walk), but in a garden.[8] Of course, continuity of screen position is an old principle in editing, and many films present movement continuity across a changing background; for a demonstration rooted in dance, see Maya Deren's

Choreography for Camera (1945) (the dancer's right foot raises in a forest, and lands in an apartment) and *At Land* (1944) (the plunging dancer becomes a falling pawn). Godard's feeling of discovery in *Breathless* may be his relief on finding that a conversation between lovers can likewise be edited according to the lovers' movement evolutions. Between cuts, the movement can take its own time. Movement is what the audience came to see.

Continuous movement in a dance composition, like *Trio A*, is obviously restricted by what Rainer calls *"actual* effort"—but film is not. The film hero's trusty horse, spliced together from several gallops, is never hungry, never balky, never winded—in the length of its phrases, this horse is more like a car. Likewise, Belmondo's always-scheming, always-smoking, always-running outlaw sustains a consistency of effort that is artificially and sometimes comically relentless. Whether or not his final run, interrupted (and therefore, prolonged) by the cut to Jean Seberg, represents a single take, when we see him on the ground, he is not winded—somehow, he is still smoking. The film's disregard for prop continuity (neckties, shirts, cigarettes in hands) is a disregard for the recuperative, caretaking stage of the effort cycle that continuous movement leaves behind.

Film is a clock that pulls images through its gears, and cuts or stretches human phrases (including the energy and fatigue of the audience) to fit mechanical and commercial periods. Lambert-Beatty sees the back-and-forth between bodily time and its mechanical modelling as a key interest of 1960s art, from works that use a snapshot or metronome-like phrasing to durational epics that "belabor the present" and implicitly pit the audience against a standard of witnessing set by the camera.[9] A symbol of this interest is the revival of Eadweard Muybridge's late-nineteenth-century movement studies—objects that can be either surveyed, as a long series of photographs, or animated, as short films—which became a template for works by everyone from Rainer and Sol LeWitt[10] to Godard and Andy Warhol. The coincidence of this trend in gallery art with Bazinian aesthetics of document-in-fiction, and with innovations in camera portability, focal range, and film sensitivity, made movement studies (think of Sam Peckinpah's gunfights, or Warhol's *Sleep* (1963), or Frederick Wiseman's cinéma-vérité, or pornography, or studies of the camera's own motion, like Ernie Gehr's *Serene Velocity* [1970]) the most typical attraction of 1960s and '70s cinema. *Breathless*— influenced by the documentary aspects of low-budget thrillers like Joseph Lewis's *Gun Crazy* (1950)—is early in using "durational" or "study" footage as a tool for storytelling. Afterward, the torch of the long-footage runner will pass to Buster Keaton, who scurries away from the camera in Samuel Beckett's *Film* (1965), just as he ran from the army of brides in *Seven Chances* (1925)—or just as Belmondo runs away from Raoul Coutard's Cineflex in *Breathless*—fate, in the succession from Keaton's Newtonian comedy to Beckett's and Godard's relativistic comedy, having become fully identified with the observer. Then, there is Dustin Hoffman, whose progress toward the observer in *The Graduate* (1967) is so attenuated by the telephoto lens that he seems to be (and, because he is an image on a screen, actually is) running in place. Hoffman replaces the running Achilles used by Zeno of Elea to illustrate the paradox of one's serial presence in the places through which one moves,[11] and this refutation of progress creates anxiety because it is framed in the story as a "race against time."

Godard's studies of running, although part of the plot, stand out for their quality of autonomy. The police have Belmondo at a disadvantage, so when he runs, unlike Hoffman, it is not toward anything that one can explain, any more than one can picture where he and Anna Karina will arrive as they run through *Pierrot le Fou* (1965). When movement defines the shot, the performer can commit to the movement like a dancer, rather than like an actor running toward a mark where he or she will deliver a line. Even if that line is to be filmed another day, everyone's consciousness of the theatre scene that is being approximated can change the quality of movement. During a 1980 interview with *Rolling Stone*, Godard, by way of explaining his Muybridge-like experiments in *Sauve qui peut (la vie)* (1979), suggests that the invention of the soundtrack pulled cinematic movement toward an average: "In silent films, there were huge differences in speed, which were determined by the actor, not the camera. Today, we've lost that and are always in the same rhythm. Silent films' rhythms were slowed down and immobilized by the lines spoken in sound movies, which is sometimes a good thing."[12] The fact that Godard's early actors were seldom filmed in sync sound thus goes a long way toward making them dancers. More generally, the compositional priority Godard has given to movement "ever since *Breathless*" makes the quality of movement in a shot at least as important as its narrative relation to other shots. When the camera watches Belmondo's actual effort without interruption, making one wonder how long the actor, and not just the character, can sustain his energy, the movement phrase per se becomes both the material and the subject, and a gangster-movie persona who is scripted to "die" is briefly installed in a mortal's body.

Trio A, too, reads as both presentational *and* representational movement. Non-referential walking, hopping, rocking, and circling sometimes throw off glimpses of Rainer's background in ballet, or Afro-Cuban, or Graham, or Cunningham technique. For Lambert-Beatty, these "images … cut into the perception of the dance as tautological, self-generating, in and of the performative moment. They freight *Trio A* with reference."[13] Since I am trying to suggest the qualities of *Breathless* that might have caught a Judson choreographer's eye, the reader may anticipate a comparison to *Breathless*'s mixture of document and pastiche. But I want to emphasize that, in both works, this mixture of "in the moment" and "freighted with reference" is not paradoxical. The more in the moment an event is, the less it can take sides that life does not take. If a professional dancer sets herself the challenge of making five minutes of constantly evolving motion, avoiding all dance postures would be kinesthetically impossible. And Belmondo's lip-rubbing quotations of Humphrey Bogart in *Breathless* are the sort of thing a moviegoer cannot help doing. A flow through *types* of movement forms the striking coherence of both works.

Considered as a human filmstrip, *Trio A* is a compilation montage of the Judson Dance Theater, which expanded the range of performable movement by treating ordinary gestures and traditional dance or theatre gestures as equals. The Judson choreographers put on stage the wide range of activity and inactivity seen offstage, in composition and rehearsal sessions. The language of improvisation "scores" by which they framed composition as performance, and its similarity to Godard's desire to "put everything into a film," will be explored in the next part of this essay.

SCORES

"Diagonals," the twelve-minute opening section of Yvonne Rainer's *Terrain* (Judson Dance Theater, 1963), promises to bring research (which in dance is kinetic, a dancer's personal exploration of movement) into performance by beginning where studio sessions and dance classes usually end, with some dancers making diagonal transits across the space while others stand against the walls, watch, and wait their turns. As Sally Banes explains in *Democracy's Body: The Judson Dance Theater 1962–1964*, the diagonal is both the "traditional path ... for the ballerina as she performs her solo variations," and, because it is "in practical terms the longest line in any room,"[14] the natural path for studio exercises that would usually not be presented to an audience.

"Diagonals" is an aleatory improvisational score, or game. The early Judson Dance Theatre events often explored the aleatory composition practices advocated by John Cage and Merce Cunningham, with whom many of the Judson dancers had performed. In some early Judson performances, dice or cards were used to pick movements from a gamut of options. Over time, social-kinetic games of decision, cooperation, and role-changing, like Tag, Simon Says, or Truth or Dare, proved to be a better template for dance performances. Such a score can include any kind of movement and any kind of mover. The choice of moderate walk, or balletic leap, is immediate, personal, and circumstantial, rather than scripted and conventional.

Dancers in "Diagonals" choose between either standing aside and watching, or obeying prompts that referred to the diagonal exercises Rainer and Simone Forti had developed in their shared studio. This menu of diagonals reflects the Judson's inventory of movement styles. The first ten diagonals could be chosen by any number of dancers who heard the call—a chorus. They included "simple options like walking, running, [or] crawling with stiff legs."[15] Three other prompts were only for solo or duet turns, and these three diagonals seem highlighted and (in two cases) more elaborately notated as "dance." The first uses a Balanchine-like vocabulary ("Right arm circles twice as l. leg chassé ..."), the second is balletic ("... End on r. plié with turned-in attitude to side"), and the third is described on Rainer's cue sheet as "Movie Death Run ('Breathless')."[16] Photographs from *Terrain* show Rainer, Trisha Brown, and Albert Reid in T-shirts and leotards, torsos bent forward and feet flying back, hands trying to cover their lower backs,[17] in an image that, while not enough by itself to trigger memories of *Breathless*, and not apparently meant to, is, in dance terms, unmistakeably "sourced" from Belmondo's posture as he ran down Rue Campagne-Première three years earlier.

Rainer's *catalogue raisonné* in *Work* includes a personal canon of "important moments as a viewer."[18] Childhood encounters with Carl Dreyer's *Passion of Joan of Arc* (in 1946, at San Francisco's Palace of Fine Arts) and Jean Cocteau's *Orphée* (unspecified screening, San Francisco, 1950), come before the influence of dance classics like George Balanchine's *Agon* or Cunningham's *Antic Meet*. When she arrived in New York in her twenties, she could have seen *Joan of Arc* again at the Judson Memorial Church, where it was the church hall's first theatrical exhibit in 1962. A week later, Brian de Palma presenting *Woton's Wake*, his first short film,[19] the dance concerts for which Judson is better known followed the screenings, and paintings, that recruited young artists to the venue. Many people in Rainer's (b. 1934) and Godard's (b. 1930) generation saw films, or at least, certain films, unproblematically as works of high art equivalent to ballet. Perhaps cheekily—but given the long run of her commitment to cinema, probably not—Rainer began her choreographic career by listing cinema as the third genre of dance.[20] In *Terrain*, the genre of Godardian cinematic movement is also the genre of "ordinary" and "phraseless" movement. Unlike precise steps noted for the "Modern" or "Ballet" diagonals, the movie death run has no sequence or end. Once one has adopted the wounded posture and lurching gait, one has to decide for oneself where to stop, just as Belmondo chose to stop short of the Boulevard Raspail in part to avoid attracting the attention of the real police.[21]

Although Al Giese's photos—which may have been taken during rehearsals—show several dancers in Belmondo's death run, the rules of "Diagonals" prohibit more than two dancers from performing a death run at the same time. This would set the death run against a landscape of other dancers who have chosen options like running, walking, or the "straight-leg waddle," yet would also create the possibility of two Belmondos colliding in the X where left and right diagonals meet. (Performers could choose either route, as long as they moved downstage.) As in the streets of Godard's cinematic Paris—where a pedestrian can peer into the camera and distract our attention from Belmondo and Seberg, in what most films would discard as a botched take—collision is part of the game: knots of dancers tracing the X of "Diagonals" would "nearly collide in the center, somehow work through each other, and find that they were comprised of new numbers" or stop at the point of collision and resolve the impasse through a secondary game called "Passing and Jostling."[22] Sidewalk traffic is game-theorized as a dance in which everyone is a choreographer. One's choices, however, come from a short menu and apply to a limited path. Following "Diagonals," the premise of stage as street is reinforced by construction-site traffic barricades (the only stage decor in *Terrain*), behind which off-duty dancers stand, visibly watching the action rather than retiring out of sight in the wings. Dancers watching from this position resemble the inadvertent "extras" in a low-budget thriller's location scenes: trying to mind their own business, not sure what kind of "score" they are seeing, not sure when to jump in; cuing and representing the involvement of the seated audience. Stage performance here reabsorbs cinema's ability to turn any street into a stage.

The dance on the pavement between intention and chance encounter had been played out many times, in many semi-documentary movie death runs, by Belmondo's predecessors, like Peter Lorre in *M* (1931), Edmund O'Brien in *D.O.A.* (1950), and Richard Widmark in *Night and the City* (1950). Soon after *Terrain*, the Judson collaborator Lucinda Childs looped the premise of stage as street back to its sources in 1964's *Street Dance*. Judson colleagues who came to a studio to see Childs perform instead encountered a tape recorder, which told them to look outside. On the street, Childs and Tony Holder went down the sidewalk at a natural pace, glanced at store windows, and strolled out of view; meanwhile, Childs's voice on the recorder described the shops she and Holder were seeing on the street.[23]

Her walk was therefore carefully timed to coincide with the tape in the studio, yet the choreography was invisible to her fellow pedestrians, as if, like Seberg and Belmondo on certain Parisian streets in 1959, Childs and Holder were being filmed "documentary style" with a long lens and then dubbed with a subjective voice-over.

Has Godard ever sourced images from the Judson Dance Theater? In the mid-1960s Godard described both *Montparnasse-Levallois* (1964) and *Pierrot le Fou* as "happenings" that he "organized" rather than directed.[24] "Happening" was a word taken up[25] to describe interactive artworks and loose, audience-participation improvisations organized by gallery artists like Jim Dine and Claes Oldenberg beginning in the late 1950s. It gained more popular currency than terms like "aleatory performance event" and is sometimes used to describe improvisation experiments by the Judson Dance Theater (although these tended not to involve the audience). "Happening" soon acquired publicity value for youth-market movies and concert events. So Godard's use of the term could be merely promotional.

However, it is easy to see how Godard might feel that *Pierrot le Fou* was a "happening." Any location shoot, with its indefinite fictional boundaries like a child's game, unpredictable periods and repetitions, planned surprises and surprises that become part of the plan, a crew of impassive documenters, and persons visibly and invisibly, consciously and unconsciously part of the show, is like a happening. This is the lesson of Lucinda Childs's *Street Dance*, a happening viewed through a screen. It is also the premise of *8½* (1963) and later films by Federico Fellini—in a way that seems distant from our era of "plot points," these films were popular precisely because of their reference to their own composition and their loose, festival-like structure. For a more political artist like Godard, the inclusion of compositional choices in a film (or *essai*) satisfies the critical mission of Bertolt Brecht's epic theatre. This kind of feature enjoys and helps the audience enjoy the improvisational aspect of all film production. Anna Karina has said that Godard's directorial method was not to give direct instructions, but to put the actor in situations that elicited the performance.[26] This is both a classic statement of the film director as gamemaster and a good description of the outcome sought by cooperative performance scores like *Terrain*.

In at least one case, Godard may have been inspired by a specific "happening" associated with the Judson Dance Theater. Carolee Schneeman's *Meat Joy* developed out of her performance choreography at Judson (like 1963's *Chromelodeon*), and was performed there in 1965. But it had premiered in Paris in 1964, causing a scandal in the popular press; descriptions and images of *Meat Joy*, if not the show itself, could have been familiar to Godard and his collaborators.

Meat Joy comes from a different history of The Judson Dance Theater than *Trio A*. Like the original happenings, it uses the stage as a living canvas of colour and motion, and like contact improvisation, the social dance form that grew out of Judson experiments by Steve Paxton and Simone Forti, it defines dances as the tactile presence and mutual contact of bodies. *Meat Joy* begins with two middle-class couples in a realistic theatrical setting under a voice-over of erotic poetry. More couples arrive, and the bourgeois setting gradually becomes a chaotic, sensual floor of ripped-up newspapers and rolling bikini-clad bodies. Almost all photos of *Meat Joy* in circulation, then and now, come from its last movements, when the giggling dancers smear themselves with raw chicken meat, sausages, and mackerels, and then are doused with paint.[27] Godard's *Week-end* (1967) resembles *Meat Joy* in its plot movement from bourgeois sexual fantasies to hippie tribalism, and in specific pictures of men carrying women on their shoulders and bodies being smeared with food and colour. Love-ins and body paint are of course icons of sixties counterculture, but Godard's image of a fish dropped into a woman's spread crotch is an unusually close match to a notorious moment from *Meat Joy*.

Although opposite in mood, *Week-end* achieves not only the shock value but the unnerving anti-style of Schneeman's work, the speechlessness before a new world. Followed from a distance in long pans, *Week-end*'s pretended and pretending guerillas ignore the lens and go about their tasks with an evenness of effort, whether it is symbolic cannibalism and rape or rowing a boat all the way across a pond. As with *Breathless* and *Terrain*, the easy integration of or convergence with another artist's work suggests not just opportunistic hipness, but a deeper sympathy with one another's methods.

NOTES

1 Yvonne Rainer, *Work 1961–73* (Halifax: Nova Scotia College of Art and Design, 1974), 63–69.
2 Carrie Lambert-Beatty, *Being Watched: Yvonne Rainer and the 1960s* (Cambridge, MA: MIT Press, 2008), 133.
3 Ibid., 130.
4 Ibid., 73.
5 Jacques Bontemps et al., "Lutter sur deux fronts: Conversation avec Jean-Luc Godard," *Cahiers du cinéma* 194 (October 1967): 16.
6 Ibid.
7 Ibid.
8 Karina's gaze and motion point to other actors, which de-emphasizes the moment of matching. If the match had been simpler and fuller—if it had been, so to speak, from crocodile to alligator—the "idea" would surface that the cut is drawing a

comparison. Like *Trio A*, film editing tries to suppress transitions and duplications. But Godard will also evince a more traditional aesthetic of dance, and a less traditional cinema, by doubling or arresting movement in jump-cuts (*Breathless*, 1960), "Eisensteinian" duplicate shots (*Les Carabiniers*, 1963), and *tableaux-vivants* (*Hélas pour moi*, 1993).

9   Lambert-Beatty, *Being Watched*, 118.

10   Ibid., 107–20.

11   "What is moving is moving neither in the place in which it is nor in the place in which it is not"—attributed to Zeno by Diogenes Laertius, *Lives of the Philosophers*, 9.72.

12   Jonathon Cott, "Godard: Born-Again Filmmaker," in *Jean-Luc Godard: Interviews*, ed. David Sterritt (Jackson: University Press of Mississippi, 1998), 95.

13   Lambert-Beatty, *Being Watched*, 153–54.

14   Sally Banes, *Democracy's Body: Judson Dance Theater 1962–1964* (Ann Arbor: UMI Research Press, 1983), 114.

15   Ibid., 113.

16   Banes, *Democracy's Body*, 113–14; Rainer, *Work*, 14–15, 28–29.

17   See Yvonne Rainer, *Feelings Are Facts: A Life* (Cambridge, MA: MIT Press, 2006), 384.

18   Rainer, *Work*, 333.

19   Banes, *Democracy's Body*, 160.

20   Most "art dance" is taught and exhibited as either "Modern" or "Classical" (i.e., ballet). Other genre tags introduced since the 1950s would include "Folk" or "World," and "Contemporary" or "Postmodern" (the category that includes the Judson choreographers).

21   Richard Brody, *Everything Is Cinema: The Working Life of Jean-Luc Godard* (New York: Metropolitan Books, 2008), 66–67.

22   Banes, *Democracy's Body*, 113–14; Rainer, *Work*, 14–15, 28–29.

23   Lambert-Beatty, *Being Watched*, 37–40.

24   Colin MacCabe, *Godard: A Portrait of the Artist at Seventy* (New York: Farrar, Straus and Giroux, 2003), 215; Jean-Luc Godard, *Godard on Godard*, ed. and trans. Tom Milne (New York: Da Capo, 1986), 217.

25   From the title of one such event, Allen Kaprow's *18 Happenings in 6 Parts* (1959).

26   Anna Karina, video interview, *Made in USA*, directed by Jean-Luc Godard (1966; London: Optimum, 2007), DVD.

27   See Carolee Schneeman, *More Than "Meat Joy"* (New Paltz: Documentext, 1979), 32–88.

BIBLIOGRAPHY

Banes, Sally. *Democracy's Body: Judson Dance Theater, 1962–1964*. Ann Arbor: UMI Research Press, 1983.

Bontemps, Jacques, Jean-Louis Comolli, Michel Delahaye, and Jean Narboni. "Lutter sur deux fronts: Conversation avec Jean-Luc Godard." *Cahiers du cinéma* 194 (1967): 12–26.

Brody, Richard. *Everything Is Cinema: The Working Life of Jean-Luc Godard*. New York: Metropolitan Books, 2008.

Cott, Jonathon. "Godard: Born-Again Filmmaker." In *Jean-Luc Godard: Interviews*, edited by David Sterritt, 91–99. Jackson: University Press of Mississippi, 1998.

Godard, Jean Luc. *Godard on Godard*. Translated and edited by Tom Milne. New York: Da Capo, 1986.

Karina, Anna. Video interview. *Made in USA*. Directed by Jean-Luc Godard. 1966. London: Optimum Releasing, 2007. DVD, 82 min.

Lambert-Beatty, Carrie. *Being Watched: Yvonne Rainer and the 1960s*. Cambridge, MA: MIT Press, 2008.

MacCabe, Colin. *Godard: A Portrait of the Artist at Seventy*. New York: Farrar, Straus and Giroux, 2003.

Rainer, Yvonne. *Feelings Are Facts: A Life*. Cambridge, MA: MIT Press, 2006.

———. *Work 1961–73*. Halifax: Nova Scotia College of Art and Design, 1974.

Schneeman, Carolee. *More Than "Meat Joy."* New Paltz: Documentext, 1979.

Part II
Godardian Politics of Representation: Memory/History

4

The Representation of Factory Work in the Films of Jean-Luc Godard: Reaching the Impossible Shore

Michel Cadé

TO WRITE ABOUT Jean-Luc Godard's relationship with factory work and its representation is first to explore a paradox. Of a hundred or so works, including moving pictures, films, videos, and television programs, representing over one hundred hours of projection, the only Godardian works devoted to the subject are two fiction films, namely *Tout va bien* (1972) co-directed with Jean-Pierre Gorin (a farewell to the Dziga Vertov Group) and *Passion* (1982), both intended for a general audience; the activist piece *British Sounds*, co-directed in 1969 with Jean-Henri Roger; *Comment ça va?* co-directed in 1975 with Anne-Marie Miéville; three episodes of *Six fois deux: Sur et sous la communication*, a television series co-directed with Anne-Marie Miéville in 1976; a few rare allusions here and there;[1] and a documentary, the director's first film, a short produced in 1953 titled *Opération béton*. Hence the filmmaker who, even before 1968, was strongly committed to the far left in a personal variation of Maoism and did not see fit to give factory work a predominant place in his works. The films in which factory work is represented as a central element, if not emphatically, span the relatively brief period from the 1968 "revolution" in France to that of *Solidarność* in Poland, two contradictory (if not opposite) moments in the worker–intellectual alliance which, in those years, so captivated Godard. Before, workers had been in the backdrop; later, they would altogether merge into the background. For Godard, with the exception of *Opération béton*, the depiction of the worker, and hence of factory work, is dated. However, it remains important in the evolution of the filmmaker's works and appears as a transitional object that enabled him to step outside the activist period and, using short films, to find anew the medium of cinema— which, if nothing else, is also a performance.

THE MOTIONS OF FACTORY AND FARM LABOUR: AN IMPOSSIBLE *MISE EN SCÈNE*

When considering the shots of labour filmed by Godard, the immediately striking aspect, aside from their brevity (with the exception of *British Sounds*), is their classical framing: long shots and medium-long shots, mostly static, revealing a workplace. This can be found both in films where work is a sort of background noise, as in *Deux ou trois choses que je sais d'elle* (1966), as well as in productions more plainly devoted to the subject, such as *Opération béton*, *British Sounds*, *Tout va bien*, a few shots of *Marcel* in *Six fois deux*, a few shots near the end of *Passion*, medium shots and medium close-ups showing motions of work in these last two films, and in *Comment ça va?* and, albeit incidentally, in *Luttes en Italie* (1969).

The second aspect that comes to mind is the importance of noise as an essential component of the representation of labour, which, with the exception of the first two work shots in *Tout va bien*, is imposed brutally on the audio track—even becoming the hallmark of this representation, whether involving factory work or other manual work, particularly in *British Sounds* and *Comment ça va?* The ubiquity of noise is central to the representation of labour in film,[2] but Godard's recourse to this *pons asinorum* for the *mise en scène* of work is all the more notable as, with the exception of *Marcel*, it abandons the famous image-audio track syncopation that can be said to constitute his trademark; apart from elements of dialogue, he only allows the coexistence, on the audio track, of noise and voice-overs. This relative respect of form in no way precludes an arresting originality in the conception of Godardian discourse on work and its motions.

To address only these motions, to begin with, I would start with Godard's refusal (except perhaps in *Opération béton*) to analyze the *process* of labour, as well as the exploitation which, for Marxists, can be read through his *mise en scène*. In the opening to *British Sounds*, featuring assembly lines for MG sports cars in the model factory of the British Motor Corporation in Oxford, he chooses a sequence-shot with medium-long framing and a slow track-sideways. In the unceasing noise, the jerky and indistinguishable movements of workers evoke a hell accompanied by a voice-over reading of Marx and Engels's *Manifesto of the Communist Party* and the recitation, by the voice of a little girl (also in voice over), of the major dates in British social history. Hence we have an exercise in style, revolutionary in tone but somewhat archaic in its choice of images.

Elsewhere[3] I have described how the entire range of shots in a back-and-forth construction between work motions captured in close-ups or even in extreme close-ups on the one hand, and long shots revealing the place of the worker in the larger organization of the workshop on the other, was able to show the viewer the *travail en miettes* or piecemeal work described by sociologist Georges Friedmann.[4] At the turn of the 1960s and 1970s this editing method was used by filmmakers such as Michel Drach in *Élise ou la vraie vie* (1969), Louis Malle in *Humain trop humain* (1972), and most notably Marin Karmitz in *Camarades* (1969) and *Coup pour coup* (1972), in which it found its fulfillment with regard to both form and activism.

Coup pour coup and *Tout va bien*, respectively filmed in 1971 and 1972, came out at almost the same time. With a screenplay in both cases built around a strike with a sit-in and sequestration of the management, and with both filmmakers belonging to the loose network of Maoism, the two films inevitably invited comparison. The verism of Marin Karmitz would draw the ire of *Cahiers du cinéma*—one need only read today the amphigoric article on the subject by the *Groupe Lou Sin d'intervention idéologique*[5]— while Godard's distanciation won him overwhelming popularity. But outside the circle of the famous journal, reception was rather cold.[6] Whereas Karmitz had chosen to film "the reality of factory work" with real female labourers on strike at Elbeuf, Godard had undertaken to show the forces in play in French society in 1972—capitalists, reformist trade unionists, leftists, the *ras-le-bol* or "fed up" in the words of Godard—and to do so via two screen giants, Yves Montand and Jane Fonda, left-wing intellectuals in life as in the works of Godard, preferring in-studio filming in an extraordinary "doll house" setting using only professional actors. He explains this modestly and with conviction on André S. Labarthe and Janine Bazin's television show *Vive le cinéma*,[7] refusing to pose as spokesperson for the workers and instead speaking in his own name. As a result, it is easy to understand Godard's refusal to recreate (by technical means used, incidentally, in factory videos) a labour *process* of which he had no direct experience. But by including, toward the end of the part dedicated to the strike, static long shots of work—generally brief, a little under one minute and thirty seconds for six fixed shots, very noisy, with commentary provided by voice-overs or intermediate shots—he introduces, in a desire for the Brechtian distancing with which he identified, an unadulterated representation of labour. The appearance of Yves Montand or Jane Fonda in these shots, drowned out in the group of workers, reinforces the intent. At the same time, the audio track contributes to bringing into focus the work conditions, a verbalization of the smell that sticks to skin, the backaches self-evidently caused by the sequence of movements shown on the screen.[8] A prior sequence in which director Guidotti (Vittorio Caprioli), held prisoner, finds himself given the same time as a worker to urinate, is just as effective as the verism of Karmitz in displaying the almost military environment created by the scientific organization of work.

In *Passion* one finds the same refusal of didacticism regarding the obviousness of the workers' successive motions, even if Godard is intent on preserving this obviousness and for example asked Isabelle Huppert to make a few factory visits to learn how to stand before a machine.[9] However, with a few brief exceptions, he renounces the supremacy of the long shot to convey meaning to labour, instead framing Isabelle (Huppert) at work in medium shots and medium close-up shots. It is true that in *Comment ça va?* he had already seen all the advantages to be had from medium close-ups and close-ups of work, namely those of a typewriter keyboard and the hands of a secretary, but in another context. In any case, there is in *Passion* a certain mockery of what was at the heart of *Tout va bien*: the strike, reduced to its preparation (but an occasion to verbalize suffering in the workplace, as in *Tout va bien*) and a powerless gesticulation; the staging of work, barely shown; the grotesque repression resulting from the meeting of a near-broke boss and a municipal police officer; and the future of the working class, with the bourgeoisie on the roads that lead to Poland.[10] Farewell, Maoists! But, as we will see, the point lies elsewhere.

The motions of work do interest Godard, but their reproduction through *mise en scène* appears impossible to him; how then can they be brought to the screen? In *Six fois deux: Sur et sous la communication*—taking advantage of the freedom afforded by the style of the television program and videos—he attempts to seize their essence without lapsing into the triviality of preconceived images. In the first two shows, *Y'a personne* and *Louison*, faced with an unemployed welder, a young woman looking for work, and a farmer, he chooses to let their hands do the talking. By asking them to go through the motions of work, stripped of all the pseudo-realism of a workshop or even of work done "for real," he joins in the tradition of Socratic maieutic by pushing his interlocutors further in their understanding of the ontological meaning of work. As usual, he has no qualms about a somewhat contradictory treatment of data but the overall coherence ends up all the stronger. In *Y'a personne*, as the small-business Grenoble boss that he is and is not, at the head of Sonimage (the video production and distribution company he started with Anne-Marie Miéville), at the business headquarters, he plays the role of a backup working for the ANPE (Agence nationale pour l'emploi) by welcoming unemployed people and job seekers. Among these, two receive preferential treatment: a young Maghrebin factory welder and a young cleaning lady. The shots between the two alternate, and he has the former carry out welding motions after having him list his tools, namely the parts to weld, the blowtorch, the welding rod, and goggles. "We made machines for sawing wood," says the welder. "Had to weld a frame. Put together two pieces, weld them so they would hold together."[11] Behind the triviality of these words, one can make out reality, but also the complexity of what is felt in this work, far from the original leftist discourse. In response to Godard's question, "If this is all you do, don't you get bored after a while?" the welder, who had a little earlier expressed his desire to "do meaningful work," answers, "The first days ... then you get used to it." Determined to explore the mystery of work, Godard talks to the worker using welding terms and leads him to compose a text, all the while showing that welding can be a mode of discourse: the filmmaker welds images, the unemployed person is welded to his condition, his family; when one writes, one welds words. Even if the welder appears to be more irritated than liberated, the most important thing is said—that manual labour is a form not only of alienation but also of creation, just like writing or film. The cleaning woman is granted specific treatment: she is prompted to use the vacuum cleaner which, from the first shots of the film, incongruously takes up a small portion of the image. The motions of housekeeping are common to all, or at least familiar to all; bringing them to the screen is less to stage them than to allow the viewer to reactivate familiar knowledge. Far from the obscenity of reconstruction, here we find ourselves in the realm of transparency. The triviality of the motion is magnified, and the young lady shocks no one when she says, "I am freer in this work than in a factory." In a relatively abstract way with the welder, filmed mostly in medium close-ups, and more concretely with the cleaning woman, filmed in close-ups, Godard takes up his discourse on labour by re-questioning it and, rather than apologizing for his Marxist convictions, he attempts to transcend labour while questioning it.

Louison, the second part of this first *Six fois deux*, confirms this impression by developing the rhetoric at work in the first part. After a lengthy long shot displaying a moving tractor, the farmer, Louison (on a few shots of fields and then over the course of a very long static shot where he is framed next to his tractor), speaks, over a sort of panorama of the audio track, of the condition of farmers and the societal choices that have led to its evolution. When he sets out to speak of his work as non-fragmented and hence distinct from factory work—yet still a kind of manual labour— Godard asks him to carry out the motions of work, right next to his tractor, even though he himself could go through these same motions, such as taking hold of the tractor's steering wheel. But through the reconstruction of the farmer's everyday motions, working, repairing a plough, welding (does this not tie in with the welder mentioned earlier?), milking cows, cleaning a milk room, picking up a pitchfork, transporting manure, Godard is able to ensure that the viewer's attention is directed to these actions only. Thus the viewer is able to overcome the barrier between the filmmaker and his subject, the absence of experience with rural and factory work that no casual initiation could make up for. He vaguely begins to see that he in fact already holds the key to eliminating the irritating mental block.

FILM AS SOLUTION

In *Numéro deux* (1975), after two minutes of opening credits and defining statements, we hear the words, "It's as if I said that in Rhône-Poulenc now, and in the chemical industry in general, women's fingers were being eaten away by acids," thus grounding the film in the problem of factory work with a long static shot that lasts seven minutes and twenty-seven seconds. Noisy machines can be heard winding up film reels and a video monitor shows the face of Jean-Luc Godard, who is leaning against the monitor, almost invisible in the darkness, speaking. In the middle of the lengthy monologue, Godard says, "This is a factory here, you see. I listen to the machine, I can hear that machine's going faster, that one's going slower. And I'm the boss, a special boss because I'm also the worker—because I'm not alone, because the workers have taken power. The others? I'll tell you about them later, they're working, I'm here listening to the factory noise."

Jean-Luc Godard had just captured what his films, since *Tout va bien* at least, had been trying to say. For a filmmaker, showing work is not to stage it, but to bring it back to what the filmmaker is familiar with: the production of films. To make films has always been to do industrial work—the thoughts of André Malraux on the subject are well known[12]—and Godard, if imbued with the artistic function of film, is well aware of what is mercilessly mechanical in the factory of image and sound, Sonimage, camera, film roll, and video.

In *Tout va bien*, the part devoted to the occupation of the Salumi factory is followed by a cut to a long static shot (one minute and nine seconds in length) of the work of filmmaker Jacques, played by Yves Montand. While the viewer's mind is still fresh with work scenes, new and different work scenes are presented. Framed in a long shot, the film set where the producer is shooting a promotional film for pantyhose reveals, albeit succinctly, the work behind the *mise en scène*. The sequence continues with a long static shot, more than six minutes long and rather reminiscent of the quasi-opening shot to *Numéro deux* three years later. Framed in a medium close-up with, at his right, a projector and a camera whose lens is aimed at the viewer, and, at his left, an unobtrusive reflector—the viewer can make out various elements of a studio in the darkness, further in the background—Montand speaks directly to the camera and hence the viewer, becoming the spokesperson of Godard, the filmmaker on his quest. His declaration ends with "I need to get back to work," words that reinforce the equating of factory work with film work, a result of the editing of sequences, intensified by the conclusion of the filming sequence with a return to the film set. This static shot, one minute and twenty-three seconds in length, frames the camera's viewfinder in a medium close-up in which one can recognize dancers that appear blurry deeper in the field, and a close-up of the arm of the operator, who is adjusting the lens. The work of the filmmaker, of the operator, framing the theoretical discourse of the former, a revelation of kinship, of what one might be tempted to call reversibility between factory work and the filmmaker's work, here stems from an affirmation of the importance of work in general in the construction of human beings and their relationships, including love relationships, as expressed by Jane when she says, "I need an image of him at work."[13]

The first section in the first part of Six fois deux, Y'a personne, clearly (if anecdotally) ties factory work to cinematic production, comparing the film producer "who welds images" with the welder and inviting the cleaning woman to join the Sonimage business[14] to make a film on her work and sell it in China; however, no correspondence can be read in the image. This is not the case in Marcel, the second section in the third part of Six fois deux. An amateur filmmaker and a watchmaker, Marcel appears from the beginning of the film framed in a medium-long shot in the workshop where he edits his films; the audio track records the sounds of machines and his conversation with Godard. In different spots, he appears at work, framed alone in a medium close-up or with women factory workers in a medium-long shot; in both cases, his eyes are on his editing table or on the parts of the watches he is assembling through a series of small motions. The effect of similarity is accentuated by the continuity of the audio track, which often does not mark a distinction between the two places, pursuing over images of factory work the discussion begun in the workshop. Shots of Marcel's film and of Marcel filming, captured by Godard, account for the remaining images used in the episode. The resemblance between the two types of work is obvious[15] and Godard drives the point home with these words to Marcel: "I saw you at work in the factory, it's like here, you have to watch really closely, make careful movements"; and he suggests to Marcel that he abandon his work and be paid to make movies. The refusal without concession of Marcel, who "would not want to make films for money" and finds the watchmaker's occupation "quite beautiful, quite varied," his work "nice"—but who is able to distinguish between factory time in which "you're absorbed in intense work" and the "simpler, more generous" work of editing films, nonetheless cannot erase the impression given by Godard's editing, namely that for a filmmaker, the only honest way to stage factory work is to relate it to that of the filmmaker, the only work of which he has inside knowledge. And this is what is at the heart of *Passion*.

Right from the second shot of *Passion*, in which a female worker is pushing a cart, the factory is obvious to the viewer, who again sees it in shot ten followed immediately by a shot of Rembrandt's *Nightwatch*, a living painting, one of the subjects of the film being produced. This back-and-forth movement between the factory and the film set comes back twice in the opening sequence. Godard seems to be telling us that working in a factory and making a movie boil down to the same thing, and in the dialogue between Jerzy (the filmmaker, played by Jerzy Radziwilowicz) and Isabelle (the factory worker), he implicitly confirms as much. Later in the film, a graphic match cut in the image of a projector's spotlight segues from a union meeting in preparation for a strike to the shooting of the film's sequences—living paintings taken from the works of Goya including his famous *Tres de mayo*, an icon of repression. As the film progresses, Godard verbalizes what is implicit in the images. First, Magali (Magali Campos), the worker who agreed to work as an extra, discovers that "you're not trustworthy, your factory and theirs are identical." If cinema is an industry, a film is a factory. Then Isabelle, in her workshop, after having declared that "sometimes I go see movies, or television, and they never show people at work," is told that "it is forbidden to film in factories," and this is more than a mere observation of the equivalence between factory work and film work: "I think that … at a deep level work is the same as … pleasure" and then in voice-off over shots of filming linked to the previous ones by the audio track, we hear music and the words, "it is the same motions as love. Not necessarily at the same speed, but the same motions."[16] This idea of a work/love homothety, already underlying the dialogues in the final part of *Tout va bien* between Jacques and Jane, sublimates Godard's solution for honestly portraying factory work in film without bringing it into question.[17]

With *Passion*, a question is answered. Running into a difficulty that seemed to him moral in nature, namely that of showing work without staging it, refusing both verism and artifice—as he is aware of his unfamiliarity with the daily practice of factory work that only a few "established" intellectuals (and, before them, Simone Weil) had had the will to know from the inside—Godard finds a solution in what he knows best, that is, film. By turning down the deception of acting as spokesperson, by making parallels between factory work and film work in images and in sound, he finds in words, in sounds, and in the images of his work a way of verbalizing and presenting the labour of factory workers. One might find this acrobatic, the posture a high-wire act, but it is impossible to deny the honesty and coherence of such an approach.

A LEGACY WITHOUT HEIRS?

Jean-Luc Godard is an artist who, like Pablo Picasso, profoundly changed his art without altogether founding a new school. While it remains an essential reference for many filmmakers, Godard's work as a whole is so original that it constitutes neither a standard to reach, nor a model to emulate. This is even more marked in the case here examined, since labour is rarely depicted in the films of Godard but nonetheless held great importance in his career as an activist. Yet it is one element, along with the elegant distance the filmmaker kept from verist representations, which in today's new social context can be considered a more or less conscious legacy of the Godardian lens for representing labour. While Marin Karmitz was underscoring the exploitation of labourers and their malaise and wretched living conditions, as well as magnifying the strike into a struggle between good and evil; and while Bernard Paul,[18] or a little later on, Maurice Dugowson,[19] with a few nuances, held views that in spite of an ideological divide were not so far removed, Jean-Luc Godard was putting forth an original vision. Without denying the exploitation of labour in the capitalist system that he sought firmly to denounce, he undertook to show the positive side of work, even the happiness the worker could find in its accomplishment. In *Tout va bien* during the discussion on work conditions between the two journalists held prisoner and the workers occupying the factory, the idea is born that beyond the objective conditions of manual work within a capitalist system, the struggle, when it leads to change—even for an instant—perhaps transforms the nature of labour and hence perhaps the labourer is not necessarily called upon to "always look grim."[20] In *Six fois deux* and then *Passion*, Godard, with the relentless drive of Isabelle struggling to keep her job, develops this idea of the dual nature of manual work as labour that is forced but nonetheless a necessary means to guarantee the worker's freedom. The economic crisis which, over the course of ups and downs spanning forty years, resulted in a calcified form of mass unemployment across society, led film to consider labour in general and factory labour in particular from the standpoint of this dual nature asserted by Jean-Luc Godard—with, in fact, a strong tendency to favour the second member of the Godardian equation.[21]

The blossoming of works (often disillusioned) following the path forged by Godard to varying degrees can hardly be considered a direct legacy of the Godardian way of portraying factory work on the screen. But if this approach cannot be said to be a direct descendant, certain convergences are too apparent for them not to be likened, in a sense, to a legacy. Hence the furious work of Rosetta in the 1999 film of the same name directed by the Dardenne brothers is not so different from that of Isabelle in *Passion*, and likewise the unsuccessful and somewhat ridiculous strike in *L'Humanité* by Bruno Dumont (1999) echoes the derisory strike led by the same Isabelle. In Dumont's film one finds the same distance, the same refusal of verism, the same tenderness mingled with irony for a working class losing its identity. The images of a boxing match to convey the violence of manual work in *État des lieux* by Jean-François Richet (1993) bears at least some relation, even if with Godard the portrayal is less naive, with the way Godard equates the work of the filmmaker with that of the labourer. But as convincing as these relations may be—and others could certainly be cited—they are only skin deep, while it seems to me this is not the case with the work of Rabah Ameur-Zaïmeche, particularly in his recent *Dernier Maquis* (2008). Already in his first film, *Wesh Wesh, qu'est-ce qui se passe?* (2002), the question of labour held an important place, involving even greater distanciation than can be found in the works of Godard. In *Dernier Maquis*, the common points (points of convergence?) with the works of Godard are numerous. First, in terms of form, there is a use of colour that the producer of *Pierrot le fou* (1965) could have adopted himself, a cutaway to a shot of the sky that may allude to the opening shot of *Passion*, shots of work more numerous than in *Tout va bien* or *Passion* but devoid of pretension to didactic realism, and a structure, as in this last film, that brings together two elements usually considered discrete: film production and labour in the one case, Islamic worship and factory work in the other. Second, in terms of ideas, the author of *Dernier Maquis*, like Godard the activist, proclaims his allegiance to Marxism; does he not declare that "class conflict is the engine of history"?[22] Like Godard, he stages a strike with a slightly distanced elegance that in no way prevents empathy, and the irony is that he gives the company boss—whose role he plays himself—the first name of Mohamed shortened to Mao, a boss who is a prophet in a dual sense; the somersault cannot but delight the hermit of Rolle. And so—is there an heir after all? Between coincidences and more or less conscious reminiscences, one thing only is clear: whether rediscovered or ascertained, Godard's lesson lives on.

Translated from the French original by Joachim Lépine

NOTES

1 For example, at the beginning of *Masculin féminin* (1966), one finds allusions to a strike, and in *La Chinoise* (1967) a few words on rural work as well as silhouettes of female workers.

2 Michel Cadé, *L'Écran bleu: La représentation des ouvriers dans le cinéma français* (Perpignan: Presses Universitaires de Perpignan, 2004), 121–25.

3 Michel Cadé, "La Représentation du travail ouvrier dans le cinéma français de fiction," in *Le travail en représentations*, ed. Patrice Marcilloux (Paris: Éditions de CTHS, 2005), 121–30.

4 Georges Friedmann, *Le Travail en miettes*, 2nd ed. (Paris: Gallimard, 1964).

5 Groupe Lou Sin, "Les luttes de classe en France: Deux films: *Coup pour coup, Tout va bien*," *Cahiers du cinéma* 238–239 (May–June 1972): 5–24.

6 Antoine de Baecque, *Godard: Biographie* (Paris: Grasset, 2010), 507.

7 Ibid. Godard's intervention on the show can be seen on YouTube.

8 On the work scenes of this film and their internal meaning, the interested reader can consult Élisabeth Boyer, "*Trop tôt, trop tard, Tout va bien, Harlan County, Les temps modernes, Rosetta, The Big One* et quelques autres ...," in "La figure ouvrière," special series, *Art du cinéma* 32–34 (2001), http://www.artcinema.org/spip.php?article67. In this text Boyer shows that Godard's (and Gorin's) foremost question in this film is the issue "of work in its relation to the subjectivity of people" (13) and that he consequently refuses any and all naturalism in his portrayal.

9 Alain Bergala, Serge Daney, and Serge Toubiana, "Propos de Godard autour de *Passion*: Le chemin vers la parole," *Cahiers du cinéma* 336 (May 1982): 9–14, 57–66. Also cited by de Baecque, *Godard*, 606.

10 And yet, according to Charles Foulon, this film is the true sequel to *Man of Marble* (1977). Foulon, "Ouvrier: Marbre vivant: *L'homme de marbre*, d'Andrzej Wajda," in "La figure ouvrière," special series, *Art du cinéma* 32–34 (2001), http://www.artcinema.org/spip.php?article72.

11 All translations of dialogue in the text are mine.

12 "Cinema is also an industry," are the final words of *Esquisse d'une psychologie du cinéma*, written in 1939, published in 1946, and republished in Denis Marion, *Le cinéma selon André Malraux* (Paris: Cahiers du cinéma, 1997), 71–78.

13 I nevertheless partly disagree with Élisabeth Boyer ("*Trop tôt, trop tard*, ..."), according to whom the question of subjectivity in this case is "not only related to the thinking of manual labour, but also to the thinking of the representation of work in general." It seems to me that, in spite of ambiguous appearances, the factory work–filmmaker work relation in Godard's work cannot be extended infinitely, and this is indicated by the rest of his work.

14 On Godard's Sonimage adventure, see de Baecque, *Godard*, 516–73.

15 The interested reader can consult Gilles Deleuze in "Trois questions sur *Six fois deux*," *Cahiers du cinéma* 271 (November 1976): 5–12.

16 Quotations taken from Jean-Luc Godard, "*Passion*," *L'avant scène du cinéma* 380 (April 1989): 28.

17 This is what Charles Foulon ("Ouvrier: Marbre vivant") expresses in his own way, taking a distance from the images of the film, in the final sentence of his article:

"Godard switches Jerzy Radziwilowicz from the position of worker to that of film-maker, a filmmaker who seeks to film the light of the [female] worker he loves."

18   In particular in *Beau Masque* (1972).

19   In *Lily, aime-moi* (1974).

20   On this subject see Steve Cannon, "Montrer la lutte, et comment les trucs changent: Godard/Gorin, commitment and intervention in *Tout va bien*," in *Cinéma et engagement*, ed. Graeme Hayes and Martin O'Shaughnessy (Paris: L'Harmattan, 2005), 65–80.

21   Michel Cadé, "Les ouvriers dans le cinéma français," in *Cinéma et engagement*, ed. Graeme Hayes and Martin O'Shaughnessy (Paris: L'Harmattan, 2005), 147–61.

22   Rabah Ameur-Zaïmeche, press conference at Cannes, May 16, 2008. Video can be viewed at: http://www.lemonde.fr/culture/son/2008/05/17/cannes-extrait-de-la-conference-de-presse-de-rabah-ameur-zaimeche-1-2_1046517_3246.html.

BIBLIOGRAPHY

Ameur-Zaïmeche, Rabah. Press conference at Cannes. May 16, 2008. Video available at: http://www.lemonde.fr/culture/son/2008/05/17/cannes-extrait-de-la-conference-de-presse-de-rabah-ameur-zaimeche-1-2_1046517_3246.html.

Bergala, Alain, Serge Daney, and Serge Toubiana. "Propos de Godard autour de *Passion*: Le chemin vers la parole." *Cahiers du cinéma* 336 (May 1982): 9–14, 57–66.

Boyer, Élisabeth. "*Trop tôt, trop tard, Tout va bien, Harlan County, Les temps modernes, Rosetta, The Big One* et quelques autres…." In "La figure ouvrière." Special series, *Art du cinéma* 32–34, (2001). http://www.artcinema.org/spip.php?article67.

Cadé, Michel. *L'Écran bleu: La représentation des ouvriers dans le cinéma français*. Perpignan: Presses Universitaires de Perpignan, 2004.

———. "Les ouvriers dans le cinéma français." In *Cinéma et engagement*, edited by Graeme Hayes and Martin O'Shaughnessy, 147–61. Paris: L'Harmattan, 2005.

———. "La Représentation du travail ouvrier dans le cinéma français de fiction," in *Le travail en représentations*, edited by Patrice Marcilloux, 121–30. Paris: Éditions de CTHS, 2005.

Cannon, Steve. "Montrer la lutte, et comment les trucs changent: Godard/Gorin, commitment and intervention in *Tout va bien*." In *Cinéma et engagement*, edited by Graeme Hayes and Martin O'Shaughnessy, 65–80. Paris: L'Harmattan, 2005.

De Baecque, Antoine. *Godard: Biographie*. Paris: Grasset, 2010.

Deleuze, Gilles. "Trois questions sur *Six fois deux*." *Cahiers du cinéma* 271 (November 1976): 5–12.

Foulon, Charles. "Ouvrier: Marbre vivant: *L'homme de marbre*, d'Andrzej Wajda." In "La figure ouvrière." Special series, *Art du cinéma* 32–34 (2001). http://www.artcinema.org/spip.php?article72.

Friedmann, Georges. *Le Travail en miettes*. 2nd ed. Paris: Gallimard, 1964.

Godard, Jean-Luc. *"Passion."* L'*Avant-scène du cinéma* 380 (1989): 28.

Groupe Lou Sin. "Les luttes de classes en France: Deux films: *Coup pour coup, Tout va bien.*" *Cahiers du cinéma* 238–239 (May–June 1972): 5–24.

Lefevre, Raymond. *Jean-Luc Godard*. Paris: Edilig, 1983.

Marion, Denis. *Le Cinéma selon André Malraux*. Paris: Cahiers du cinéma, 1997.

5

Godard, Spielberg, the *Muselmann*, and the Concentration Camps

Junji Hori

GODARD AND SPIELBERG

IN A 1997 television interview with the popular French journalist Paul Amar, Godard is shown a demo of a filmmaking simulation computer game released under the title *Steven Spielberg's Director's Chair*. When asked whether Spielberg is still a filmmaker or if he has now become a businessman, Godard responds by reciting from memory a short poem by Bertolt Brecht entitled "Hollywood," which he also quoted through Fritz Lang's character in the film *Le Mépris* (1963). Then, unperturbed by a provocative question about whether a collaborative filmmaking project between himself and Spielberg would be possible, Godard evokes his favorite dichotomy between *culture* as rule and *art* as exception, and considers the fellows of Hollywood, who gleefully join the ranks of people selling their wares in "the market where lies are bought" (Brecht), as a typical form of *culture*—an accumulation of products that circulate in a capitalistic sense. It is as if Godard himself approved the simplistic schematic that serves the purpose of dividing the two filmmakers according to the dichotomy between high-class and low-class culture, art and entertainment, or modernism and kitsch.[1]

Although Godard and Spielberg certainly differ on a number of points, it is easy to see from a brief glimpse at their respective filmographies that the two, in fact, share a common interest in film history and twentieth-century history. When Godard first clearly depicted his interest in World War II in his short film *Le Dernier mot* (1988), Spielberg was filming his *Empire of the Sun* (1987). Furthermore, Hanns Zischler, an actor who plays a dual role in *Le Dernier mot* as a German officer and his son, also cooperated closely with Godard's *Allemagne année 90 neuf zéro* (1991) and played the role of a document forger named Hans in Spielberg's *Munich* (2005). In addition, Godard's preparation and production periods for *Histoire(s) du cinéma* (1988–98), which features the death and resurrection of cinema during World War II, particularly the Holocaust, overlap with those of Spielberg's *Empire of the Sun*, *Schindler's List* (1993), and *Saving Private Ryan* (1998), all of which also focus on World War II. For that matter, it is almost as if Spielberg's filmography was moving upstream against Godard's filmography. For instance, the Black September Organization links Spielberg's *Munich* (2005), whose story begins from the terrorist incident caused by this group, and Godard and Jean-Pierre Gorin's project *Jusqu'à la victoire*, which was left unfinished because of the Black September incident of September 1970. It is also true that the 1968 Chicago Conspiracy Trial, the subject matter for one of Spielberg's new projects, is a theme also handled by Godard and Gorin's film *Vladimir et Rosa* (1971).

If we keep in mind this affinity between the two directors, Godard's repeated criticisms of Spielberg come to resemble a type of defence mechanism. For instance, take the 1998 interview conducted by the magazine *Les Inrockuptibles*.[2] From the very outset, Godard tossed around remarks such as "I can't say that I'm envious of Spielberg" and "There's no need for me to get on my knees for him." And, aside from the opening scene depicting the invasion of Normandy, he levelled a negative evaluation toward the then just-released *Saving Private Ryan* in the name of Anthony Mann's *Men in War* (1957). Psychoanalytically speaking, it is not difficult to note a sort of denial on Godard's part when he abruptly mentions a famous commercial director's name without being asked about it, and avoids the confrontation with the recent film by taking refuge in the cinephilic past.

We focus here on the fact that this kind of rash and even envious renouncement of Spielberg by Godard was rather pronounced in the 1990s, when his critical rhetoric against the United States was also prominent. For example, the question of why people would prefer to go watch a bad American movie rather than a bad Bulgarian movie—a clever quip that only Godard would make regarding the overwhelming supremacy that Hollywood enjoys in the global market—frequently came up during interviews at that time.[3] In fact, Godard's criticisms of Spielberg were also connected with this context. In other words, Spielberg was singled out by Godard as the representative of insincere filmmakers who naively cling to the circumstances surrounding the hegemony of Hollywood (recall that Godard has always been interested in the economic, cultural, and political situation of film production). This connection reached its peak in Godard's *Éloge de l'amour* (2001) in which Godard attacks Spielberg almost farcically as a representative of a Hollywood/America that appropriates other people's memories—memories of the Resistance in particular. However, viewed from a different perspective, Godard's complacency here in simply providing sarcastic banter prevents him from directly facing Spielberg's films.

It does not require psychoanalysis to recognize that Godard *denies* Spielberg because, for him, the latter's films are objects of desire. For Godard, the most haunting object of desire is almost certainly *Schindler's List*. In 1995, when the New York Film Critics Circle attempted to bestow a special award upon him, he rejected it. The foremost reason for doing so was that "JLG was never able through his whole movie maker/goer career to prevent M. Spielberg from rebuilding Auschwitz."[4] Why in the world would Godard express such heated animosity—an animosity close to an infantile aggression—towards *Schindler's List*? Perhaps it is because, in a manner of speaking, *Schindler's List* was a film that usurped some of Godard's ideas as to how to represent concentration camps.

A TRUE FILM TO BE MADE ABOUT CONCENTRATION CAMPS

Concentration camps and the Holocaust were not only *leitmotifs* in *Histoire(s) du cinéma* but also one of Godard's persistent objects of interest from early on, as evidenced by the allusion to the then ongoing Frankfurt Auschwitz Trial (from December 20, 1963, to August 1, 1965) by the protagonists of *Une femme mariée* (1964). In a 1963 article in which Godard responds to each piece of negative criticism being directed toward *Les Carabiniers* (1963), he envisions "the only real film to be made" about concentration camps—which could never be made "because it would be intolerable"—a film that would depict the realistic hardships that the "torturers" faced every day. These problems would include "how to get a human body measuring two meters into a coffin measuring fifty centimeters," "how to load ten tons of arms and legs on to a three-ton lorry," and "how to burn a hundred women with petrol enough for ten." Godard adds that "one would also have secretaries making lists of everything on their typewriters." What would make such situations particularly intolerable in such scenes is, according to him, not "their horror," but "their very ordinary everydayness."[5]

One thing to consider here is the fact that Godard's interest lies, at least in these statements, not so much in the unprecedented process of the *extermination* of European Jewry, as in the peculiar place that is the *concentration camps*. It should, therefore, be noted that Godard does not share the same starting point with Claude Lanzmann, for whom the impossibility of providing a representation of the extermination process would constitute the keystone in realizing *Shoah* (1985).[6] Instead, Godard's attempt to focus on the torturers' monotonous daily routine in the concentration camps brings to mind Adolf Eichmann, an innocuous bureaucrat thoughtlessly engaged in the deportation of the Jews by efficiently performing his daily routine, portrayed as a perfect embodiment of "the banality of evil" by Hannah Arendt.[7]

Another important thing to note is that Godard in this period seemed to find it inappropriate to straightforwardly show the atrocities in the concentration camps. In the roundtable discussion on Alain Resnais's *Hiroshima mon amour* (1959), he complains about one aspect of this otherwise admirable film:

> One thing that bothers me a bit in *Hiroshima*, which had also bothered me in *Nuit et brouillard*, is the ease with which he shows horrible scenes, for [when confronted with such scenes] we go immediately beyond the aesthetic. I mean, whether it is beautifully shot or not—it doesn't matter—such scenes leave a terrible impression on the spectator anyway. If a film about concentration camps or torture is signed by [Emile] Couzinet or by Visconti, I think it is almost the same thing for me…. The problem that arises when showing horrible scenes is that the director's intention automatically goes beyond our comprehension, and we are shocked by these images, almost in the same way that we are shocked by pornographic images.[8]

Here, Godard wonders if the effect of directly confronting the spectator with "horrible scenes," such as the atrocities in the concentration camps and torture, amounts to that of showing obscene, thought-numbing "pornographic images"—a fundamental question concerning the ethics of representation.[9] The idea of looking instead at the management of a concentration camp may have resulted from his choice of approaching the subject without easily resorting to any "horrible scenes."

GODARD AND *SCHINDLER'S LIST*

While a film about concentration camps was nothing more than a figment of Godard's imagination in the 1960s, it takes a more specific form during a series of lectures held at Montreal in 1978:

> There is another film that I always wanted to make…. No, that I have often intended to make. Now I'd like to make it, not with unknown actors, but with top-class stars and immense sums of money because it would be a spectacular blockbuster…. It's a film about concentration camps, but I'd like to make it as a spectacular super-production, although it will never be made. I will never make it because it would be very expensive, just as it really was very expensive…. Killing six-million people, or even killing four-hundred people a day, costs a lot. Everything has to be well organized, it really is a super-

production. [...] And telling the story of a secretary who typed "four gold teeth, five-hundred grams of hair" and came back the next day.... She knew and didn't know at the same time.[10]

What interests us here is that, in addition to his insistence on telling the story of a typist, he conceives the film as being "a spectacular super-production." Now, do we not have a super-production movie on the subject of the Holocaust, made with a relatively big budget using several "top-class stars"? Are we not tempted to say that Spielberg's *Schindler's List* is none other than the film that Godard had imagined?

In fact, in Spielberg's film, during the course of which typewriters appear as frequently as in Godard's *Histoire(s) du cinéma*, is there not a scene in which the contents of a large number of suitcases, belonging to Jewish people being transported to Krakow, are carefully separated and classified by the Jewish prisoners? Is it not also true that potential difficulties raised by Godard in another interview—"How to find twenty thousand extras who weigh thirty kilos? What's more, one would have to really beat them. But what assistant would be willing to beat up a skeletal extra?"[11]—were overcome by *Schindler's List* in a number of cruel scenes that are almost unbearable to watch?

There are also additional points from which we can ascertain that *Schindler's List* is precisely one of Godard's films "which might have existed" ("qu'il y aurait"). Godard frequently mentions Andrzej Munk's posthumous work *Pasażerka* (1963) as one of the few films ever created about concentration camps.[12] The reason he praises this work is not only because it is one of the earlier films on this subject but also because of its unique portrayal of the complex psychological and emotional relationship between a female jailor and a female prisoner in a death camp. Along with his interest in the bureaucracy of concentration camps, Godard also seems intrigued by the irregular human relations (including homosexual emotions) that occurred within the camps. That is why he was equally interested in André Lacaze's true-life story *The Tunnel* (1978). This novel vividly depicts a group comprised of members from various strata of society, including hoodlums, peasants, and teachers under the control of a homosexual German *Kapo*, who are all taken from the Mauthausen Concentration Camp in order to construct a tunnel in an even more remote mountainous area. In a 1980 interview, he describes the book as "zippy" to the point where "we forget completely that it is a camp and that it is awful and horrible." He even says that it would have been better than *La Grande Illusion* (1937) had it been adapted by Jean Renoir. In a 1985 interview, he returns to this novel, considering the possibility of adapting it with Gérard Depardieu, obviously a "top-class star" in French cinema.[13] However, we must remember here that *Schindler's List* also powerfully depicts the irregular human relations that occur in the unusual place that is the concentration camp. The opportunistic businessman Oskar Schindler (Liam Neeson), who is reminiscent of the main character of *The Tunnel*, a hoodlum, was himself saved in the end, so to speak, by the Jewish workers he thought he had saved. The portrayal of the pathological SS officer Amon Göth (Ralph Fiennes) also leaves a strong impression. The sadomasochistic relationship shared between Göth and his Jewish maid is also reminiscent of the jail-or-prisoner relationship depicted in *Pasażerka*.

The reason Godard focuses on irregular human relations in the concentration camps is that, to him, there exists a parallel relationship between filmmaking and death camps. The only place that one may find authority on a par with that of a film director would have to be in a concentration camp. According to Godard, in the exact same way that a film is "a product of this kind of authority in which a single person wields absolute authority over other individuals," the concentration camps "were managed from above by big SS bosses."[14] We can say that Spielberg's film also implicitly links Schindler's enamel factory (incidentally, factories are one of Godard's most recurrent themes), which is contrasted with concentration camps in their roles as death factories, to a film studio, thus reminding us of Hollywood's Jewish origin. In this way, *Schindler's List* is again coloured by overtones of Godardian notions.

It should be remembered here that *Schindler's List* results from thorough research on previously made Holocaust films. In a roundtable discussion on the film, Gertrud Koch posits that Spielberg "recycled every little slip of film that was made before to produce this film."[15] Yosefa Loshitzky remarks more specifically that *Schindler's List* is "a visually spectacular and eclectic text, quoting from styles as diverse as film noir, German Expressionism, Italian Neorealism, World War II newsreels, and CNN news coverage."[16] To this list, we can now add some of Godard's long-standing ideas on the concentration camps, even if Spielberg had no intention of appropriating them.

Schindler's List is thus a *Godardian* film on a number of different fronts, although Godard, who had no means other than to turn his own home into a studio, could never have possibly made it. It is more than just a conjecture that Godard, who had once attempted and failed to make "a Hollywood film" in affiliation with Francis Coppola's American Zoetrope company, could not find peace when faced with this film. Godard and Spielberg are not exact opposites of each other, although they seem to be at first glance.

On the contrary, they are uncannily similar on a number of points concerning the motif of concentration camps. However, despite the several unexpected affinities between them, it is also true that *Schindler's List* is no more than a partial and superficial appropriation and embodiment of Godard's ideas. Indeed, many considerable differences exist between the two filmmakers. One such difference involves the fundamental standpoint from which each of them approaches genocide in the death camps. To elucidate it, we have to consider another idea arising from concentration camps that Godard has embraced for over thirty years.

THE *MUSELMANN* AND THE REPETITION OF HISTORY

As early as the 1970s, Godard began to develop a particular interest in the so-called *Muselmann*, literally "the Muslim," which was the term widely used in the concentration camps to refer to prisoners close to dying from exhaustion, starvation, and hopelessness. This extreme state between life and death, and between the human and the inhuman, has thus far prompted pathological, psychiatric, ethical, political, and philosophical reflections.[17] However, Godard is exclusively interested in the term *Muselmann* itself. He emphasizes the fact that, in the Nazi concentration camps where most of the prisoners were Jewish, the weakest ones were called "Muslim" rather than terms for other races or religions. According to him, the power relationship among the three parties implicated in this appellation foreshadows the postwar Israeli–Palestinian conflict. "The current war in the Middle East was born in a concentration camp on the day when a large Jewish tramp (*"un grand clochard juif"*) on the verge of dying was also called 'Muslim' by some SS or other."[18] This passage from his letter to Elias Sanbar, dated July 19, 1977, coupled with a famous photograph from April 1945 of a starving prisoner sitting with his mouth half-open at the Bergen-Belsen camp, makes it abundantly clear why Godard pays such attention to this name.

The first instance in which Godard mentions the term in his films can be found in the latter half of *Ici et ailleurs* (1974).[19] Anne-Marie Miéville states the following in a voice-over commentary: "I noticed something, you know, when reading books about concentration camps. When prisoners were no longer standing, when they were really useless, at the final stage of physical decline, they were called a 'Muslim.'" In terms of the image, we see a photograph of a group of survivors behind barbed wire, taken by Margaret Bourke-White at the liberation of the Buchenwald camp, followed by documentary footage (through the TV monitor that the French family residing *here* is supposed to be watching) that shows two female ex-guards carrying an emaciated body to a mass grave in the Bergen-Belsen camp, and a close-up of a decayed corpse in the Mauthausen camp. This sequence is preceded by television footage in which the bodies of four fedayeen are defenestrated and burned by furious inhabitants of a Mizrahi town, with Miéville's voice commenting that "when we see these images, we only have one thing to say, one sound to use," and is followed by a part of a Hebrew elegy reciting "Auschwitz, Majdanek, Treblinka ..." These sequences illustrate straightforwardly the classical thesis of the French pro-Palestinian and anti-Zionist ultra-left, which can be formulated as "the Jews are doing to the Arabs what the Nazis did to the Jews."[20] Accordingly, the term *Muselmann* here is regarded exclusively as a convenient word that neatly condenses the viewpoint that the origin of the Palestinian difficulties had something to do with the concentration camps.

This somewhat rash and hasty historical viewpoint reflects clearly Godard's avowed pro-Palestinian, anti-Zionist position in the 1970s. However, in my view, his continuous reflection on the term *Muselmann* over the next three decades has tempered its sharp ideological overtones, thus turning it from a provocative weapon to denounce Israel's policies toward the Palestinians into an emblem of an unfortunate repetition of history in a larger context. For instance, in 1995, Godard explains his interest in the term in the following way:

> This word "Muslim" was associated with the word "Jew" in a very particular place, that is, in the concentration camps. According to the books, what the Germans called "Muslim" was the final stage of an inmate, when he could no longer even move, devoid even of the strength to live. They could have called him "Indian," "Gypsy," or "Russian" because, at that time, there was no shortage of people for them to look down on. At the time, I said that Beirut started there. Today, we can say that Sarajevo also started there. People don't make a comparison [*rapprochement*].[21]

It is important to note here that the term "Muslim" is not only related to "Beirut" but also to "Sarajevo" because it no longer simply evokes a naive view that equates Israel with Nazi, but rather designates a primal scene of repetitive calamities that Muslims have suffered in Lebanon, in Algeria, or in Sarajevo, albeit in completely different historical situations.[22]

Godard's insistence that not only the Palestinian difficulties but also all of the tragedies that Muslims have undergone originate in the appellation of "Muslim" in the concentration camps clearly echoes his idiosyncratic historical imagination, which always highlights the *repetitive* aspects of historical events, regardless of their accuracy or preciseness. His interest in history has indeed centred less on historical events themselves than on how they are connected to each other. Put differently, what has always attracted him is to "make a comparison" between several histories, that is, to practise a montage between them in his idiosyncratic sense. Conversely, the cinematographic technique of montage does require such a viewpoint on history. At any rate, his persistent interest in the term *Muselmann* is perfectly compatible with his fundamental historical imagination based on the notion of montage.[23]

To look at an interstice between historical incidents also means, at least theoretically, the withdrawal from directly taking sides with any party in their representations. In claiming the importance of the appellation "Muslim," Godard does not identify himself with the Jews in the concentration camps or with the Muslims in Palestine or in Sarajevo. He simply calls attention to their potential relations by making them collide from the (meta-)vantage point where he no longer manifestly supports the Palestinian cause. He has recently even started calling himself a "Jew of the cinema,"[24] but this does not imply that he is willing to identify himself with the Jewish people. In the light of a specific sense of belonging among the Jews in the Diaspora, he seeks to act differently in terms of national, ethnic, and cultural identity.

In the first movement of *Film socialisme* (2010), a woman's voice reads a (modified) passage of Hannah Arendt's epistolary retort to Gershom Scholem, who accused her of lacking "love of the Jewish people" after the publication of *Eichmann in Jerusalem* in 1963: "You are quite right. I don't love any people—neither the French, nor the North American, nor the Jewish people, nor the Blacks. I love only my friends." This citation could also be interpreted as a manifestation of Godard's wish as to how to mobilize a category of identity; he claims that his actions are not based on love of any particular people or nation, thus locating himself in the gap between several identities and out of any ordinary identity politics.

The biggest difference between Godard and Spielberg is precisely concerned with the question of identity. Spielberg, who was raised in an Orthodox family and whose grandfather was a Jew from Odessa, belatedly becomes fully conscious of his Jewish identity, dedicating *Schindler's List* to "six-million Jews murdered." Furthermore, the final scene in which the Schindler survivors and the actors and actresses who incarnated them visit Schindler's grave together in Israel to put pebbles on it is explicitly Zionistic, to which even Claude Lanzmann expressed his strong disagreement.[25] Godard, on the contrary, attempts to consider history from a standpoint detached from his own identity. Given that historiography based on identity politics tends to exclude those who do not share the same identity, Godard's attempt to conceive history without taking sides with any particular identity, or, which amounts to the same thing, by assuming various identities at once, is exceptionally valuable. Rather than accusing him of lacking accurate and coherent historical knowledge (recent debates on his alleged anti-Semitism do not appear from nowhere, but are based on the misunderstanding of his fundamental ideas), we should fully explore the potential of his historiographic methodology.

NOTES

1   For a partial transcription of this interview, see Jean-Luc Godard, *Jean-Luc Godard par Jean-Luc Godard, tome 2: 1984–1998*, ed. Alain Bergala (Paris: Cahiers du cinéma, 1998), 408–22.

2   Jean-Luc Godard, Frédéric Bonnaud, and Arnaud Viviant, "La légende du siècle," *Les Inrockuptibles* 170 (1998): 23–24.

3   "I prefer, like everyone else, a bad American movie to a bad Bulgarian movie." Ibid., 23.

4   Jean-Luc Godard, "Letter from Jean-Luc," *Village Voice*, February 14, 1995, 49. Duncan Wheeler reflects on Godard's disapproval of Spielberg's film in "Godard's List: Why Spielberg and Auschwitz Are Number One," *Media History* 15, no. 2 (2009): 185–203.

5   Jean Narboni and Tom Milne, eds., *Godard on Godard* (New York: Da Capo Press, 1972), 198. In a 1965 interview, Godard also shows interest in filming "the life of a short-hand typist at Auschwitz," and relates it to Mikhail Romm's *Ordinary Fascism* (ibid., 225). Godard's comments on the concentration camps and the Holocaust are well documented in Richard Brody, *Everything Is Cinema: The Working Life of Jean-Luc Godard* (New York: Metropolitan Books, 2008), 509–13, with a particular relation to Claude Lanzmann's *Shoah* (1985).

6   For a detailed confrontation between the two filmmakers, see Libby Saxton, *Haunted Images: Film, Ethics, Testimony and the Holocaust* (London: Wallflower Press, 2008), 46–67. In discussing the possible proximity and complementarity between Godard and Lanzmann, Saxton evokes Spielberg as their common adversary (64–65). But I think that "Godard's hostile reaction to *Schindler's List*" (65) should not be taken literally. I also suggest that the neat and convincing Godard/Lanzmann confrontation could be relativized by interpolating the former's hidden affinities with Spielberg.

7   Hannah Arendt, *Eichmann in Jerusalem: A Report on the Banality of Evil* (New York: Viking Press, 1963). For that matter, Rony Brauman and Eyal Sivan's reconstitution of the footage of the Eichmann trial in 1961, *Un spécialiste* (1999), inspired chiefly by Arendt's book, could be fruitfully compared with Godard's remark on the concentration camps.

8   Jean Domarchi et al., "Hiroshima, notre amour," *Cahiers du cinéma* 97 (July 1959): 11.

9   Interestingly enough, contrary to Godard's hesitation toward the "horrible scenes" in *Nuit et brouillard*, Truffaut provides a contrasting view on the film. "Resnais'

work, which combines color in the present with documentary black-and-white footage, subtracts from the latter all macabre theatricality, all staged horror, and thus forces us to react with our heads rather than with our nerve endings." See François Truffaut, *The Films in My Life*, trans. Leonard Mayhew (New York: Simon and Schuster, 1978), 303.

10 Jean-Luc Godard, *Introduction à une véritable histoire du cinéma* (Paris: Albatros, 1980), 259.

11 *Le Matin Magazine*, May 10–11, 1980, cited in Brody, *Everything Is Cinema*, 510.

12 See, for instance, *Godard par Godard, tome 2*, 172. This film is also mentioned in Chapter 3A of *Histoire(s) du cinéma*, together with *La Dernière Étape* (*Ostatni Etap*, directed by Wanda Jakubowska, 1948), as "two expiatory films" by the Poles, followed by Godard's narration that "they [the Poles] ended up welcoming Spielberg when 'never again' ('plus jamais ça') became 'it's better than nothing' ('c'est toujours ça')."

13 Jean-Luc Godard, *Jean-Luc Godard par Jean-Luc Godard, tome 1: 1950–1984*, ed. Alain Bergala (Paris: Cahiers du cinéma, 1998), 453, 603.

14 Godard, *Introduction à une véritable histoire du cinéma* (Paris: Albatros, 1980), 221–22.

15 Jim Hoberman et al., "*Schindler's List*: Myth, Movie, and Memory," *Village Voice*, March 29, 1994, 25.

16 Yosefa Loshitzky, "Holocaust Others: Spielberg's *Schindler's List* versus Lanzmann's *Shoah*," in *Spielberg's Holocaust: Critical Perspectives on "Schindler's List,"* ed. Yosefa Loshitzky (Bloomington: Indiana University Press, 1997), 109.

17 Giorgio Agamben, *Remnants of Auschwitz: The Witness and the Archive* (New York: Zone Books, 1999), 45–48.

18 *Cahiers du cinéma* 300 (May 1979): 17.

19 Richard Brody reports that Godard had already introduced the term to Yasser Arafat out of the blue in 1970, when he and Gorin were preparing the finally unfinished *Jusqu'à la victoire* in Palestine, explaining to the bewildered Chairman of the PLO that there is "a direct relationship" between the Palestinian difficulties and the concentration camps. Brody, *Everything Is Cinema*, 352–53.

20 This formulation is borrowed from Antoine de Baecque, *Godard, biographie* (Paris: Grasset, 2010), 531.

21 *Godard par Godard, tome 2*, 311. In a 1998 interview with Alain Bergala, Godard also relates the term "Muslim" to "what is happening in Algeria." Elsewhere, the connection between this name and Sarajevo is associated mysteriously with André Bazin's famous formula "montage forbidden [*montage interdit*]." Ibid., 11, 346.

22 Although the term "Muslim" begins to reappear in his films from the 1990s (particularly in Chapter 4B of *Histoire(s) du cinéma* [1998], *Notre musique* [2004], and *Film socialisme* [2010]), the underlying idea here is unclear as opposed to that in his statements in interviews—which sometimes led to confusion. The slightly, but decisively, different contexts in which the term appears in the form of the written text on the screen in each film should be carefully analyzed in detail.

23 For an analysis on Godard's method of representing history through montage, see Junji Hori, "Godard's Two Historiographies," in *For Ever Godard*, ed. Michael Temple, James S. Williams, and Michael Witt (London: Black Dog, 2004), 334–49.

24 Jean-Luc Godard, Jacques Mandelbaum, and Thomas Sotinel, "À Sarajevo, le 'juif du cinéma' cultive l'optimisme," *Le Monde*, May 13, 2004.

25 "Although many regard me as a Zionist, I would never dare to deliver such 'sledge-hammer blows' as those Spielberg gives at the end of his *Schindler's List*. [...] Israel is not the redemption of the Holocaust. The six million did not die so that Israel could exist." Claude Lanzmann, "Holocaust, la représentation impossible," *Le Monde*, March 3, 1994, 7.

BIBLIOGRAPHY

Agamben, Giorgio. *Remnants of Auschwitz: The Witness and the Archive*. New York: Zone Books, 1999.

Arendt, Hannah. *Eichmann in Jerusalem: A Report on the Banality of Evil*. New York: Viking Press, 1963.

Brody, Richard. *Everything Is Cinema: The Working Life of Jean-Luc Godard*. New York: Metropolitan Books, 2008.

Cahiers du cinéma 300 (May 1979).

De Baecque, Antoine. *Godard, biographie*. Paris: Grasset, 2010.

Domarchi, Jean, Jacques Doniol-Valcroze, Jean-Luc Godard, Pierre Kast, Jacques Rivette, and Eric Rohmer. "Hiroshima, notre amour." *Cahiers du cinéma* 97 (July 1959): 1–18.

Godard, Jean-Luc. *Introduction à une véritable histoire du cinéma*. Paris: Albatros, 1980.

———. *Jean-Luc Godard par Jean-Luc Godard, tome 1: 1950–1984*. Edited by Alain Bergala. Paris: Cahiers du cinéma, 1998.

———. *Jean-Luc Godard par Jean-Luc Godard, tome 2: 1984–1998*. Edited by Alain Bergala. Paris: Cahiers du cinéma, 1998.

———. "Letter from Jean-Luc." *The Village Voice*, February 14, 1995.

Godard, Jean-Luc, Frédéric Bonnaud, and Arnaud Viviant. "La légende du siècle." *Les Inrockuptibles* 170 (1998): 20–28.

Godard, Jean-Luc, Jacques Mandelbaum, and Thomas Sotinel. "A Sarajevo, le 'juif du cinéma' cultive l'optimisme." *Le Monde*, May 13, 2004.

Hoberman, Jim, Wanda Bershen, Richard Goldstein, Annette Insdorf, Ken Jacobs, Gertrud Koch, Art Spiegelman, and James Young. "*Schindler's List*: Myth, Movie, and Memory." *Village Voice*, March 29, 1994, 24–31.

Hori, Junji. "Godard's Two Historiographies." In *For Ever Godard*, edited by Michael Temple, James S. Williams, and Michael Witt, 334–49. London: Black Dog, 2004.

Lanzmann, Claude. "Holocaust, la représentation impossible." *Le Monde*, March 3, 1994, 1, 7.

Loshitzky, Yosefa. "Holocaust Others: Spielberg's *Schindler's List* versus Lanzmann's Shoah." In *Spielberg's Holocaust: Critical Perspectives on "Schindler's List*," edited by Yosefa Loshitzky, 104–18. Bloomington: Indiana University Press, 1997.

Narboni, Jean, and Tom Milne, eds. *Godard on Godard*. New York: Da Capo Press, 1972.

Saxton, Libby. *The Haunted Images: Film, Ethics, Testimony and the Holocaust*. London: Wallflower Press, 2008.

Truffaut, François. *The Films in My Life*. Translated by Leonard Mayhew. New York: Simon and Schuster, 1978.

Wheeler, Duncan. "Godard's List: Why Spielberg and Auschwitz Are Number One." *Media History* 15, no. 2 (2009): 185–203.

6

"The Obligations of Memory": Godard's Underworld Journeys

Russell J.A. Kilbourn

Memory has no obligations.

—*Éloge de l'amour*

IN HIS *VILLAGE Voice* review, J. Hoberman suggests that Godard's *Éloge de l'amour* (*In Praise of Love*, 2001) can be seen "as a fragmentary remake of Jean Cocteau's *Orphée* [1949]—a movie about the attempt to retrieve a lost love that haunts *Alphaville* [1965] and is itself haunted by France's German occupation."[1] In this essay I have space only to sketch a reading of the critique in *Éloge de l'amour* of Steven Spielberg's *Schindler's List* (1993) through the lens of Cocteau's transposition of the Orpheus myth, by way of *Alphaville*, which, in many ways, is Godard's answer to Cocteau. There is more than a little of the underworld journey in Lemmy Caution's (Eddie Constantine) "strange adventure" in the de-humanized dystopia of the titular Alphaville.[2] By the same token, *Orphée* is far more than a modern cinematic resetting of the katabasis narrative chronotope of classical myth and epic.[3]

Filmmakers from across the spectrum have long exploited cinema's available resources in the representation of memory as visual-spatial construct. For example, *Orphée*'s otherworldly underworld setting—called "the Zone"—is filmed in part on location in the ruined St. Cyr military college at Yvelines, France.[4] Jacques Aumont views "the Zone" as a "space where time escapes time, memory is frozen and history is abolished. As such, it represents the recent Holocaust, the *Lager* of death, amnesia and forgetting."[5] Of these four films, however, *Éloge de l'amour* is most properly a memory film, in its narrative, structure, and themes, the last third being an extended flashback sequence in saturated colour digital video, following abruptly upon the first section, shot in rich, grainy black-and-white 35 mm. As Amy Taubin reminds us, "the literal translation of '*éloge*' [in the French title] is *eulogy*—praise bestowed on the dead. In *In Praise of Love*, love is almost entirely couched in the past tense, inextricable from mourning, guilt, and regret."[6] In this respect, theme intersects with the image in its iconic and indexical aspects, corresponding to digital video and film, respectively.

Elsewhere I have treated Cocteau's *Orphée* as a kind of modernist ur-text for the memory film sub-genre, as it thematizes memory, desire, mourning, and death in a modernist resetting of the Orphic myth.[7] In transposing aspects of this story, *Alphaville* too offers a meditation on time, desire, and identity in a near-future (but utterly mid-'60s) dystopian Paris controlled by a faceless but all-too-human technology. One can already see in the earlier film Godard's fascination with a constellation of ideas around the meta-theme of time and memory; in *Éloge de l'amour* this finds a highly evocative, complex cinematic form that (not surprisingly) goes against the grain of the representation of memory in a classical Hollywood cinema predicated on the manufactured desires and identifications constitutive of the regime of the gaze.[8] In this light, Spielberg's *Schindler's List* exemplifies the big-budget, high-quality Hollywood film emblematic of the broader cultural-industrial matrix that for most of us constitutes the only truly collective, even global, prosthetic memory, in a way that resonates far

Fig. 6.1 *Still from* Orpheus, *directed by Jean Cocteau, and performed by Jean Marais and Marie Déa. An André Paulvé Film, 1950. (Criterion Collection, 2000, DVD)*

beyond Holocaust studies. Spielberg's film also exemplifies the contemporary extension and intensification of a classical film idiom calculated to seduce, satisfy, and give pleasure as much as to educate or memorialize:

> the relationship of mass culture to memory has often addressed concerns about how popular culture and mass media can co-opt memories and reconfigure histories in the name of entertainment—what has become known, for better or for worse, as the "Spielberg style" of history, in which simplistic narratives are deployed to evoke particular empathetic responses in viewers, and through which memory texts are fashioned. Thus, the relationship between mass culture and entertainment forms and memory has been fraught from the early years of modernity with a fear that memory can be transformed, co-opted, and appropriated through popular culture forms.[9]

For Stuart Klawans, "'Spielberg' is the name Godard gives to a false universalism: the omnipresent culture of Hollywood, which unites people by offering them all the same fantasies."[10] In *Histoire(s) du Cinéma*, Chapter 3A, Godard (in voice-over) declares: "Cinema was first made for thinking. That was soon forgotten. But that's another story. The flame went out for good at Auschwitz."[11] This is followed by a sequence of images from the Occupation, the Resistance, and Liberation of France. Then Godard invokes Spielberg's sojourn in Poland to make *Schindler's List*: "'Never again,'" remarks Godard, "became 'It's better than nothing.'"[12]

Éloge de l'amour asks "how can we maintain this link to the past, to history, in a world that seems to deny history, in the perpetual present of a corporate culture conforming to a model provided by America, that is to say, a country without a history?"[13] As Edgar (Bruno Putzulu), in the film's first half, comments to Berthe (Cécile Camp), the object of his rather tepid desire, regarding the so-called Spielberg Associates' attempt (in the second half) to purchase the memories of French Resistance fighters: "The Americans have no real past. [...] They have no memory of their own. Their machines do, but they have none personally. So they buy the past of others. Especially those who resisted."[14] But to reduce the film's argument, as the film itself tempts us to do, to one that says that "America has no history of its own and hence must appropriate history from others,"[15] is to overlook the film's more complex, even contradictory, critical position. "'The Americans are everywhere, aren't they, sir?' a Vietnamese chambermaid asks [Edgar's patron, Mr. Rosenthal, adding:] 'Who remembers Vietnam's resistance?' Resistance, for Godard, is a factor of memory."[16] In fact, the film makes explicit its own contradictory politics of memory in the repeated claim that "there can be no resistance without memory or universalism." Hoberman implies that *Éloge de l'amour* is Godard's own act of resistance, after the fact.[17] But Godard had confronted this past in film long before; in *Alphaville*, after all, dissident citizens of the titular city are arrested and shot for expressing individual will and irrational desire: speech crimes intolerable in a panoptic world run according to the binary logic of a giant analog computer invented by a Bondian super-villain named either "Nosferatu" or "Von Braun" (who also bears more than a passing resemblance to Godard).

But the debate around *Schindler's List* is also always a debate about the representation of the Holocaust:

> For many audiences, Spielberg's vision will constitute their sole, or primary, encounter with the Shoah and will, as such, overdetermine their relationship to this traumatic event. In its attempts to conceal its own partiality and subjectivity, the film implicitly signposts its own status as a master text for collective remembrance. Godard evokes the spirit of resistance in an attempt to ward off American imperialists such as Spielberg who attempt to provide the last word on the Holocaust.[18]

What Spielberg (and post-classical Hollywood) obscures, and Godard repeatedly lays bare, is that eyewitness testimony of past events is always already subject to, indeed constituted by, pre-existing structures: the genres, clichés, and tropes of memory, dominated by variations on the flashback:[19] *this* is how memory should be recounted; *this* is how the past should look; etc. Cocteau's idiosyncratically allegorical engagement in *Orphée* with the memory of WW II and the Resistance in France finds a curious complement in Godard, whose preoccupation with the question of representing such events resurfaces in his 2001 film, whose black-and-white first section seems to address *Schindler's List* on the visual-stylistic level, even as its colour-saturated final third—for Godard an exceedingly rare extended flashback sequence—ups the ante with a direct satire of Spielberg's aggressive (and wholly fictional) bid to buy the rights to an elderly French couple's story of fighting in the Resistance. Here Godard's ongoing critique of the commodification of the image merges with the question of representing certain aspects of the war (or twentieth-century history per se) in a dialectical analysis of the relation between commodities and memory, in an attempt to resist what Richard Terdiman calls the necessary forgetting behind reification: the cultural amnesia at the heart of late capitalist modernity.[20] On the one hand, then, there is the pseudo-messianic model of "redemption" *through* the commodified image, exemplified by Hollywood and *Schindler's List*.[21] On the other hand, there is the infernal or perhaps more properly modernist "purgatorial" model (what Derrida calls "messianicity without messianism")[22]—not really a coherent model at all—involving the redemption *of* the commodified image, represented by the international art film (as it persists into the twenty-first century), and by a film like *Éloge de l'amour*.[23] In other words, if the image is to save us, first we must save the image. It is therefore also necessary to consider how Godard's critique of the relation between commodities and memory has changed since the mid-'60s: has it softened with time, becoming more "elegiac"? The film's much-remarked melancholia is itself a modality of a self-conscious or reflexive memory that resists utterly the siren song of unreflective nostalgia and the melodramatic trappings of contemporary Hollywood narrative symptomatic of the commodification and globalization of individual and collective traumatic memory; the aesthetics of appropriation and sentimentalization characteristic of late or postmodern pop culture. At the same time, Godard's film thematizes an ethical critique of such notions as "collective" memory or trauma even as it foregrounds yet again what I call cinema's general status as pre-eminent prosthetic memory for the twentieth century.[24]

To objections that *Éloge de l'amour* is not "about" the Holocaust—even in a sense wholly other than *Schindler's List*—one can answer with Edgar's observation to Berthe, late in the first half: "When I think about something, I'm really thinking about something else. You can only think about something if you think of something else. For instance, you see a landscape new to you. But it's new to you because you mentally compare it to another landscape, one which you know." (These words are a repetition of another speech later in the film but earlier in time; that is, at the end of the flashback of which the second part is comprised.) In this view, thinking, thought itself, always involves memory; without memory there is no thought—just as this film engages the viewer's memory in its very structure. Therefore, although the French Resistance, and not the Holocaust, is the major wartime event referenced in the film, some critics suggest that the Holocaust is the film's real, albeit secret, subject;[25] a European or international subject, while the Resistance is of course a specifically French subject. As evidence, Michael Sofair points to "a fleeting scene in which we see Edgar waiting for a train that stops at a platform with the sign 'Drancy Avenir.'"[26] During a telephone conversation with Berthe, Edgar asks in voice-over: "Whoever connected Drancy [site of a transit camp from which Jews were transported from France for extermination] with the future?" (Fr. *avenir*: future). Berthe replies: "Some upright family man. He came home from the office, kissed his children, and told his little girl he'd worked well." This brief exchange marries the spirit of the scathing critique of bourgeois family values from *Orphée*'s final scene[27]—such values constitute a primary target of much political postwar art cinema—with Godard's oblique but non-allegorical analysis of France's involvement in what became the Final Solution.

Therefore, according to Michael Sofair, "understanding the relation between the past evoked by Drancy and the future is also our challenge in trying to relate the two halves of *In Praise of Love*, as its first half is future to the second, which more explicitly recalls the time of which Drancy was a part."[28] The manner in which it does this also affords a more explicit instance of the film's oblique engagement with the Holocaust. First, it should be noted that where the second half addresses wartime France primarily in its story, the first half does so as much on the level of the image (the black-and-white; Paris as cinematic city;[29] old European and Hollywood films). In the second half, over a videotape of archival footage of what appear to be extermination camp corpses, Berthe quotes a line misleadingly attributed to Georges Bataille's 1935 anti-Fascist novel *Blue of Noon*:[30] "The state is the very antithesis of the image of a loved one, whose sovereign reason negates that of love."[31] Later in the scene she continues, quoting Maurice Blanchot's work on friendship: "The image, alone capable of denying nothingness, is also the gaze of nothingness upon us."[32] A typically complex intertextual patchwork, Berthe's dialogue here is at the same time an *intra*-textual borrowing from *Histoire(s) du Cinéma*, Chapter 4B, in which Blanchot's words are intoned by Godard in voice-over. The key to reading this scene may be the earlier sequence by the Seine, the inverse of this conversation in the second half about the image as "the gaze of nothingness upon us," in which Edgar (always recalling one thing by thinking of another) is the one to express hope. In the earlier conversation, ironically, near the film's mid-point, close to her own end, Berthe seems at her most hopeful:

BERTHE (sitting by the river): What are you thinking about?

EDGAR (looking across the river at the abandoned Renault factory): The empty fortress.

B: That sounds familiar.

E: I was thinking of the Communist trade union.

B: There is no emptiness. There is always a voice somewhere.

E: What about silence?

B: Even in silence.

E: What about death?

B: There is no death. When it comes, there is always a sense of self.

This dialectic, in fact a chiasm, of hope and voice, silence and hopelessness, reflected in the shift from black and white to colour, never resolves within the diegesis, which ends almost where it began. (A running joke in the film has Edgar leafing through a book with blank pages, as if in ironic homage to Cocteau's Orpheus, who at one point is presented with the latest issue of a new avant-garde poetry journal titled *Nudisme*, whose pages are comparably empty.) As Edgar explains, his never-to-be-realized project embraces every aspect of love, including its antitheses and failures, where the French Resistance might be seen as proof that collective desire as engine of "History" can achieve liberation even as individual relationships and memories are betrayed.

The obvious dialectic in the film is that between the vestiges of Western European "high culture" and mass or popular cultural forms, especially Hollywood. But the later Godard's less-than-subtle critique of Spielberg, of Hollywood, and of American culture generally must be taken with a grain of salt if only because of his own long-standing love affair with American cinema and its iconography of stars and auteurs; witness the highly subjective *Histoire(s) du cinéma*.[33] Alongside his almost anachronistic attachment to the monuments of high culture, one can see in these recent works a kind of nostalgia, not always ironic, for American cinema. Where *Alphaville* provides one example of Godard's mid-'60s "postmodern" contradictory infatuation with popular culture,[34] a post-Marxist, twenty-first-century film like *Éloge de l'amour* demonstrates how far Godard has

Fig. 6.2 *Still from* In Praise of Love, *directed by Jean-Luc Godard and performed by Bruno Putzulu and Cécile Camp. Avventura Films, 2001 (New Yorker Video, 2003, DVD)*

travelled from this proto-postmodernist aesthetic toward a kind of renewed modernism, eschewing in classical Godardian style the very popular culture with which his early cinema was deeply engaged. After all, what could be further from the agential secret agent Lemmy Caution (or, for that matter, Jean-Paul Belmondo's Michel in *À bout de souffle*) than Edgar, the passively melancholic protagonist of the more recent film? (On the other hand, Edgar is a bit like a grown-up version of Jean-Pierre Léaud's Paul in 1966's *Masculin féminin*; they even dress the same way: a young man trying to be an adult.)

In contrast to *Alphaville*, where Lemmy Caution in the end does manage to take Natasha with him to what is presumably a better world ("Don't look back," he cautions her), *Éloge de l'amour* more faithfully modernizes *Orphée* in the protagonist's failed quest to find and understand the elusive woman, Berthe, who goes unnamed in the first, black-and-white, section, and whose face is rarely shown in a frontal shot—as if the viewer, like Edgar, were constrained by an unspoken prohibition upon looking lest in being seen she be lost a second time and for good. As Douglas Morrey suggests, "this approach to filming a heroine [may] simply [reproduce] in a different way the traditional gender division of narrative cinema, with Berthe as the elusive, enigmatic woman[35] and Edgar as the questing subject of the narrative. But it should be pointed out that Godard's filming of Cécile Camp definitively denies the spectator any kind of fetishistic appropriation of her body,"[36] just as it denies conven-

Fig. 6.3 *Still from* In Praise of Love, *directed by Jean-Luc Godard and performed by Bruno Putzulu and Cecile Camp. Avventura Films, 2001. (New Yorker Video, 2003, DVD)*

tional spectatorial identification. This failure to *see* the beloved properly—the film's seeming "failure" to *show* her properly—is at the heart of the film's elegy to love redoubled within the story in Edgar's unfinished project on the three stages of life: youth, adulthood, and old age—coupled with the four stages of love: meeting, passion, separation, reconciliation.[37] (As Colin McCabe points out, Edgar's ideal seems to be courtly love: the protagonists of his never-to-be-realized project are named Percival and Eglantine, while the proposed title of the film Spielberg would make from the life story of the elderly Resistance fighters is "Tristan and Iseult," from their wartime code names.)[38]

According to *Schindler's List* cinematographer Janusz Kaminski: "We wanted people to see this film years from now and not realize when it was made."[39] For Godard, "this approach serves to make *Schindler's List* both 'out of date' and 'indecent.'"[40] Just as he inverts the narrative in *Éloge de l'amour*, Godard also inverts cinematic conventions around the representation of the diegetic present, typically in colour, and the past, whose association with black and white is traceable on one level to the fact that cinema's first forty or fifty years is overwhelmingly monochromatic.[41] According to Godard: "I thought it would be more appropriate to work against the generally accepted idea of showing the present in color and the past in black-and-white, as in newsreels. On the contrary, I wanted to find a way of intensifying the past."[42] It is all the more appropriate that Godard (long before *Histoire(s) du cinéma*) should have been among the first to recognize this past as cinema's own history—a recognition that coincided with the emergence of the New Wave in France and the full flowering of the international art cinema movement whose very existence depends on this self-awareness.

In Taubin's view: "The obvious comparison in *In Praise of Love* is between film and video. Godard pushes each of them in a different direction to highlight their radically different textural and expressive qualities. Film, as the older medium—the bearer of twentieth-century history[43]—comes with built-in memory. The images of Paris in the first half of the film invite comparisons not only to Godard's own early black-and-white work but to Bresson, Renoir, to an entire tradition of representation,"[44] which is explicitly intertextualized in the film. "Video, on the other hand, particularly as Godard uses it with the colour over-saturated and the contrast over-loaded, has virtually no history. But paradoxically, since video images are less articulated and more mutable than film images … they are inherently correlatives of memory."[45] Taubin's "inherently" requires further thought, insofar as it implies that what we mean by "memory" is colonized by cinema; that the interiority once implied by personal individual memory

Fig. 6.4 *Still from* Schindler's List, *directed by Steven Spielberg and performed by Liam Neeson and Ben Kingsley. Universal Pictures, 1993. (Universal Studios, 2009, DVD)*

has given way irredeemably to the radical exteriority of memory as "art" or prosthetic technique for which notions like "authenticity" and "origin" demand redefinition.[46]

Duncan Wheeler identifies the difference between what he calls "Spielberg's historical realism" and Godard's Brechtian tendencies,[47] which presuppose a radical self-reflexivity as guarantor of a fundamentally polit-ical cinema committed to an engagement with the present, even in the iron-ically elegiac register that pervades *Éloge de l'amour*. There is one potentially defamiliarizing post-production effect in *Schindler's List*, however, in which colour is introduced into the lustrous black-and-white imagery in the form of a little girl's red coat.[48] This effect, and the two sequences in which it occurs, affords a revealing point of comparison to Godard's attitude to the general question of the cinematic narrativization and subjectivization of historical trauma. In this sequence Oskar Schindler is shown in medium shot and then close-up atop a hill gazing down upon the liquidation of the Krakow ghetto from what Mary Louise Pratt in a post-colonial context names the "monarch of all I survey" perspective,[49] a position of visual mas-tery. That Schindler is clearly affected by what he passively witnesses does nothing to mitigate the fact that this sequence aligns the viewer's with Schindler's perspective, just as the type of shot is aligned intertextually with countless others in which a typically masculine protagonist (or if merely the camera, still a gendered look) gazes down imperiously upon the world from on high.[50] In Donald Reid's words, "collectivities outside an experience, like later generations, identify with an experience ... through personalized individual narratives."[51] Nowhere does this process function more smoothly or invisibly than in Hollywood films, like *Schindler's List*, that purport to depict a specific historical moment or event with some degree of accuracy, authenticity, or "truth." This qualifies therefore as what Alison Landsberg defines as prosthetic memories, externalized and artificial, which "enable individuals to have a personal connection to an event they did not live through, to see through another's eyes ... to make possible alliances across racial, class and other chasms of difference."[52]

CONCLUSION

For Douglas Morrey, *Éloge de l'amour* "at times appears so preoccupied with *images of the past* that the creation of new images comes to seem a virtual impossibility.... Godard's film is haunted by other images from the history of cinema."[53] Morrey is careful to parse a key distinction here, in order to highlight a key inversion in the relation of past and present: "There is a sense in which Godard, after such a lengthy absorption in film history, has become so infused with past images (and images of the past) that images in the present can only act as ghosts of those that have gone before."[54] This is not simply a more poetic way of talking about Godard's extraordinary intertextuality; following Morrey's logic, cinema's past images are haunted by the superfluity of images in its epigonal present. For Godard, present images, especially *American* ones, are at once too abundant, too late, and the wrong kind, whereas those that we truly need, or perhaps truly desire, are absent. This paradox goes some ways toward clarifying the film's utterly un-metaphysical evocation of both past and present in the terms of a cinematic underworld or afterlife, not to speak of its inverted—or *chiastic*—relation of past and present, of index and icon.

"To what extent does memory help us reclaim our lives?" asks Edgar. In Ricciardi's view, "[Godard] suggests that, by virtue of its nonchalance of retrospection, film makes it possible to rewrite the myth of Orpheus in a less tragic key than literature permits: 'Cinema authorizes Orpheus to turn back without killing.'"[55] In the beautiful, digitally manipulated concluding scene (the actual middle of the story), Edgar sits on a train, leafing through not a blank book but Chateaubriand's autobiography, *Memoirs from Beyond the Grave* (1848).[56] "Thus everything in my story wanes. As I am left with only images of what happened so quickly, I will go down to the Elysian fields with more shades than a man has ever taken with him."[57] At this point in the story, Edgar does not know what we do, that Berthe probably has tuberculosis, and will take her own life, the off-screen event with which the first part concludes. Whether or not Berthe is among these "shades," then, depends on the perspective in which one views their relationship, having gone from meeting to separation (passing over passion) to the second, absolute separation of death. And here can be seen the link between work and love which Morrey identifies as a central concern, connecting the theme of love to the theme of the three ages of man.[58] Godard's conclusion (as such) to this Orphic underworld journey could not be further either from that of *Alphaville* or from Cocteau's *Orphée*. In the latter's extraordinarily ironic conclusion, after all, Death in the form of a beautiful woman sacrifices herself and her love for the hero by rewinding time to send him back to his Eurydice and to blissful bourgeois contentment, a little nuclear family on the way. Whether a vision of hell or of paradise, this is a world from which Edgar is forever exiled.

NOTES

1   J. Hoberman, "Invisible Cities," *Village Voice*, September 3, 2002, http://www.villagevoice.com/2002-09-03/film/invisible-cities/1.
2   *Alphaville, une étrange aventure de Lemmy Caution.*
3   *Katabasis*, Greek for "a going down, a descent," refers to an underworld journey undertaken by a hero in quest of special knowledge. See Erling B. Holtsmark, "The *Katabasis* Theme in Modern Cinema," in *Classical Myth and Culture in the Cinema*, ed. Martin M. Winkler (New York: Oxford University Press, 2001), 25.
4   James S. Williams, *Jean Cocteau* (Manchester: Manchester University Press, 2006), 110.
5   In Williams, *Jean Cocteau*, 128. Cocteau's more obviously allegorical "zone" owes a direct debt to the "division of France during the war into two administrative zones: the *Zone Libre* and the *Zone Occupée*" (Williams, 124–25).
6   Amy Taubin, "In the Shadow of Memory," *Film Comment* 38, no. 1 (January/February 2002): 50.
7   Russell J.A. Kilbourn, *Cinema, Memory, Modernity: The Representation of Memory from the Art Film to Transnational Cinema* (New York: Routledge, 2010), 51–55.
8   For Isabelle McNeill, *Éloge de l'amour* "is structured, both formally and thematically, around questions of memory, history and the way the past is reinscribed in the present." "Phrases, Monuments and Ruins: Melancholy History in *Éloge de l'amour*," *Studies in French Cinema* 3, no. 2 (2003): 111.
9   Marita Sturken, "Memory, Consumerism, and Media: Reflections on the Emergence of the Field," *Memory Studies* 1, no. 1 (2008): 75.
10   Stuart Klawans, "Auteur, Auteur!" *The Nation* 275, no. 8 (2002): 35, http://www.thenation.com/article/auteur-auteur.
11   "It could even be argued that by turning his attention away from the horrors of the present day to create a simulacrum of past horrors, Spielberg is replicating, in

microcosm, the moment when, for Godard, cinema committed its original sin in failing to show the camps to the world." Duncan Wheeler, "Godard's List: Why Spielberg and Auschwitz Are Number One," *Media History* 15, no. 2 (2009): 193; see also 201.

12 "'Plus jamais ça' est devenu 'C'est toujours ça.'" Elsewhere Godard remarks, "The expression 'Never forget' annoys me. I would prefer to say that [memory] has certain rights and that it is a duty to not forget these rights. Without justice, the work of memory can't be done." "Hope Springs Eternal," *Film Comment* 38, no. 1 (2002): 53.

13 Douglas Morrey, "History of Resistance / Resistance of History: Godard's *Éloge de l'amour* (2001)," *Studies in French Cinema* 3, no. 2 (2003): 122.

14 "The Aubracs' story became in turn the subject of an American comic book immediately after the war (*True Comics*, 1946). The Americans bought the Aubracs' story long before Godard suggested they wanted to buy the memory." Donald Reid, "The Grandchildren of Godard and the Aubracs: Betrayal, Resistance, and the People without a Memory," *French Cultural Studies* 15, no. 1 (2004): 82.

15 Hoberman, "Invisible Cities."

16 Ibid.

17 Ibid. Or, as Donald Reid puts it: "*Éloge de l'amour* is Godard's own act of resistance to the imperial aggression he sees himself confronting today in the form of Hollywoodization.... *Éloge de l'amour* addresses the memory of the French Resistance and the nature of resistance today, not the Resistance as an historical event" ("The Grandchildren of Godard," 76–77).

18 Wheeler, "Godard's List," 192.

19 See Maureen Turim, *Flashbacks in Film: Memory and History* (New York: Routledge, 1989), 1–20.

20 Richard Terdiman, *Present Past: Modernity and the Memory Crisis* (Ithaca, NY: Cornell University Press, 1993), 11–12. See also Kilbourn, *Cinema, Memory, Modernity*, 145.

21 James Cameron's *Titanic* (1997) is also mentioned unfavourably in the film as another excellent example of this apotheosis of the melodramatic mode. By the same token, just because *The Matrix* (1999) is intertextualized in the form of a movie poster does not necessarily imply, as many critics claim, that this or other contemporary films are being singled out for abuse. After all, right next to this poster, in the same shot, is the poster for Robert Bresson's *Pickpocket* (1959). On the other hand, there is a subsequent scene in which two girls dressed in traditional costume come to the door with a petition to dub *The Matrix* into Breton ...

22 Jacques Derrida, *Archive Fever: A Freudian Impression*, trans. Eric Prenowitz (Chicago: University of Chicago Press, 1996), 72.

23 See also Alessia Ricciardi on Godard's *Histoire(s) du cinéma* (1998) in "Cinema Regained: Godard between Proust and Benjamin," *Modernism/Modernity* 8, no. 4 (2001): "Playing the role of Virgil, Godard guides us on our meandering way through an inferno of images while commenting in voice-over on the past as if from beyond the grave" (644). For Proust, "'the true paradises are the paradises that we have lost.' *Histoire(s)* ends on a freeze-frame of a rose superimposed over a still image of Godard himself" (657). In this concluding image, evocative of the end of the *Paradiso*, Godard makes explicit the connection between his magnum opus and Dante's *Divina Commedia*.

24 In Douglas Morrey's words, "*Éloge* shares the concern of *Histoire(s) du cinéma* with the responsibility of cinema towards the memory of the twentieth century." *Jean-Luc Godard* (Manchester: Manchester University Press, 2005), 230.

25 John Drabinski sees "indications" in *Éloge de l'amour* "of the centrality of the Holocaust for his … work, in particular the shot of Vladimir Jankelevitch's *L'imprescriptible.*" *Godard between Identity and Difference* (New York: Continuum, 2008), 140.

26 Michael Sofair, "*In Praise of Love (Éloge de l'amour),*" *Film Quarterly* 58, no. 2 (2005), 41. See also Morrey, *Jean-Luc Godard*, 232.

27 See Kilbourn, *Cinema, Memory, Modernity*, 54.

28 Sofair, "*In Praise of Love,*" 41.

29 See Morrey *Jean-Luc Godard*, 233; and James Quandt, "Here and Elsewhere: Projecting Godard," in *For Ever Godard*, ed. Michael Temple, James S. Williams, and Michael Witt (London: Black Dog, 2004), 134.

30 According to Roland-François Lack, this line is actually from the text "L'amour d'un être mortel," first published in 1951 in *Botteghe Oscure*, and included in volume 8 of Bataille's *Oeuvres Complètes* (email communication, 3 July 2011, courtesy of Douglas Morrey). See also Leslie Hill, "'A Form That Thinks': Godard, Blanchot, Citation," in *For Ever Godard*, ed. Michael Temple, James S. Williams, and Michael Witt (London: Black Dog, 2004), 408.

31 In the first part Edgar remarks to Philippe (in voice-over) that "two years ago [he] met someone…. Not very attractive, but she dared speak her mind. I wonder what became of her? P: What's your definition of an adult? E: She really had something to say about the state, and the impossibility of the state falling in love. Actually, I'm dreaming. What I'd like is someone like Simone Weil and Hannah Arendt." On the significance of Weil for Godard, see Morrey, *Jean-Luc Godard*, 142.

32 See Maurice Blanchot, *Friendship*, trans. Elizabeth Rottenberg (Stanford, CA: Stanford University Press, 1997), 40.

33 There isn't space here to examine the irony of Jean-Luc Godard's helping to rehabilitate the very cinema he helped to deconstruct during the New Wave. As Ricciardi puts it, "If, early in his career, the director's bold experiments helped establish the 'amnesic' style of the New Wave, they now permit him to rehabilitate the tatters of our past." "Cinema Regained," 645.

34 Allen Thiher observes of *Alphaville*'s protagonist, for example: "[Lemmy] Caution is … an ambivalent figure, both a creation of pop irony and a subversive force that defines itself as sheer energy in revolt against the canons of repressive culture…. The ironic glorification of popular myth thus turns not only against the myths themselves, but also against the enshrined cultural values of modernism." "Postmodern Dilemmas: Godard's *Alphaville* and *Two or Three Things That I Know about Her*," *boundary 2* 4, no. 3 (Spring 1976): 953.

35 Physically, Berthe (Cécile Camp) much more closely resembles Orphée's female nemesis Aglaonice (Juliette Gréco) in Cocteau's film, rather than either Eurydice or the Princess.

36 Morrey, "History of Resistance," 127.

37 This is itself a project he conceived after first meeting Berthe and abandoning a cantata on the Resistance activities of Simone Weil, who was Jewish, but who, like

Berthe's grandmother, the Resistance heroine, embraced Catholicism—albeit for different reasons. Weil died of tuberculosis at thirty-four; Berthe, ill with tuberculosis, commits suicide while still a young woman (Sofair, "*In Praise of Love*," 50). Interestingly, Weil moved within the same Resistance circles as Georges Bataille, whose anti-Fascist novel *Blue of Noon* is referred to at one point in the film.

38 Colin MacCabe, *Godard: A Portrait of the Artist at Seventy* (New York: Farrar, Straus, and Giroux, 2003), 326.

39 Janusz Kaminski, quoted in Wheeler, "Godard's List," 187.

40 Wheeler, "Godard's List," 187.

41 See, for example, McNeill, "Phrases, Monuments and Ruins," 115–16; and Wheeler Winston Dixon, "In Praise of Godard's *In Praise of Love*," *Film Criticism* 27, no. 3 (Spring 2003): 30.

42 Godard, quoted in Dixon, "In Praise of Godard's *In Praise of Love*," 30. Speaking of *Éloge de l'amour* as memory film, for Dixon, "the second half of *In Praise of Love* ... gathers great emotional force as it moves toward its conclusion; its use of vibrant color suggests that for Edgar, the past is more real, more alive than the present. As the film begins, Edgar is dead, searching for actors to recreate his emotions. By the end of the film, which is really the beginning, we can see how his quest went awry" (28).

43 In Jeffrey Pence's words, "cinema ... carried the burden of memory in modernity." "Postcinema/Postmemory," in *Memory and Popular Film*, ed. Paul Grainge (Manchester: Manchester University Press, 2003), 237.

44 Taubin, "In the Shadow of Memory," 52.

45 Ibid. Morrey points out, however, that in *Histoire(s)* Godard repeatedly refers to black and white "as the colours of memory and mourning" (*Jean-Luc Godard*, 231).

46 As McNeill points out, however,

> this is no ordinary flashback, for the film never returns to the 'present,' and our sense of time is further confused by the intertitles in the second part, which sometimes say 'two years previously,' sometimes 'already a long time ago,' and sometimes simply 'archives.' The effect of this lengthening of time is to create a sense of distance, and combined with the saturated colour of the digital video, this gives the second half a slightly unreal quality. It creates the impression of a fleshing-out of the experience of memory through film." ("Phrases, Monuments and Ruins," 119)

"One consequence of this structure is that past and present must communicate across a break in time without ever falling into place on some continuous narrative timeline" (Sofair, "*In Praise of Love*," 36).

47 Wheeler, "Godard's List," 189.

48 Despite the visual parallels, the effect could not be further from the opening shots of Godard's *Une femme est une femme* (1961), in which Anna Karina moves through Paris cafés and streets in stockings and scarf coloured Godard's signature red.

49 Mary Louise Pratt, *Imperial Eyes: Travel Writing and Transculturation*, 2nd ed. (New York: Routledge, 2008), 197.

50 One thinks, for example, of the famous opening shots of Leni Riefenstahl's *Triumph of the Will* (1935), where the film camera shows us Hitler's godlike point of view from the aeroplane in which he descends through the clouds to Nuremburg in 1934, at the other end of the historical process whose issue we see dramatized in this scene.

51 Reid, "The Grandchildren of Godard," 79.
52 Alison Landsberg, "Prosthetic Memory: The Ethics and Politics of Memory in an Age of Mass Culture," in *Memory and Popular Film*, ed. Paul Grainge (Manchester: Manchester University Press, 2003), 156.
53 Morrey, *Jean-Luc Godard*, 232.
54 Ibid., 233.
55 Ricciardi, "Cinema Regained," 657, quoting *Histoire(s) du cinéma*, Chapter 2A.
56 Chateaubriand grew up in Brittany, the very place in which Edgar and Cécile first meet.
57 "Elysian fields," the place of the blessed dead in Greek mythology, in French of course also suggests the Avenue des Champs-Élysées in Paris, one of the most famous streets in the world and in world cinema.
58 Morrey, *Jean-Luc Godard*, 237.

BIBLIOGRAPHY

Bataille, Georges. *Blue of Noon*. Translated by Harry Mathews. London: Marion Boyars, 2006.

Blanchot, Maurice. *Friendship*. Translated by Elizabeth Rottenberg. Stanford, CA: Stanford University Press, 1997.

Derrida, Jacques. *Archive Fever: A Freudian Impression*. Translated by Eric Prenowitz. Chicago: University of Chicago Press, 1996.

Dixon, Wheeler Winston. "In Praise of Godard's *In Praise of Love*." *Film Criticism* 27, no. 3 (Spring 2003): 18–39.

Drabinski, John E. *Godard between Identity and Difference*. New York: Continuum, 2008.

Hill, Leslie. "'A Form That Thinks': Godard, Blanchot, Citation." In *For Ever Godard*, edited by Michael Temple, James S. Williams, and Michael Witt, 396–415. London: Black Dog, 2004.

Hoberman, J. "Invisible Cities." *The Village Voice*, September 3, 2002. http://www.villagevoice.com/2002-09-03/film/invisible-cities/1.

Holtsmark, Erling B. "The *Katabasis* Theme in Modern Cinema." In *Classical Myth and Culture in the Cinema*, edited by Martin M. Winkler, 23–50. New York: Oxford University Press, 2001.

"Hope Springs Eternal." *Film Comment* 38, no. 1 (2002): 53.

Kilbourn, Russell J.A. *Cinema, Memory, Modernity: The Representation of Memory from the Art Film to Transnational Cinema*. New York: Routledge, 2010.

Klawans, Stuart. "Auteur, Auteur!" *The Nation* 275, no. 8 (2002): 35. http://www.thenation.com/article/auteur-auteur.

Landsberg, Alison. "Prosthetic Memory: The Ethics and Politics of Memory in an Age of Mass Culture." In *Memory and Popular Film*, edited by Paul Grainge, 144–61. Manchester: Manchester University Press, 2003.

McCabe, Colin. *Godard: A Portrait of the Artist at Seventy*. New York: Farrar, Straus, and Giroux, 2003.

McNeill, Isabelle. "Phrases, Monuments and Ruins: Melancholy History in *Éloge de l'amour*." *Studies in French Cinema* 3, no. 2 (2003): 111–20.

Morrey, Douglas. "History of Resistance / Resistance of History: Godard's *Éloge de l'amour* (2001)." *Studies in French Cinema* 3, no. 2 (2003): 121–30.

———. *Jean-Luc Godard*. Manchester: Manchester University Press, 2005.

Pence, Jeffrey. "Postcinema/Postmemory." In *Memory and Popular Film*, edited by Paul Grainge, 237–56. Manchester: Manchester University Press, 2003.

Pratt, Mary Louise. *Imperial Eyes: Travel Writing and Transculturation*. 2nd ed. New York: Routledge, 2008.

Quandt, James. "Here and Elsewhere: Projecting Godard." In *For Ever Godard*, edited by Michael Temple, James S. Williams, and Michael Witt, 126–43. London: Black Dog, 2004.

Reid, Donald. "The Grandchildren of Godard and the Aubracs: Betrayal, Resistance, and the People without a Memory." *French Cultural Studies* 15, no. 1 (2004): 76–92.

Ricciardi, Alessia. "Cinema Regained: Godard between Proust and Benjamin." *Modernism/Modernity* 8, no. 4 (2001): 643–61.

Sofair, Michael. "*In Praise of Love (Éloge de l'amour)*." *Film Quarterly* 58, no. 2 (2005): 36–44.

Sturken, Marita. "Memory, Consumerism, and Media: Reflections on the Emergence of the Field." *Memory Studies* 1, no. 1 (2008): 73–78.

Taubin, Amy. "In the Shadow of Memory." *Film Comment* 38, no. 1 (2002): 50–52.

Terdiman, Richard. *Present Past: Modernity and the Memory Crisis*. Ithaca, NY: Cornell University Press, 1993.

Thiher, Allen. "Postmodern Dilemmas: Godard's *Alphaville* and *Two or Three Things That I Know about Her*." *boundary 2* 4, no. 3 (Spring 1976): 947–64.

Turim, Maureen. *Flashbacks in Film: Memory and History*. New York: Routledge, 1989.

Wheeler, Duncan. "Godard's List: Why Spielberg and Auschwitz Are Number One." *Media History* 15, no. 2 (2009): 185–203.

Williams, James S. *Jean Cocteau*. Manchester: Manchester University Press, 2006.

7

Jean-Luc Godard's *Histoire(s) du cinéma* Brings the Dead Back to the Screen

Céline Scemama

THE MONUMENTAL FILM *Histoire(s) du cinéma* opens the way to the final period in Godard's works. The film, four hours and twenty-five minutes in length, comprises eight chapters containing images that by and large pre-date the production. It is a work of montage and mixing. Everything—photography, painting, engraving, sculpture, literature, archives, philosophy, poetry, discourse, history, and ... cinema—is edited and mixed. The voice-over of Godard over a large portion of the film is sepulchral in tone, and the work as a whole creates an apocalyptic effect and yields a hopeless vision of all things.

Since the appearance of the production, the films of Jean-Luc Godard have been like tentacles of *Histoire(s) du cinéma*. Indeed, the form Godard invents for the film invites the use of a morbid, animal-like, and monstrous lexical field. And yet, what beauty in the horror! This horror is not in the form itself, but in the fact that the form is apt to evoke horror, to bring back the worst of what is held prisoner *Dans le noir du temps*.[1] The film's beauty lies in the invention of a form that is able to bring back to the screen all that is buried in the darkness of history. *Histoire(s) du cinéma* forces the viewer to delve into the darkness. This beautiful and complex film does not allow itself to be summarized and, worse, it does not allow itself to be seen.

The film's heterogeneous content appears by way of interferences, flashes, or continuous digression. The form brings about moments of indescribable beauty, but what is perceived cannot be directly translated into discourse. In view of such a flood of superimposed, clashing, or intertwined references, it appears that a discursive and unifying "reading" is no longer appropriate. Godard *dares* to offer up a complex film that refuses to be consumed. This daring is part of the immense and hopeless enterprise of the work.

One can endure not immediately understanding a text and not mastering all of its references. Cinema, for its part, seems to be constrained to perform an entertainment role. *Histoire(s) du cinéma*, on the contrary, defends the idea that cinema is "primarily for thinking" but that "this will immediately be forgotten."[2] It shows and demonstrates that cinema is made for thinking through all of its available forms: images, sound, voices, texts, everything, and even everything combined.

It is thus in a literal sense that *Histoire(s) du cinéma* resists viewing. It resists viewing because there is too much to hear and too much to see. This excess can be likened to an infected wound, an abscess. But the most dreadful thing is that the abscess will not burst; it reveals itself, but nothing is released. Calm is never restored because whatever comes out only comes out in image. And the image, together with the audio track, undertakes to show that all the pain and injustice suppressed by time remains a prisoner of time, forever in suffering. What explodes on screen does not escape the screen; the explosions are therefore implosions. The screen brings no relief, saves nothing—it only shows the way things are and how they fall back in time. Their only way to return is to come back in the form of images. And so they come back however they can, in terrible convulsions. The sounds and images of *Histoire(s) du cinéma* are like electric shocks, audiovisual bursts, groans, convulsive jolts. The overall effect is a ghastly impression of agony without end, eternal agony.

Nothing really begins or ends; eyes and ears are unable to follow anything stable because it is all in continual, lightning-fast transformation. The images and sounds are, as it were, breathless. The sounds, images, and words momentarily capture the viewer's attention, only to evaporate like mirages. And as they disappear, other visual and auditory cataclysms are already produced, flooding the viewer's memory, so that most often it is impossible to make out everything that takes place in a given shot. The shot itself as a unit of cinema loses its contours and its unity. In fact, nothing creates unity: dispersion, explosion, overflow, and tearing away are all forms consistent with Godard's vision of history. This history finds neither unity, nor harmony, nor completion. No sooner do the images appear than they fly off like shooting stars. What can be seen can thus only be seen as what has already disappeared, much like dead stars that continue to shine from another time: "when I look to the sky and the stars, I can see only what has disappeared, a man said" (*Dans le noir du temps*).[3]

"The true picture of the past flits by. The past can be seized only as an image which flashes up at the instant when it can be recognized and is never seen again," writes Walter Benjamin.[4] The images of *Histoire(s) du cinéma* sparkle like long-dead stars whose glow persists as the glimmer of a bygone era.

The four hours and twenty-five minutes of images and sounds are like the final hours of Hermann Broch's Virgil,[5] the final hours of a poet overcome by fever and immersed in the deepest and most deeply buried reminiscences. However, the reminiscences resurrect nothing; everything dies. What can come back to the screen comes back to the screen only.

It is in this light that one must understand the phrase of Saint Paul that has misled certain commentators of Godard's film. *Histoire(s) du cinéma* demonstrates, literally, that cinema has the ability to bring back images the same way the dead are brought back. It is the editing and mixing, "the thought of cinema"[6] in the words of Godard—that is, the principle of *rapprochement*—that enables this resurrection in image. Montage is "a resurrection of life," wrote Godard in his beautiful article "Le montage, la solitude et la liberté."[7] But editing can neither save nor resurrect the dead; it can only make them come back in images, and thereby still "save the honour of all the real."[8] "Bringing back" the oppressions of the past in image is how Godard reads the precept of Saint Paul: "The image will come at the time of resurrection."[9]

THE RISE OF BODIES TO THE SCREEN

A very well-known moment in the film eloquently illustrates this phenomenon of resurrection in image. We refer to shot 35[10] of Chapter 1A—"Toutes les histoires"—which can be titled "Martyrdom and resurrection of the documentary" following Godard's formulation. The shot brings together four images: two from a documentary by George Stevens on Nazi camps (*D-Day to Berlin*, 1944), a shot from the fiction film *A Place in the Sun* (1951) by the same filmmaker, and a detail from Giotto's *Noli me tangere*.[11] The fragment of the Giotto painting is completely transformed by a 90-degree rotation of the biblical scene. In the original painting, Christ is on the right and Mary Magdalene, the former sinner become saint, is at his feet. Her arm is reaching out to the one who has just been resurrected, while Christ is pushing her away with his hand. He must ascend to God the Father and is not to be touched by a mortal. This hand that pushes away mortals in Giotto is an imploring hand in Godard's painting. The pivoted image has Mary Magdalene above, reaching down to Christ (now underground), of whom only an outstretched hand remains. In this transformation of the image Christ is not yet out of the ground, but is seeking help—and Mary Magdalene's hand will never be able to reach or save him.

In this constellation, several images come together:

First, the same wandering heads in the darkness of a Goya painting[12] cross-fade to the piled corpses from the Stevens documentary. The images are similar. The paintings of Goya have contemplated the worst possibilities for mankind.

Second, the superimposed body of Elizabeth Taylor appears basking in the sun, looking to her beautiful lover lying beneath her.

Third, in alternation, beneath the body of the star, a corpse appears frozen in a convulsive movement; it, too, is from the Stevens documentary.

Fourth, the metamorphosized detail from the Giotto painting is superimposed on the image of the two lovers. The Hollywood star rises up in a beautiful slow-motion movement, a deceleration added by Godard. The Hindemith sonata[13] ceases during the star's ascent and produces an effect of suspension, but one that appears to be definitive, creating an undeniable effect of death. The halt in the music freezes the picture, which seems to remain forever repressed in time. At this moment, Angela (Elizabeth Taylor) is thus located exactly between the hand of the imploring Christ and that of Mary Magdalene who is attempting to reach his hand, a feat that will forever remain impossible.

Jacques Rancière sees an "angel of resurrection" in the star's body: "Elizabeth Taylor stepping out of the water is a figure for the cinema itself being reborn from among the dead. The angel of the Resurrection and of painting descends from the heaven of Images to restore to life both the cinema and its heroines."[14] But although her name is Angela in the fiction of Stevens, she is not an angel in this painting of Histoire(s) du cinéma. "To describe precisely"[15]—such is the work of the historian for Godard in Histoire(s) du cinéma. And so what do we see in this image? A body that entirely resembles a wound, with a mouth that seems to be endlessly screaming in a void black as the underworld. The image gives the frightening impression of a man buried alive. His entire being stretches toward the shining star, sun shimmering on her wet skin. What is she resurrecting? Is there even the slightest hope in this image? The desire-filled lovers lie just above this mutilated body buried underground; the shot is one of the darkest despair. There is no resistance, reconciliation, or divine transcendence to be found here. Even Christ does not ascend to God the Father in this image, but remains underground imploring help in Godard's version of the painting.

"As Rancière has rightly stated," writes James S. Williams, "in the case of Giotto's Noli me tangere, Godard has effectively divorced the figures from their plastic and dramatic context (whose meaning, after all, was absence, separation, and the empty tomb) in order to impose an absolute image, that of cinema's redemption."[16] This idea that Godard tears an element away from its dramatic and plastic context can also be found in Rancière's analysis of the long passage devoted to Hitchcock in *Histoire(s) du cinema*.[17] But the idea cannot be applied in the same way to the shot organized around Giotto's *Noli me tangere* as it can to the Hitchcockian images. When it comes to the shots taken from films by Hitchcock in *Histoire(s) du cinéma*, Rancière considers that Godard divorces images from the "film fable" by "dissociating things that are indissociable."[18] "Hitchcock's cinema, Godard is saying, is made of images whose power is indifferent to the stories into which they've been arranged. We remember the glass of milk Cary Grant takes to Joan Fontaine in *Suspicion*, but not the financial problems the character thinks he might solve by coming into his wife's life insurance ..."[19] Rancière considers that, by showing things outside their narrative situations, Godard "is dissociating things that are indissociable," but Hitchcock precisely succeeds in transferring the narrative situation into objects, and this is what Godard illustrates: Hitchcock imprints his vision on an object that constitutes the narrative, and not vice versa. The filmmaker does not say that "the power of images is independent of the stories to which they are bound." Nor does he say that only images remain in our memory. He does not say, "One remembers only," but rather "but one remembers."

The problem posed by the Rancière interpretation of the Stevens/ Giotto shot is slightly different. By thus manipulating the Giotto painting, Godard proposes a vision of history. And although it is true that this vision consists of things divorced from their contexts, it is not in view of turning them into an "absolute image" but perhaps even, quite to the contrary, of presenting things in a state of disconnection and wandering. "The only connection to be made is between the *unspeakable* horror of the Nazi crimes and that which remains *inexpressible* in this image."[20] But there is no possibility of salvation here. Between the extended hand of Christ and that of the saint, there is the Hollywood star separating heaven and earth and preventing any form of communication between screaming mortals and the celestial spheres, with the angels and saints powerless to relieve the suffering of the lowly world. No beyond can heal the wounds of humanity. *Histoire(s) du cinéma* returns to the very beginnings of a civilization and skews it, as with the scene painted by Giotto. If Christ was a martyr, he remains a martyr in *Histoire(s) du cinéma* in which there is neither resurrection nor ascension of Christ. Mary Magdalene can neither touch nor save him; there is no rescue for martyrs.

In Godard, Rancière sees salvation, in the reconciliatory divine heights, for all the atrocities committed on earth; but in *Histoire(s) du cinéma*, those who scream underground will scream until the end of time because nothing can save them. There is no resurrection for the dead in this image; but there is a resurrection in image, which is another matter altogether. What the images bring back to life in this painting is not the dead, but the image of the dead contained in the eyes of George Stevens. It is the images of cinema that remember:

> The Voice-over by Godard breathlessly declares: "O what wonder to look at what one cannot see / O sweet wonder of our blind eyes." Montage! ... Godard's belief in the testamentary powers of the cinema—"neither an art nor a technique but a mystery" [ni un art ni une technique, un mystère][21]—does not imply an attitude of mystification, however. While quite capable of attaining a moral, existential or spiritual rigour, the focus of his activity in Histoire(s) du cinéma is an historical and political understanding of 'montage.'[22]

The American filmmaker has elaborated his fiction with the memory of the dead seen in extermination camps or in wagons of the Buchenwald-Dachau train that he filmed. The drowned, never recovered from the lake by which lovers meet, come back in image in Histoire(s) du cinéma. The dead "we cannot see, but which Godard makes visible through his montage."[23] They come back in image and it is only in this way that Godard understands the precept of Saint Paul.

Williams wonders if this might have to do with the "European nostalgic melancholy for the impossible"[24] displayed by Godard in Histoire(s) du cinéma. This sense of the impossible indeed corresponds to what is at play in this shot in which any form of redemption and help is made utterly impossible. This expression of the impossible is very subtly observed through the lens of Lacanian thought by Alan Wright:

> The Real, as Lacan was fond of saying, is the Impossible.... The impossible task of montage as imagined by Godard is to make visible the abysmal structure at the heart of cinematic representation, the absence that haunts every film image, i.e. the traumatic kernel of the Real. Montage shows that which a narrowed range of vision renders imperceptible in the image, the unspeakable fact of an unrepresentable Thing. The name of that Thing is Auschwitz. Traditionally, documentary aims to record reality, to act as a witness to events.... [Godard's] version of montage produces an apparition of the Real, a sublime recognition of the impossibility of doing justice to reality.[25]

When the world has forgotten and beautiful films are made with beautiful stars, Godard shows that beneath and just behind, in the memory of the world, the dislocated corpses, the terrorized faces, the darkness of history remains engulfed. The coloured image of the George Stevens documentary preceding the image of the star, that of the dislocated corpses piled in a freight wagon, persists behind that of Elizabeth Taylor in black and white; and beautiful Angela saves no one.

"And if George Stevens hadn't been the first to use the first 16 mm colour film at Auschwitz and Ravensbrück, Elizabeth Taylor's happiness would doubtless never have found a place in the sun."[26] Godard here shows that the filmmaker has "death in his eye"[27] when filming the body of the star. Beneath this body of such beauty lies another, screaming in pain and crying out for help. It has been forgotten, no one hears it—but the image remembers.

THE REMINISCENCES OF CINEMA, THE TESTAMENT OF GODARD

Another form of resurrection in images is undertaken in *Histoire(s) du cinéma*. Within Godard's lifetime, the term "resurrection" is not entirely appropriate because it is premature, but when considering the film's dimension of legacy and death, the term finds legitimacy.

Godard gives himself a strange role in *Histoire(s) du cinéma....* His attributes—cigar, glasses, three-day-old stubble, visor—and his trembling, gravelike voice are a signature. This omnipresence of the filmmaker is surprising from the one who said, "history, not the one who relates it"[28] and "first the works, then the men."[29] But on closer inspection, it appears that Godard is no longer really Godard in his film; he carries something greater than himself.

The substitution between Godard and cinema primarily takes place through his transformation of the famous Cartesian precept. The passage from Descartes's "cogito ergo sum" to Godard's "cogito ergo video"[30] reveals that Godard's thought does not exist outside the images that meet on the screen: he thinks, that is, he sees.

The editing room is where Godard projects images, sounds, and words. All that happens on the screen undergoes a transformation by being divorced from its context. When he is not in his editing room, Godard can often be seen standing in front of his library reciting book titles out loud with an inspired air. His library, too, is a place of cinema, a place from which he does cinema.

The projection is the engine of the production; substitution is another. The projection/substitution principle also applies to Godard. Whether at his editing table, in his office, or before his library, his eyes are the focal point of the projection. But since what is projected on the screen is the object of substitution, Godard himself becomes a subject of substitution and this is perhaps one of the great singularities of *Histoire(s) du cinéma*. Godard substitutes himself for cinema and dares to substitute cinema for art and then history, more precisely the eye of history.

In the opening of Chapter 2B,[31] Godard appears on the screen with his famous visor and a big cigar between his teeth. One could almost laugh— but no, nothing in *Histoire(s) du cinéma* provokes laughter. It is impossible to laugh faced with his image associated with a series of women in distress: the print of a woman with a fist sunk into her eye; disturbing shots of dead or passed-out women in Lang's first *Mabuse* (1922) and then in L'Herbier's *L'Inhumaine* (*The Inhuman Woman*, 1924); and a poem, "Palabras para Julia" (a letter from a father to his daughter), whose sadness is accentuated by the music and voice of Paco Ibañez. Godard looks straight ahead with a grave and enlightened look. Then he pronounces the words, "*Les Grandes espérances* [*Great Expectations*],[32] *L'homme sans qualités* [*The Man without Qualities*]."[33] "Montage my beautiful care" and "a new wave"[34] are displayed on the screen between the two titles pronounced out loud. These two expressions reflect Godard the filmmaker and not the man. The "*Great Expectations*" of cinema, those it could have borne, in no way correspond to "*The Man without Qualities.*" Indeed, Godard bows his head.

The pre-eminence of art over man can also be found in the form of the museum attendant,[35] a role he plays in *Nouvelle vague* (1990). The attendant no longer speaks for himself or for the authors, but for the works. "We're closing, we're closing, children!" the attendant warns. Custodian of cinema, the museum keeper also finds himself answering for art in general since cinema, the last-born of the arts, appears to carry with it the entire heritage of art: "That's it, it started long before, it's the meaning of the word *Histoire(s)* in the plural."[36] The young visitors to the museum reflect and debate. Audrey, the young woman, does not understand this strange place where one sees artwork of all kinds: "What about Daumier, what does he have to do with the New Wave?" "Ask the attendant," the young man answers.[37] On the screen, a strange white sheet is waved about over a stage (the Mummenschanz), and a woman with bared breasts and a finger on her lips (*Passion*),[38] the gesture calling for silence as the word *murmure* appears on the screen. And then the shot of a forest filmed from a high angle (*Valley of the Giants*),[39] a forest with trees so tall that they exceed the frame. A slow camera movement slides from the tops of the trees down to the trunks, gradually revealing, way at the bottom, two characters made insignificant by these gigantic trees. Here the images show how large works are and how small men are by comparison. The title of the film itself, *Valley of the Giants*, indicates in this context that it is not the creators that are so big, but rather the works. The young lady visiting the museum does not like it, she complains about seeing "endless photographs, works, but never people." Her friend explains to her that "that's what the New Wave was about: the auteur-policy, not the authors, the works."[40] Godard the attendant, who had been impassively reading on a bench, speaks up and agrees with the young man: "Your friend is right, miss—first the works, then the men."[41] But this museum is even larger, in fact much larger, because the works contain the world and the museum of which Godard is here the attendant is nothing less than the "museum of the real,"[42] a title that comes up eight times, like the number of chapters in the film. While on the screen a series of black-and-white photographs are presented in succession—Becker, Rossellini, Melville, Franju, Truffaut, Demy—Audrey asks, "You knew them all?" To which Godard the attendant answers, "Yes, they were my friends."[43]

Godard's ego is thus not so big; he is no more than the humble guardian of the museum. But it is not just any museum. It is the museum of the real.

Cinema, with its striking ability to see, foresee, and glimpse ahead, has nevertheless been unable to prevent the worst from happening, even going as far as crimes against humanity. If Godard substitutes himself for cinema in this dark film, it is thus as a dying person, agonizing like Hermann Broch's Virgil in his final hours, haunted by the most terrible reminiscences.

The reminiscences of cinema have thus become those of Godard. This is why certain archived images come back so frequently now in his films that they have become Godardian. But they come back with his vision, his marks, his writing, his style. As he says concerning Hitchcock, "Ultimately it is forms that tell us what is at the bottom of things, and what is art if not that by which forms become style, and what is style if not man?"[44] And so when we systematically see an image repeated, like the frightful image of an emaciated woman's corpse being dragged across the ground by two kapos, we see a fragment of history surging back up to the screen; however, this piece of history is no longer separable from the one showing it. The image appears as a reminiscence of cinema, but also the reminiscence of a man who is none other than what he sees.

Translated from the French original by Joachim Lépine

Appendix A

(Table 7.1)

Excerpt from *Histoire(s) du cinéma*,[a] Chapter 1A—"Toutes les histoires" (All the [Hi]stories)

TIME[b]	IMAGES	VOICE OVER / OFF	AUDIO TRACK	TEXT
46'52"	Blackout / detail of the flight of the monsters from *Bon Voyage* (the *Caprices*, Goya, 1799) / cross-fade to corpses piled onto an open wagon (the image, which seems to be painted over in bright red, belongs to those of the Buchenwald-Dachau convoy filmed by George Stevens on April 29, 1945, *D-Day to Berlin*) and E. Taylor in *A Place in the Sun* (George Stevens, 1951)	and if George Stevens hadn't been the first to use the first 16 mm colour film at Auschwitz and Ravensbrück Elizabeth Taylor's happiness doubtless wouldn't have found *A Place in the Sun*		
47'06	E. Taylor id. alternating with the face of a corpse whose eyes are filled with terror (the image, coloured in red and blue, also belongs to those of the Buchenwald-Dachau convoy filmed by G. Stevens) / detail of *Noli me tangere* (*Resurrection*), rotated 90 degrees, from *Scenes from the Life of Christ* (Giotto, 1304–1306, Scrovegni Chapel) with E. Taylor, in slow motion, superimposed between the hands of Mary Magdalene (above) and the hand of Christ (below)	thirty-nine forty-four martyrdom and resurrection of the documentary "O what wonder to look at what one cannot see O sweet wonder of our blind eyes" [*Le Journal d'un curé de campagne* (*Diary of a Country Priest*), Bernanos, 1936; Bresson, 1951]	First movement (*Fantasy*) from the Hindemith *Sonata in F major for viola and piano*, Op. 11, No. 4 (1919): the music stops with the sudden disappearance of the shot of Elizabeth Taylor rising	

a The "score" of *Histoire(s) du cinéma* can be consulted online at: http://cri-image.univ
-paris1.fr/celine/celine.html.

b Times are indicated based on the Japanese edition of Godard's film (Imagica, 2001).
They may vary slightly from those in other editions.

Appendix B

(Table 7.2)

Excerpt from *Histoire(s) du cinéma*, Chapter 2B—"Fatale beauté" (Deadly Beauty)

TIME	IMAGES	VOICE OVER / OFF	AUDIO TRACK	TEXT
1'53"	JLG in white with his tennis visor and a cigar in his mouth looking straight ahead and slightly up, with a very inspired look …		Typewriter only [Ibáñez continues] no puedo más y aquí me quedo Typewriter only [Ibáñez continues] Entonces siempre acuérdate de lo que un día yo escribí Ibáñez continues + typewriter	Id. / fatal beauty / the coin of the absolute / the reply of darkness / montage my beautiful care [superimposed]
2'26"	Id.	*Les Grandes espérances* [*Great Expectations*] [Dickens, 1860–1861; Davis Lean, 1946]	pensando en tí	a new wave [superimposed]
2'31"	Id. then he writes on the typewriter	*L'Homme sans qualités* [*The Man without Qualities*] [Musil, 1930–1942]	como ahora pienso silence—then applause, then typewriter	Id. / the control [superimposed] of the universe [superimposed]

(continued next page)

TIME	IMAGES	VOICE OVER / OFF	AUDIO TRACK	TEXT
2'46"	Id., still looking up into the air with a slight smile	*Les mariés de la tour Eiffel* [*The Marriage on the Eiffel Tower*] [Cocteau, 1924]	Id.	The signs among us
2'54"	Blackout / Ava Gardner playing piano, *Pandora and the Flying Dutchman*, (Lewin, 1950) / blackout / JLG id. in a flash, his mouth open / blackout		Typewriter + *Pandora* played on piano and sung right from blackout 1	do ré mi fa tal [over blackout 1] / id. [in red over shot] fatal fatal[a] beauty [over blackout 2]
3'09"	Rapid alterna-tion-flashing between JLG (mouth still wide open) id., a beautifully framed and very brief shot of a pretty woman smiling in the middle, a sleeping baby in the lower left corner and a man in the lower right corner, and Mitchum and Joan Fontaine, against the light, looking at each other, *The Locket* (Brahm, 1946)		Id. piano/singing	

a A more accurate rendering of *beauté fatale* would be "deadly beauty"; the term "fatal beauty" is used here to preserve the double entendre (original text: "do/ré/mi/fa/tale").

TIME	IMAGES	VOICE OVER / OFF	AUDIO TRACK	TEXT
3'19"	Blackout		Id.	always the fatal [superimposed] moment [green]
3'24"	Curtains in the wind, a single shot and then the entire hallway with the beauty at the end of the hall, a bigger close-up, the beauty looking to the right, then to the left, *La Belle et la bête* [*Beauty and the Beast*] (Cocteau, 1946)	there was a short film the commentary was narrated by Jean Cocteau it explained how a film is made the voice said [*Le Rouge est mis (Speaking of Murder)*, Gilles Grangier, 1957] I entered fraudulently [Igor Barrère and Hubert Knapp, 1953]		
3'39"	Blackout / two brief shots of the beauty / blackout / close-up photograph of a young Cocteau wearing a hat, pointing a weapon at the viewer		Silence, then *Symphony* in three movements, first movement (Stravinsky, 1945; cf. 1b, 30'26)	always the fatal [superimposed] moment / will come to distract [superimposed] us [Queneau, *L'Instant fatal*, 1946] [green on blackout 1 and blackout 2 and on shot]

(continued next page)

TIME	IMAGES	VOICE OVER / OFF	AUDIO TRACK	TEXT
3'55"	Image split in two: on the right, JLG, stupefied; on the left, (1) Jennifer Jones on the ground in *Duel in the Sun* (Vidor, 1948)		Id.	
3'58"	(2) Young woman running, *The Fury* (De Palma, 1978)		Id.	
3'59"	(3) Anna Magnani running, assassination sequence, *Roma, città aperta* [*Rome, Open City*] (Rossellini, 1945)		Id	
4'01"	(4) Jennifer Jones id.		Id	
4'06"	(5) Close-up of a gun, then a man at the wheel being shot (*The Fury*?)		Id	
4'08"	(6) Shirley MacLaine before being killed in *Some Came Running*, (Minnelli, 1958)		Id	
4'10"	(7) The running woman from *The Fury*		Id	
4'12"	(8) Anna Magnani in a wider shot (9) MacLaine looking (she seems to be looking at Magnani running)		*Trivium* for organ (Arvo Pärt, 1976) Shot fired	

TIME	IMAGES	VOICE OVER / OFF	AUDIO TRACK	TEXT
	(10) Magnani near collapse			
	(11) Another woman from *The Fury*			
	(12) Magnani's collapse			
	(13) The other woman from *The Fury*			
	(14) A man shoots			
	(15) MacLaine assassinated			
	(16) A man killed and thrust backward			
	(17) The man falling on the hood and windshield of a car in slow motion (*Fury?*)			
4'24"	(18) Death of a resistance fighter after torture in *Roma, città aperta* (19) Shot of his fiancée with German officers, laugh followed by scream and JLG disappears with the shot of the fiancée falling to the ground	Pärt id.		
4'35"	Sinatra with MacLaine dead in his arms, he looks at his hand covered in his young wife's blood (large cinemascope, blurred) / blackout	Id.		fatal [over the cinemascope track below]

(continued next page)

TIME	IMAGES	VOICE OVER / OFF	AUDIO TRACK	TEXT
4'44"	Gretchen walking in the wind and snow, collapsing to the ground, then closer shot (Madonna-like) from *Faust* (Murnau, 1926)	but when I was born	Id.	fatal
4'58"	Blackout	did I also enter fraudulently	Id.	only the hand
5'01"	Man writing an M on the palm of his hand, *M* (Lang, 1931) / blackout	into my mother's blood I wanted to be an engineer I don't even know whether I succeeded	Id.	that erases
5'05"	Man turning his camera's winding handle and woman in white, terrified (long shot), *King Kong* (Cooper and Schoedsack, 1933)	in being ingenious all these stories that are now mine how to tell them perhaps show them	Id.	/ that erases can write [Meister Eckhart, XIII/XIV; cf. 1a, 42'28]
5'15"	Blackout		Id.	the fatal moment
5'16"	Man jumping up and down as if electrified, with hand in the foreground, *The Fury* id. the link shot gives the impression that the woman from *King Kong* is scared of him; he thus substitutes for the gorilla)		Id.	(hi) stories of cinema

TIME	IMAGES	VOICE OVER / OFF	AUDIO TRACK	TEXT
5'18"	Flames in Murnau's *Faust* (appearance of Mephistopheles)		Id.	Id.
5'22"	Women on the backs of men in *Rancho Notorious* (Lang, 1952)	the invention of the scenario		Fatal beauty
5'28"	Blackout / woman smiling with cigarette case and man at his desk, *Sunset Boulevard* (Wilder, 1950)	is a small-time mafia accountant some order had to be made of the disorder of the innovations		beauty [over blackout]
5'32"	Rapid alternation (over the rhythm of the typewriter) pinup and man with a moustache (held by a young woman) wringing another man's neck, *Barney Oldfield's Race for a Life* (Mack Sennett, 1913)	of Mack Sennett	Typewriter	
5'39"	Blackout		Id.	history of cinema [in white] [superimposed on:] cinema / (Hi)stories [superimposed on:] of cineme [*cinémoi*] to whom did it belong [yellow]

(continued next page)

TIME	IMAGES	VOICE OVER / OFF	AUDIO TRACK	TEXT
5'42"	JLG in a closer shot (bare-chested, at a table, cigar, typewriter, tennis visor)	*The Magic Mountain* [Thomas Mann, 1924]		
5'50"	Cross-fade: mountain on a lake (long shot)			
6'01"	Slow cross-fade to Monica Vitti on a cliff before the sea, *L'Avventura* (Antonioni, 1960)	*La Dame aux camélias* [*The Lady of the Camellias*] [repeated] [Alexandre Dumas, 1852] and Friedrich Murnau and Karl Freund		
6'11"	JLG id. he writes, then looks at his hands at the end and turns them over	they invented Nuremberg lighting while Hitler couldn't yet afford a beer in a Munich café *Les Mains sales* [*Dirty Hands*] [Sartre, 1948]	*Te Deum* (Arvo Pärt, 1984–1986)	
6'38"	Both hands turned over (same movement as JLG), a man on his knees, his hands on the naked back of a woman in *Un Chien andalou*, then a disturbing face looking at his hands, Orlacs Hände [*The Hands of Orlac*] (Wiene, 1924)	*To Have and Have Not* [the Hawks film, 1945; the Hemingway novel, 1937]	Id.	

TIME	IMAGES	VOICE OVER / OFF	AUDIO TRACK	TEXT
6'45"	Blackout		Typewriter	thinking with your hands [de Rougemont, 1936] [yellow]

Appendix C

(Table 7.3)

Excerpt from *Histoire(s) du cinéma*, Chapter 3B—"Une vague nouvelle" (A New Wave)

TIME	IMAGES	VOICE OVER / OFF	AUDIO TRACK	TEXT
23'11"	On a theatre set, a man behind a white sheet (probably the Mummenschanz)	den Gott ihm vorgezeichnet hat ["one can hardly criticize a people when it has turned away from the path God has traced for it"] [woman's voice:] the path God has traced for it [JLG also integrates the dialogue of *Nouvelle vague* in his "blue book":] [A woman:] what are these museums?	Id.	we have ceased to be / up to the level of basic truths /
23'28"	Superimposed sheet id. and flashing shot of a man against the light in a bedroom	T-shirts [Boy:] new wave, Audrey new wave.	motor	and yet they do not cease to be
23'43"	Woman in *Nouvelle vague* (JLG, 1990) rapidly alternating with a T-shirt featuring the words "Torlato Favrini Industrias"		Museum bell	

118

TIME	IMAGES	VOICE OVER / OFF	AUDIO TRACK	TEXT
23'47"	Sheet id. flashing with woman / angel and child scene, camera moves past several figures, ends with a woman with breasts bared holding up a finger to her lips (over "murmur") and woman playing cello with iris around moving sheet, from *Passion* (JLG, 1981)	[JLG, low:] we're closing we're closing, children. [Girl id.:] and Daumier, what relation to the new wave? [Boy:] Ask the attendant.	Music id.	mur muring now and again
24'11"	High-angle shot of forest (JLG camera movement over still image) with two characters at the bottom of the trees, *Valley of the Giants* (William Keighley, 1938)		Brief, tense string passage (Vivaldi?)	
24'20"	The cross-fade remains superimposed: JLG seated with a book in hand, a young man comes toward him, then the girl, the boy leaves and then so does the girl, Godard begins to read (*Nouvelle vague*)	[In: bell] [JLG:] please, did you like it? [Boy:] oh yes, there are interesting things [Girl:] I don't agree we keep seeing photos of the works but never of the people [Boy:] that was the new wave, the auteur-policy not the authors, the works	Birds at the end (when the forest takes over)	

(continued next page)

TIME	IMAGES	VOICE OVER / OFF	AUDIO TRACK	TEXT
24'20" cont'd		[JLG:] your friend is right, young lady, first the works, then the men. [Girl:] have you no heart, sir? [JLG:] one can film work, young lady, not hearts. [Girl:] I don't know, work is scarce in these times, sir [JLG reading:] and who is without work, young lady there are times with too many hands and not enough hearts yes, heartless times but not without work when an era is sick and doesn't have work for all hands		
25'18"	Slow camera movement over a house and a very green lawn, *Nouvelle vague* id. with a child in the middle, detail from *La Laveuse* [*The Laundress*] (Daumier, 1868–1860) / blackout / id. with the laundress and child / blackout	It's a new exhortation she is making of us the exhortation to work with our hearts instead of using our hands and I know of no era not yet that did not have work enough for all hearts	Birds and someone knocks on the door more and more insistently (in)	a new wave

TIME	IMAGES	VOICE OVER / OFF	AUDIO TRACK	TEXT
25'43"	JLG seated with his book id., seen in profile from the right		More knocking at the door	
25'47"	Slow cross-fade to photograph of Jacques Becker with camera, same profile	[Girl:] So Becker Rossellini		
25'52"	Photograph of Rossellini with a monkey in his arms and a camera at his side	Melville Franju Jacques Demy		
25'55"	Photograph of Franju during the shooting of *Yeux sans visage* [*Eyes Without a Face*] (1960)	you knew them		not ceased to be [below]
25'58	Shot of Melville / blackout	[JLG:] yes, they were my friends [Melville seems to answer for JLG]		Id.

NOTES

The text in this essay partly draws from ideas developed by the author in *"Histoire(s) du cinéma" de Jean-Luc Godard: La force faible d'un art* (Paris: L'Harmattan, 2006).

1   Jean-Luc Godard, 2001, episode of the film *Ten Minutes Older: The Cello*.

2   *Histoire(s) du cinéma*, Chapter 3A—"La monnaie de l'absolue"—(12'20"). Times are indicated based on the Japanese edition of Godard's film (Imagica, 2001). This may vary slightly from other editions. Original text: *"Que le cinéma soit d'abord fait pour penser, on l'oubliera tout de suite."*

3   Jean-Luc Godard, 2001. Original text: *"Quand je regarde le ciel avec les étoiles, je ne peux voir que ce qui a disparu, dit un homme."*

4   Walter Benjamin, "Theses on the Philosophy of History," in *Illuminations*, ed. Hannah Arendt, trans. Harry Zohn (London: Fontana, 1992), 247.

5   Hermann Broch, *The Death of Virgil*, 1945.

6   Jean-Luc Godard, interview by Pierre Jacerme, *Revue Internationale de Psychanalyse*, 1, "Le refoulement des lois," (1992): 139. Godard's formulation is "le dire propre au voir."

7   "Le montage, la solitude et la liberté," in *Jean-Luc Godard par Jean-Luc Godard*, vol. 2 (1984–1998), ed. Alain Bergala (Paris: Cahiers du cinéma, 1998), 242–48.

8   *Histoire(s) du cinéma*, Chapter 1A—"Toutes les histoires"—(32'40"–32'55"). The "score" of *Histoire(s) du cinéma* can be consulted online at http://cri-image .univ-paris1.fr/celine/celine.html. Original text: "Sauver l'honneur de tout le réel."

9   Saint Paul, "First letter to the Corinthians" (the quote is changed by Godard), in *Histoire(s) du cinéma*, Chapter 1B—"Une histoire seule"—(21'23"). Godard's version reads, "*L'image viendra au temps de la résurrection.*"

10   *Histoire(s) du cinéma*, Chapter 1A—"Toutes les histoires"—(47'06"). See Appendix A.

11   *Resurrection (Scenes from the Life of Christ)*, Giotto, 1304–1306, Scrovegni Chapel.

12   Flight of the monsters detail, from *Bon Voyage (Los Caprichos)*, Goya, 1799.

13   Hindemith, first movement (*Fantasy*) from the "Sonata in F major for viola and piano," Op. 11, No. 4, 1919.

14   Jacques Rancière, *Film Fables*, trans. Emiliano Battista (Oxford: Berg, 2006), 184.

15   *Histoire(s) du cinéma*, Chapter 2A—"Seul le cinema"—(1'27"). Original text: "Faire une description *précise.*"

16   James S. Williams, "European Culture and Artistic Resistance in *Histoire(s) du cinéma* Chapter 3A, La monnaie de l'absolu," in *The Cinema Alone: Essays on the Work of Jean-Luc Godard, 1985–2000*, ed. Michael Temple and James S. Williams (Amsterdam: Amsterdam University Press, 2000), 136.

17   *Histoire(s) du cinéma*, Chapter 4A—"Le contrôle de l'univers"—(11'59"–15'33").

18   Rancière, *Film Fables*, 172.

19   Ibid.

20   Douglas Morrey, *Jean-Luc Godard* (Manchester: Manchester University Press, 2005), 226.

21   *Histoire(s) du cinéma*, Chapter 1B—"Une histoire seule"—(10'11"); Chapter 2B—"Fatale beauté"—(10'36" and 23'08").

22   Alan Wright, "Elisabeth Taylor at Auschwitz: JLG and the Real Object of Montage," in *The Cinema Alone: Essays on the Work of Jean-Luc Godard, 1985–2000*, ed. Michael Temple and James S. Williams (Amsterdam: Amsterdam University Press, 2000), 59. "O what wonder to look at what one cannot see/O sweet wonder of our blind eyes" (*Ô quelle merveille que de pouvoir regarder ce qu'on ne voit pas, Ô doux miracle de nos yeux aveugles*), in *Le Journal d'un curé de campagne*, Bernanos, 1936; Bresson, 1951.

23   Morrey, *Jean-Luc Godard*, 227.

24   Williams, "European Culture and Artistic Resistance," 136.

25   Wright, "Elisabeth Taylor at Auschwitz," 54–55.

26   Original text: "Et si George Stevens n'avait utilisé le premier, le premier film en seize en couleurs à Auschwitz et Ravensbrück, jamais sans doute, le bonheur d'Elizabeth Taylor n'aurait trouvé une place au soleil."

27   Original text: "La mort dans l'œil."

28 *Histoire(s) du cinéma*, Chapter 1B—"Une histoire seule"—(9'47", 10'25", and 33'29"). Original text: "L'histoire, pas celui qui la raconte."

29 *Histoire(s) du cinéma*, Chapter 3B—"Une vague nouvelle"—(24'20"). Original text: "D'abord les œuvres, les hommes ensuite."

30 *Histoire(s) du cinéma*, Chapter 1B—"Une histoire seule"—(0'13").

31 *Histoire(s) du cinéma*, Chapter 2B—"Fatale beauté"—(0'10"–7'33", Godard appears at 1'53").

32 Charles Dickens, *Great Expectations* (1860–1861).

33 Robert Musil, *The Man without Qualities* (*Der Mann ohne Eigenschaften*, 1930–1942).

34 Original text, respectively: "Montage mon beau souci," "une nouvelle vague."

35 *Histoire(s) du cinéma*, Chapter 3B—"Une vague nouvelle"—(23'11"–25'58"). See Appendix C.

36 *Histoire(s) du cinéma*, Chapter 2A—"Seul le cinéma"—(3'42"). Original text: "C'est ça, ça avait commencé bien avant, c'est le sens du mot *Histoire(s)* au pluriel."

37 Original text: "Et Daumier, quel rapport avec la Nouvelle Vague?"—"Tu demande-ras au gardien."

38 Jean-Luc Godard, *Passion* (1982).

39 William Keighley, *Valley of the Giants* (1938).

40 English translation from Michael Temple and James S. Williams (eds), *The Cinema Alone: Essays on the Work of Jean-Luc Godard, 1985–2000* (Amsterdam: Amsterdam University Press, 2000), 9. Original text: "c'était ça la Nouvelle Vague, la politique des auteurs, pas les auteurs, les œuvres."

41 Original text: "Votre ami a raison mademoiselle, d'abord les œuvres, les hommes ensuite."

42 *Histoire(s) du cinéma*, Chapter 3B—"Une vague nouvelle"—(23'11"–25'58"). Original text: "Le musée du réel."

43 Original text: "Quand même vous les avez connus?"—"Oui, c'étaient mes amis."

44 *Histoire(s) du cinéma*, Chapter 4A—"Le contrôle de l'univers"—(14'21"–14'43"). Original text: "Ce sont les formes qui nous disent finalement ce qu'il y a au fond des choses, or qu'est-ce que l'art sinon ce par quoi les formes deviennent style, et qu'est-ce que le style sinon l'homme?"

BIBLIOGRAPHY

Benjamin, Walter. *L'Homme, le langage, la culture*. Translated by Maurice de Gandillac. Paris: Gonthier, 1971.

———. "Theses on the Philosophy of History." In *Illuminations*, edited by Hannah Arendt, translated by Harry Zohn, 245–255. London: Fontana, 1992.

Godard, Jean-Luc. Interview by Pierre Jacerme. *Revue internationale de psychanalyse* 1 (1992): 139.

———. *Jean-Luc Godard par Jean-Luc Godard, Tome 2: 1984–1998*. Edited by Alain Bergala. Paris: Cahiers du cinéma, 1998.

Morrey, Douglas. *Jean-Luc Godard*. Manchester: Manchester University Press, 2005.

Rancière, Jacques. *Film Fables*. Translated by Emiliano Battista. Oxford: Berg, 2006.

———. "La Sainte et l'héritière: A propos des *Histoire(s) du cinéma.*" *Cahiers du cinéma* 536 (1998): 58–61.

Scemama, Céline. *"Histoire(s) du cinéma" de Jean-Luc Godard: La force faible d'un art.* Paris: L'Harmattan, 2006.

Temple, Michael, and James S. Williams, eds. *The Cinema Alone: Essays on the Work of Jean-Luc Godard, 1985–2000.* Amsterdam: Amsterdam University Press, 2000.

Williams, James S. "European Culture and Artistic Resistance in *Histoire(s) du cinéma* Chapter 3A, 'La monnaie de l'absolu.'" In *The Cinema Alone: Essays on the Work of Jean-Luc Godard, 1985–2000*, edited by Michael Temple and James S. Williams, 113–39. Amsterdam: Amsterdam University Press, 2000.

Wright, Alan. "Elizabeth Taylor at Auschwitz: JLG and the Real Object of Montage." In *The Cinema Alone: Essays on the Work of Jean-Luc Godard, 1985–2000*, edited by Michael Temple and James S. Williams, 51–60. Amsterdam: Amsterdam University Press, 2000.

Part III
Godardian Legacy in Philosophy

8

Jean-Luc Godard and Ludwig Wittgenstein in New Contexts

Christina Stojanova

> Progress is ambiguous, isn't it?
>
> —Jean-Luc Godard

> The trouble about progress is that it always looks much greater than it really is.
>
> —Johann Nestroy

IN AN INTERVIEW for *New York Times Magazine*, given in the wake of the 9/11 tragedy, Jean-Luc Godard voiced his perennial anxiety "about the invasion of technology and false memory, created by the media to replicate or explicate the past,"[1] stating: "I suppose that's a feeling many people in the world have today—a kind of incoherent rage against all things technocratic. It comes from being powerless."[2]

Godard's concerns with the very real dangers brought on by what Slavoj Žižek calls the "unchecked invasion of technology and media"—and its potential to reduce humans to "abstract subjects devoid of all substantial content, dispossessed of our symbolic substance"[3]—informs his whole oeuvre. And yet, as a filmmaker, Godard has widely availed himself of technological innovations from the early portable cameras in the 1950s to cellphone imaging and digital editing, used for his latest *Film socialisme* (2010).

Godard's ambiguous attitude towards technology and new media could be interpreted in light of Ludwig Wittgenstein's philosophy, or more specifically, in light of its reading by Ray Monk, one of Wittgenstein's most versatile interpreters and biographers. In an early draft of his foreword to *Philosophical Remarks* (1930), quoted by Monk, Wittgenstein expresses his own strand of technological pessimism: "Our civilization is characterized by the word 'progress.' Progress is its form rather than making progress being one of its features.... And even clarity is sought only as a means to this end, not as an end in itself. For me on the contrary clarity, perspicuity are valuable in themselves.... So I am not aiming at the same target as scientists and my way of thinking is different from theirs."[4]

The ambiguity of Wittgenstein's and Godard's attitude towards technological progress is not the only similarity that brings them together. This chapter foregrounds other striking examples of conceptual and structural affinities—or "family resemblances" as Wittgenstein would have it—displayed in their key works. While both Wittgenstein and Godard sought to fundamentally redesign their respective fields conceptually and artistically, their efforts betray a major concern about the fate of the arts vis-à-vis the encroachment of technology and consumerism—a concern made all the more paradoxical in light of consistent attempts at appropriation of their oeuvres by new-media theorists and practitioners.

GODARD AND TECHNOLOGY: *ALPHAVILLE* AND BEYOND

Godard's 1965 film *Alphaville, une étrange aventure de Lemmy Caution*, declared programmatic, even prophetic in many ways within and without Godard's body of work, reveals concisely the controversy at the heart of Godard's work. David Sterritt, for example, sees *Alphaville* as programmatic in terms of its "fundamental stance toward the influence of entertainment, diversion, and spectacle on everyday social and political life,"[5] indicative of Godard's notorious ideological contradictions and artistic ambiguities. More to the point, Richard Brody considers *Alphaville* as the "end of a certain road" for Godard, marked by films "reminiscent of those made within the mainstream of the industry," before "venturing dangerously far into the cinematic wilderness"[6] towards "complex and maddeningly cryptic essay-films," as a recent review of *Film socialisme* for the fashionable lifestyle Montreal weekly *Mirror* has it.[7]

Godard's journey away from anything that remotely resembles artistic compromise could be defined as one of his most consistent authorial characteristics. It is also his unique way of fighting consumerism and commodification in the name of giving "humanity back a 'place in the world.'"[8] And while his film *2 ou 3 choses que je sais d'elle* (1966)—where he flatly equates consumerism with prostitution, prompted however "not out of necessity … but to pay for consumer items … considered [until recently] luxuries"[9]—becomes his anti-consumerist manifesto for the 1960s, *Histoire(s) du cinéma* (1988–1998) passionately solicits resistance against commercialization and marginalization of arts and culture that have been growing exponentially over the last three decades. Yet being fully aware that consumerism, coupled with commercialization, has the power to nullify criticism and resistance by turning them also into commodities, Godard has kept reinventing his technological, aesthetic, and ideological allegiances, thus sabotaging any and all attempts at being himself commodified (or rather, pigeonholed). Indeed, to quote from Aristotle's famous definition of a complex character, Godard has remained surprisingly consistent in his inconsistencies.

In this line of thought, the story of Lemmy Caution, an American private eye, and his trip to Alphaville—a city of the future from another galaxy, ruled by the ominously powerful computer Alpha 60—has become, along with Chris Marker's *La Jetée* (1962), something of an originary text in the dystopian cinematic tradition, highlighted by such iconic—and commercially successful—films as *2001: A Space Odyssey* (Stanley Kubrick, 1968) and *The Matrix* (Andy and Larry Wachowski, 1999). By playing up various facets of Alphaville's legacy, these films corroborate what Sterritt calls the "existence of different 'Godards.'"[10] And while *2001* stays close to the "sociocultural criticism"[11] of *Alphaville*'s modernist art-cinema narrative, epitomized by HAL 9000, the much more potent heir of Alpha 60 as yet another misanthropic *Heuristically programmed ALgorithmic computer*, always already balancing on the edges of the digital "cinematic wilderness," *The Matrix* runs away with *Alphaville*'s commercial potential. By exploiting the existential theme of a computer-dominated mythological reality as the ultimate "failing of modern civilization,"[12] the Wachowskis' most successful film simultaneously profits commercially by "indulging"[13] the viewers with its sophisticated CGIs.

Alphaville is also explicitly indicative of the paradoxical interrelatedness of Godard's philosophical and pragmatic engagements with technology and media. According to Brody, the film is inspired by the dark prophecies of Georges Bernanos' book *La France contre les robots (France against the Robots)*, which "considers mechanization and technology to be the avatars of [a] new universal tyranny."[14] The inevitability of the "alienation through technology"[15] is made uncannily contemporary, since *Alphaville* is shot entirely on location in Paris, in and around coldly functionalist, concrete-and-glass buildings from the 1960s.

Yet while it is easier to place Godard's philosophical stance on technological progress within the long line of socially pessimistic thinkers, starting with Georg Simmel and Wittgenstein and ending with Žižek and Zygmunt Bauman who, not unlike Bernanos, see the unchecked technological evolution as the core reason for what Charles Taylor calls the "malaise of modernity,"[16] it is much more intriguing to view Godard's practice as a filmmaker in light of the neo-Luddism of the 1960s New Left movement, with which he passionately identified. One of the early media theorists and advocates, Hans M. Enzensberger, defines the New Left aversion to all things techno- logical as "cultural archaism,"[17] which he illustrates with the refusal of the student organizers of the 1968 strikes in Paris to avail themselves of new printing techniques. And, in order to conduct "their agitation among the workers with a modern offset press, [they] printed their posters on the hand presses of the École des Beaux Arts."[18] Moreover, he writes, the "favourite target for aggression" of their colleagues from Berkeley "at the very beginning of the student revolt, during the Free Speech Movement ... was the university computer."[19] Enzensberger explains the New Left oppo- sition to new media—albeit packaged as resistance against its ubiquitous "manipulation"—with "old bourgeois fears ... of 'the masses' ... along with equally old bourgeois longing for pre-industrial times dressed up in progressive clothing." Without mincing words, Enzensberger accuses the "comrades" of double-standards and even downright hypocrisy vis-à-vis new-media politics, pointing to the "split between the puritanical view of political action ... roughly corresponding to the historical situation in 1900" and the "area of private 'leisure,'" when the activists "listen to the Rolling Stones, watch ... television, and go to cinema to see a Western or a Godard" [sic!].[20]

In his bold ventures into the "cinematic wilderness" of ideological and aesthetic experimentation after *Alphaville*, Godard moves beyond what Enzensberger defines as the Leftist double standard. And while, as a true Marxist-Leninist, he remains critical of the growing exploitation and alien- ation of the masses through technological advancement of the capital- ist-owned means of production, as a film practitioner—while privileging newest sound-image technologies whether in front, behind, or instead of the (traditional 35 mm) camera, or in post-production—he never does so without sound political and practical motivation, neither does he com- pletely abandon the older technologies. In fact, the pieces of cinematic equipment, indeed technology itself, has been moving towards the centre of Godard's narrative system since the 1960s. It is enough to mention the professional tape-recorder, featured prominently in *Made in USA* (1966) as an avatar of the diseased journalist, yielding taped messages and political statements as the only leads Anna Karina's character Paula finds to the political intrigue that led to his disappearance; or the earpiece Marina Vlady wears in *2 ou 3 choses que je sais d'elle* (1966) to mask the fact that her lines were in fact responses to Godard's questions and statements, although those are made at times quite audible.

Certainly, the audiovisual experiments in *Le Gai Savoir* (1968) and in the subsequent Groupe Dziga Vertov films, made between 1970 and 1972, are amongst the most radical attempts to problematize not only the aesthetic and ideological aspects of the interaction between image, sound, and text, but also the technology behind them. Thus, in the introduction of *Vladimir et Rosa* (1971), the voice-over narration meticulously dissects the restaging of the Chicago Eight trial, throwing into high relief the scientific progressivity of the filming process. The Marxist-Leninist discourse, the male voice-over energetically claims, is built on the dialectical interaction between "theory" and "practice," thus ensuring its "scientific truthfulness." The means of production—a portable French-made camera and a Nagra tape recorder—are then introduced with the same passionate urgency, thus seriously blurring the boundaries between self-reflexivity and self-irony.

By way of exception, in *Tout va bien* (1972), the expensive broadcast equipment in the Parisian studio of the American network that Suzanne (Jane Fonda) works for is shown as stifling her creative journalistic fervour—maybe because the studio is American and she is a dissident. On the other hand, the professional 35 mm camera perched next to Jacques (Yves Montand) during his interview-like statements—with Jacques addressing directly the viewer, or rather, the director filming him—is cast as an abstraction of the inherently ethical cinematographic process. The camera suggests the "semi-autobiographical,"[21] even confessional nature of these self-reflective statements, where Jacques's revolutionary disillusionment can be read in light of Godard's own post-1968 fatigue. The presence of the 35 mm camera, on the other hand, intensifies the meta-cinematic and meta-ideological function of the episode, underscoring the ethical gap between its potential to reveal "the truth 24 frames per second"[22] and its current use in a shoot of a pantyhose commercial, which Jacques is directing "to pay the bills."

The most recent instalment in the ongoing argument about Godard's complex allegiances to new-media technologies comes from Brody's blog on the *New Yorker* website (January 12, 2011). Reminiscing about a decade-old interview with Godard, Brody brings up the director's "dissatisfaction with something that did not yet exist: e-books" and recalls him saying that he "preferred to edit video with analog rather than digital technology." With "digital," Godard explains, "time no longer exists … there's less thought, there's more time, therefore there's less cinema … and all movies resemble each other [despite] some very beautiful images, some very beautiful things … it's harder to make good movies than before."

And, in light of this statement, Brody concludes by noting—not without sad irony—the growing intervals between Godard's films since the time this interview was taken in 2000: "There were three years between the completion of *In Praise of Love* and *Notre Musique*, six years between the latter film and *Film Socialisme*.... He's using digital technology now—and, filling the time that's saved with thought, making the past reappear ..."[23]

WITTGENSTEIN IN *ALPHAVILLE*

The foreword to *Philosophical Remarks*, quoted above, was amended by Wittgenstein to further clarify the "spirit" of his engagement with issues of progress and modernity: "*This* spirit is different from the one which informs the vast stream of European and American civilization in which all of us stand. *That* spirit expresses itself in an onward movement, in building ever larger and more complicated structures; the other in striving after clarity and perspicuity in no matter what structure."[24] Its new version clearly suggests that his philosophy is "in sympathy" with Godard's artistic "spirit" in more ways than their shared ambiguity towards scientific progress. Indeed, Godard and Wittgenstein are fluid, multi-faceted geniuses, resistant to facile interpretations and intellectual commodification, who nonetheless share similarly messianic aspirations, or "family resemblances," when striving to redesign fundamentally their respective fields of cinema and philosophy "in no matter what structure." And it is really strange that so little has been done so far to link their work. The first publication to relate Godard to Wittgenstein[25] is Robert MacLean's well-informed, albeit somewhat chaotic, essay "Opening the Private Eye: Wittgenstein and Godard," published in *Sight and Sound* more than three decades ago.[26] As pointed out elsewhere,[27] MacLean's article sustains the argument that *Alphaville* is profoundly Wittgensteinian, both in letter and in spirit.

In light of *Tractatus Logico-Philosophicus*, *Alphaville* adds new dimensions to Godard's concerns with the "invasion of technology and false memory, created by the media." As Bertrand Russell's preface to the *Tractatus*—Wittgenstein's "first and only" completed book—states, it was "supposed to be the last word on philosophical problems ... and bring philosophy to an end"[28] by demonstrating that "old philosophical questions were ill-informed and arose from 'the misunderstanding of the logic of our language.'"[29] Wittgenstein's propositions, bordering on the nonsensical, expose in a merciless manner the brazen logic of our postmodern moment. And, in light of two of the most quoted ones, numbers 5.6 and 7,[30] Godard's futuristic nightmare acquires an unexpectedly contemporary meaning.[31] Taken at face value, the propositions "manifest themselves" in the "pictorial forms" of an eerily familiar totalitarian world of ubiquitous surveillance, obedience, and dread. Proposition 5.6—"the limits of my language mean the limits of my world"—is "pictured" by the fearful manner in which Alphaville's citizens observe their strict and ever-changing language code, whose trespassing means quite literally the end of one's world. Proposition 7—"what we cannot speak about, we must pass over in silence"—defines the limits of the language by yielding an existential and quasi-religious depth to the axiomatic interdiction against anything considered illogical by Alphaville officials. The dystopian world of Alpha 60 seeks not only to restrict the rejuvenating powers of language—defined by the later Wittgenstein as a human "form of life"—in favour of "assertoric sentences," but also to curb human emotions, which might upset the "crystalline purity" of its instrumental reason. Therefore both words and feelings, pertaining to the forbidden realms of "ethics, religion, the meaning of life, logic and philosophy"[32] are punishable by death, like the man who "behaved illogically" by grieving over the passing of his wife, or the one who keeps "uttering the unutterable" by repeating "conscience, conscience" on his death-bed.

The attempt to remake reality in the image of Hegel's rationality—"What is real is rational, but not everything that is rational is real"—has been the philosophical foundation of every totalitarian creative destruction, which centres on the full rationality of absolute knowledge, in this case epitomized by Alpha 60. Not unlike the Hegelian state, Alpha 60 is the exclusive bearer of "the ethical idea in history."[33] And when Lenny insists that he is a "free man," Alpha 60 responds that this "reply is meaningless.... [W]e know nothing ... we record ... we calculate ... and we draw conclusions.... Your replies are difficult to code and sometimes impossible." For any mentioning of the "unutterable" is enough to bring Alpha 60 to a standstill and ultimately to self-destruction since it is programmed to endorse only those human activities that can be computed. The objectives of the "electronic tyrant" Alpha 60 are made explicitly clear in its hoarse-voiced statement: "In the so-called capitalist world or communist world there is no malicious intent to suppress men through the power of technology and materialism, but rather the natural aim of all organizations to increase their natural structure."[34] In other words, what cannot be computed cannot be spoken about, and if spoken, it destroys either the speaker or the computer. It is enough to recall the quick disintegration of Soviet power as a result of Gorbachev's misguided attempts to improve totalitarianism "from above" through introducing freedom of speech in a country that has never known such, in order to realize the scope of Godardian prophecy. Furthermore, the current "minification"[35] of computer languages, which precludes attempts at expressing anything "higher"[36] on strictly technological grounds, tends to undermine democracy and freedom of expression "from below," which could easily result in some form of self-imposed informational totalitarianism.

In this sense, the explanation Godard's heroine from *2 ou 3 choses que je sais d'elle* gives to her boy—by quoting another modern language theorist, Martin Heidegger—about language being "the house in which man lives,"[37] ominously alludes to the kind of computerized Newspeak we now "live in," enclosed by the limited number of signs one could text or tweet with. Despite Enzensberger's vehement rejection of the "Orwellian fantasy" as an "undialectical and obsolete" media model,[38] it seems that on this curve of social and technological development, marked by the meteoric rise of information empires—and determined by "the natural aim of all organizations to increase their natural structure"—the Orwellian model has reclaimed its urgency. The power of media empires to manipulate public opinion dwarfs anything that Orwell—and maybe even Godard![39]— might have imagined, for it will be up to the owner of what Tim Wu has called "the master switch"[40] to determine the future not only of the house we live in, but also of the world as we know it.

WITTGENSTEIN AND GODARD: RECONTEXTUALIZING THE "PICTURE" IN *HISTOIRE(S) DU CINÉMA*

Nonetheless, "the deepest mystery at the heart of the *Tractatus*,"[41] as Monk concisely sums it up, is that Wittgenstein believed, at least partially, that "nonsensical propositions ... can indeed show what they fail to say."[42] For, as long as you "do not try to utter what is unutterable, then nothing gets lost ... [although] the unutterable will be—unutterably—contained in what has been uttered!"[43] For Godard, the ultimately "unutterable ... contained in what has been uttered" is the impossible love, whose various dimensions he has been exploring since the early 1980s. In this, his endeavours are again "in sympathy" with the "spirit" of the later Wittgenstein, more specifically with the latter's growing opposition to the rigour of logic and philosophy in favour of "language games," understood by Monk as "producing the kind of emotional understanding that consists in seeing connections."[44]

According to Monk, in *Philosophical Investigations*, which was published in its entirety only posthumously in 1953, Wittgenstein abandons the idea that "propositions are a logical picture of reality"[45] and invites us to carefully reconsider the ever-changing uses of the picture instead of being "held captive" by it. By turning to the language games of "ordinary language" and its various "contexts," we are encouraged to "enrich our imagination" by "replacing [the old picture] with another."[46] Aware of Wittgenstein's respect for Freud as creator of a new and powerful mythology, Monk describes this knowledge through imagination—often "overlooked" by Wittgensteinian scholars—as therapy rather than philosophical argument.[47]

In a similar fashion Godard has been urging his viewers to turn away from the commercialized "pictures of reality," supplied by the Hollywood-dominated media. With growing intensity, he has been offering an arsenal of creative ways for reclaiming and "enriching our imagination, held captive for so long" by the entertainment industry. Among his most influential attempts to put the "old picture" to new uses are the eight instalments of *Histoire(s) du cinéma* (1988–1998), whose cognitive emotionality is hailed by Jacques Rancière as a "neo-symbolist and neo-humanist tendency in contemporary art."[48] In Douglas Morrey's succinct summary, *Histoire(s)* is a "history of cinema, made of cinema, constructed from the images and sounds of cinema itself. A mythical and very personal history [of] the medium within the wider history of art as well as in the political history of the twentieth century."[49] Indeed, as Walter Benjamin writes in the *Arcades Project*, "history breaks down into images, not stories."[50] And the most efficient tool in this breaking down of history and putting it together again on screen, is montage, which Godard considers "cinema's unique contribution to the history of art" and a "new form of critical thought."[51] Meant to redesign what Rancière calls "imageness"—that is, the "particular regime of articulation between the visible and the sayable"[52]—the montage in *Histoire(s)* uncannily evokes Wittgenstein's "language games." Like words, released from the metaphysical constraints of the philosophical language into new contexts of "ordinary" and "private" languages, so the images of *Histoire(s)*, emancipated from the narrative hierarchies of cinematic storytelling are being reassembled in new contexts and in unseen formations, according to what Wittgenstein called "family resemblances." For episode 1B of *Histoire(s)*, for example, Godard designs the "visible" via associative montage techniques, that is, superimposition, insets, and bleaching, which allow him to compare and collide both linearly and vertically scenes from classical Hollywood films and from his own oeuvre, documentary found footage, stills from modern and Renaissance paintings, text, and intertitles. The articulation of the "sayable" and the "audible" is even more complex, featuring his own voice-over commentary, dialogues from the film excerpts, eerie sounds of wind and war, as well as added music track, varying from rock to classical music. Flickering words on the screen—"girl," "cry," "flower"—serve as meaning-making "prototypes" at the centre of these clusters, loosely connected to the emotional world of popular imagination.

More coherent statements—"industry of escapism," "the only place where memory is held captive"—although conceptually more lucid in channelling of the associative flux, do not, as Roland Barthes has it, "naturalize the meaning of the image into a definite sense that is ideologically determined in advance."[53]

The mesmerizing effect of this unique "imageness" is, in Wittgensteinian terms, "imponderable"—that is, subliminal and irrational—evidence for understanding people and their history. This *non-scientific* form of understanding" of the unfathomable, Monk claims emphatically, is "characteristic of the arts [which Wittgenstein] sought to protect from the encroachment of science and scientism."[54] Indeed, as Wittgenstein writes in *Culture and Value*, "People nowadays think that scientists exist to instruct them; poets, musicians, etc., to give them pleasure. The idea that these have something to teach them—that does not occur to them."[55] The thing Godard teaches us *sub specie aeternitatis* through this powerful "fusion of images" is the "community-building power" of the "autonomous world of images."[56] Media scholar Richard Dienst further clarifies the link between Godard's emotive cognition and the heightened responsibility of the viewer, defining *Histoire(s)* as an "insistent demonstration of the connections between spectatorship and citizenship, castigating the political system for poverty, incivility, and war, while insisting that all of us are responsible for what has been put to view."[57]

GODARD, WITTGENSTEIN, AND NEW MEDIA

The aesthetic, philosophical, and civic potential of *Histoire(s)* has not been lost on new-media scholars, and was almost immediately declared as an exemplary new-media artifact (or object, as prominent new-media theorist Lev Manovich has it) in terms of format, politics, and above all—because of its montage aesthetics—as a truly "new form of critical thought." Dienst remarks that, at the time of its completion in 1998, *Histoire(s)* was an accomplished multi-media piece, delivered in "video, printed book, and audio CD," presenting "different 'variations' of the material, calling for a different kind of attention." He also points out that Godard's success in making the multi-media transition of text and images smooth and natural, is rooted in his versatile "montage technique, grounded in superimposition, onscreen captioning, and an arrhythmic conception of mixing."[58] In his seminal work, *The Language of New Media*, Manovich cites Godard as one of the pioneers of the new-media "electronic montage," which replaced his explorations in "temporal montage" from the 1960s. For *Histoire(s)*, he writes, Godard developed "a unique aesthetic of continuity that relies on electronically mixing a number of images together within a single shot …

creating a very slow cross-dissolve between images … that seems never to resolve in a singular image…. [The camera] oscillates between two separate flickering images as if hesitating until the second image finally replaces the first."[59] Manovich's discussion of Godard's technique not only proves its relevance to new-media arts, but also discloses the manner in which it grasps the "imponderablility" of "inner processes." By imitating the way "ideas or mental images float around in our minds, coming in and out of mental focus," Godard's montage suggests the "basis of our mental life," whose main task, according to "Locke and other associationist philosophers," is "forming associations."[60]

Indeed, like Wittgenstein, whose philosophy has been subjected to recurring attempts at appropriation by new media in its striving for legitimacy—despite his deep opposition against "the worship of science and progress, characteristic of our age"[61]—Godard has become something of a reluctant new-media guru. Time and again, in support of his theory on the dynamics between database and narrative in new-media arts,[62] Manovich summons Godard, claiming that "Godard's *History of Cinema* represents an important step towards database cinema. Godard treats the whole history of cinema as his source material, traversing this database back and forth, like a virtual camera flying over a landscape made from old media."[63] Yet again, true to his nature, Godard resists this new attempt at intellectual commodification, and turns to some semblance of linear, although still wilfully obscure, narratives for the three feature-length films he made after *Histoire(s)*. Apparently weary "within the vague and complicated system that the whole world is continually entering and watching,"[64] as he describes the new-media universe, he even shot *Film socialisme* from a stubbornly static camera ("the chemist doesn't do tracking shots in front of his microscope nor petrol companies when drilling into the sea bed," as he explains in the press kit, published on the Cannes film festival website).[65]

As Brody writes, Godard "was and remains a conservative revolutionary, whose utopian visions are moralistic and aesthetic"[66]—and, one is tempted to add, a romantic-revolutionary, who strongly believed and believes in the possibility to counter the "invasion of technology and false memory, created by the media to replicate or explicate the past" on its own turf—just consider his two latest films, shot on 3D!—by reaching for the "unutterable" and the "imponderable" through poetry—that "light which the modern world is lacking"—and conscience, which for Godard "has the sacred status of faith and transcendent moral law."[67] Seen in this light, Godard's humanism is a *monumentum aere perennius*[68] not only to Wittgenstein's Proposition 6.121,[69] which compellingly asserts the transcendence of poetry and conscience, claiming that "ethics and aesthetics are one and the same," but to his entire philosophy.

NOTES

1   Wheeler Winston Dixon, *Visions of the Apocalypse: Spectacles of Destruction in American Cinema* (London: Wallflower Press, 2003), 106.

2   Quoted in Dixon, *Visions of the Apocalypse*, 106 (from Lawrence Osborne, "An Enfant Terrible at 70," *New York Times Magazine*, September 30, 2001, 52–53.

3   Slavoj Žižek, *First as Tragedy, Then as Farce* (London: Verso, 2009), 92.

4   Quoted in Ray Monk, *How to Read Wittgenstein* (New York: W.W. Norton, 2005), 95.

5   David Sterritt, *The Films of Jean-Luc Godard: Seeing the Invisible* (Cambridge: Cambridge University Press, 1999), 10.

6   Richard Brody, *Everything Is Cinema: The Working Life of Jean-Luc Godard* (New York: Holt, 2008), 236.

7   Malcolm Frazer, "*Master's Mess: Film Socialisme* Is Another Puzzling Essay-film from Ageing Auteur," *Mirror* (Montreal), April 21, 2011.

8   Quoted in Jacques Rancière, *Dissensus: On Politics and Aesthetics*, trans. Steven Corcoran (London: Continuum, 2010), 194.

9   Douglas Morrey, *Jean-Luc Godard* (Manchester: Manchester University Press, 2005), 62.

10 Sterritt, *The Films of Jean-Luc Godard*, 13.

11 Ibid.

12 Ibid.

13 Ibid.

14 Brody, *Everything Is Cinema*, 231.

15 Ibid., 230.

16 In his celebrated, concise work *Malaise of Modernity* (1991), renowned Canadian philosopher Charles Taylor discusses the issue of (post)modern self-actualization—or what he calls "authenticity"—as being bogged down by narcissism, the unavoidable side effect of unchecked technological progress.

17 Hans Magnus Enzensberger, "Constituents of a Theory of the Media" (originally published in *New Left Review* 64 [1970]: 13–36), in *The New Media Reader*, ed. Noah Wardrip-Fruin and Nick Montfort (Cambridge, MA: MIT Press, 2003), 263.

18 Ibid., 264.

19 Ibid.

20 Ibid.

21 Morrey, *Jean-Luc Godard*, 97.

22 *Le Petit soldat* (Jean-Luc Godard, 1961).

23 Richard Brody, "Godard on E-Books," *The Front Row: Notes on the Cinema* (blog), website of *The New Yorker*, January 12, 2011, http://www.newyorker.com/online/blogs/movies/2011/01/godard-e-books.html.

24 Ludwig Wittgenstein, "Foreword," in *Philosophical Remarks*, trans. Rush Rhees (Oxford: Blackwell, 1998), xi.

25 The second publication, referring to both Wittgenstein and Godard is Stanley Cavell's reflections on *Je vous salue, Marie*, Godard's 1985 contemporized rendition of the Virgin Mary's relationship with God the Father and Joseph, her husband. Cavell summons Wittgenstein's *Philosophical Investigations* (section 118)—"Where does our investigation take its importance from since it seems only to destroy everything interesting, that is, all that is great and important?"—in order to interpret their

story as one of "psychic trauma and of scepticism." It however remains unclear whether Cavell refers to the gospel story of the Virgin Mary as "all that is great and important" that is "destroyed by investigation" or Godard's version of it. Stanley Cavell, "Foreword," in *Jean-Luc Godard's Hail Mary: Women and the Sacred in Film*, ed. Maryel Locke and Charles Warren (Carbondale: Southern Illinois University Press, 1993), xvii.

26   Robert MacLean, "Opening the Private Eye: Wittgenstein and Godard," in *Sight and Sound* 47, no. 1 (1977–78): 46–49.

27   Christina Stojanova, "Beyond Text and Image: Péter Forgács and His *Wittgenstein Tractatus*," in *Wittgenstein at the Movies: Cinematic Investigations*, ed. Béla Szabados and Christina Stojanova (Lanham, MD: Lexington Books, 2011), 122.

28   Quoted in Monk, *How to Read Wittgenstein*, 16.

29   Ibid., 17.

30   Ludwig Wittgenstein, *Tractatus Logico-Philosophicus* [1921], trans. D.F. Pears and B.F. McGuinness (London: Routledge Classics, 2002).

31   MacLean mentions also Propositions 5.63, 5.641, 6.42, and 6.421. "Opening the Private Eye," 46, 48.

32   Monk, *How to Read Wittgenstein*, 21.

33   *Hegel's Philosophy of Right*, trans. T.M. Knox (Oxford: Oxford University Press, 1977), 279.

34   Brody, *Everything Is Cinema*, 231.

35   A computer programming term, signifying "the process of removing all unnecessary characters, used to add readability to the source code, without changing its functionality. Minified source code is especially useful for interpreted languages (such as JavaScript), deployed and transmitted on the Internet, because it reduces the amount of data that needs to be transferred." *Wikipedia*, s.v. "Minification (programming)," http://en.wikipedia.org/wiki/Minification_%28programming%29.

36   Wittgenstein, *Tractatus Logico-Philosophicus*, Proposition 6.42.

37   Martin Heidegger, *Pathmarks*, trans. William McNeil (Cambridge: Cambridge University Press, 1998), 254.

38   Enzensberger, "Constituents of a Theory of the Media," 262.

39   Godard's latest film, to be released in 2013, is prophetically called *Goodbye to Language 3D (Adieu au langage)*.

40   Tim Wu, *The Master Switch: The Rise and Fall of Information Empires* (New York: Alfred A. Knopf, 2010).

41   Monk, *How to Read Wittgenstein*, 27.

42   Ibid., 29.

43   Wittgenstein, quoted in Monk, *How to Read Wittgenstein*, 25.

44   Monk, *How to Read Wittgenstein*, 72.

45   Ibid., 47.

46   Ibid., 79.

47   Ibid.

48   Jacques Rancière, *The Future of the Image*, trans. Gregory Elliott (London: Verso, 2009), 67.

49   Morrey, *Jean-Luc Godard*, 221.

50   Walter Benjamin, quoted in Gerhard Richter, *Walter Benjamin and the Corpus of Autobiography* (Toronto: Scholarly Book Services, 2002), 199.

51 Quoted in Morrey, *Jean-Luc Godard*, 221.

52 Rancière, *The Future of Images*, 11.

53 Roland Barthes, paraphrased in Morrey, *Jean-Luc Godard*, 85.

54 Monk, *How to Read Wittgenstein*, 101–2.

55 Ludwig Wittgenstein, *Culture and Value*, trans. Peter Winch (Chicago: University of Chicago Press, 1984), 36.

56 In a recently published collection in English, Jacques Rancière outlines the trajectory of Godard's montage techniques from the political and aesthetic "collage" to civic "fusion"—that is, from a "clash of contraries" between "'high culture' and the world of commodity" in the 1960s and a "principle of linking heterogeneous elements" in the 1980s, to a "fusion of images" in *Histoire(s)*. Rancière, *Dissensus*, 194.

57 Richard Dienst, "Breaking Down Godard's Histories," in *New Media, Old Media: A History and Theory Reader*, ed. Wendy Hui Kyong Chun and Thomas Keenan (London: Routledge, 2006), 131.

58 Ibid., 126.

59 Lev Manovich, *The Language of New Media* (Cambridge, MA: MIT Press, 2001), 151–52.

60 Ibid., 152.

61 Monk, *How to Read Wittgenstein*, 96.

62 Manovich, *The Language of New Media*, 225–29.

63 Lev Manovich, "Old Media as New Media: Cinema," in *The New Media Book*, ed. Dan Harries (London: BFI Publishing, 2002), 217.

64 Jean-Luc Godard, quoted in Manovich, *The Language of New Media*, 152.

65 "JLG Film Socialism: Ideas Separate Us, Dreams Bring Us Together," Festival de Cannes press kit for *Un Certain regard*, 2010, 16, http://www.festival-cannes.fr/assets/Image/Direct/033107.pdf.

66 Brody, *Everything Is Cinema*, 231.

67 Ibid., 232.

68 The full quote is *Exegi monumentum aere perennius* (I have raised a monument more lasting than bronze), from the eponymous ode by Horace (Book III), *Exegi Monumentum*.

69 "It is clear that ethics cannot be put into words. Ethics is transcendental. (Ethics and aesthetics are one and the same.)" Wittgenstein, *Tracatus*, Proposition 6.421.

BIBLIOGRAPHY

Brody, Richard. *Everything Is Cinema: The Working Life of Jean-Luc Godard*. New York: Holt, 2008.

———. "Godard on E-Books." *The Front Row: Notes on the Cinema* (blog). *The New Yorker*. January 12, 2011. http://www.newyorker.com/online/blogs/movies/2011/01/godard-e-books.html.

Cavell, Stanley. "Foreword." In *Jean-Luc Godard's Hail Mary: Women and the Sacred in Film*, edited by Maryel Locke and Charles Warren, vii–xxiii. Carbondale: Southern Illinois University Press, 1993.

Dienst, Richard. "Breaking Down Godard's Histories." In *New Media, Old Media: A History and Theory Reader*, edited by Wendy Hui Kyong Chun and Thomas Keenan, 125–32. London: Routledge, 2006.

Dixon, Wheeler Winston. *Visions of the Apocalypse: Spectacles of Destruction in American Cinema*. London: Wallflower Press, 2003.

Enzensberger, Hans Magnus. "Constituents of a Theory of the Media." In *The New Media Reader*, edited by Noah Wardrip-Fruin and Nick Montfort, 259–76. Cambridge, MA: MIT Press, 2003.

Frazer, Malcolm. "Master's Mess: *Film Socialisme* Is Another Puzzling Essay-film from Ageing Auteur." *Mirror* (Montreal), April 21, 2011.

Hegel, G.W.F. *Hegel's Philosophy of Right*. Translated by T.M. Knox. Oxford: Oxford University Press, 1977.

Heidegger, Martin. *Pathmarks*. Translated by William McNeil. Cambridge: Cambridge University Press, 1998.

"JLG Film Socialism: Ideas Separate Us, Dreams Bring Us Together." Festival de Cannes press kit for *Un Certain regard*. 2010. http://www.festival-cannes.fr/assets/Image/Direct/033107.pdf.

MacLean, Robert. "Opening the Private Eye: Wittgenstein and Godard." *Sight and Sound* 47, no. 1 (1977–78): 46–49.

Manovich, Lev. *The Language of New Media*. Cambridge, MA: MIT Press, 2001.

———. "Old Media as New Media: Cinema." In *The New Media Book*, edited by Dan Harries, 209–18. London: BFI Publishing, 2002.

Monk, Ray. *How to Read Wittgenstein*. New York: W.W. Norton, 2005.

Morrey, Douglas. *Jean-Luc Godard*. Manchester: Manchester University press, 2005.

Rancière, Jacques. *Dissensus: On Politics and Aesthetics*. Translated by Steven Corcoran. London: Continuum, 2010.

———. *The Future of the Image*. Translated by Gregory Elliott. London: Verso, 2009.

Richter, Gerhard. *Walter Benjamin and the Corpus of Autobiography*. Toronto: Scholarly Book Services, 2002.

Sterritt, David. *The Films of Jean-Luc Godard: Seeing the Invisible*. Cambridge: Cambridge University Press, 1999.

Stojanova, Christina. "Beyond Text and Image: Péter Forgács and His *Wittgenstein Tractatus*." In *Wittgenstein at the Movies: Cinematic Investigations*, edited by Béla Szabados and Christina Stojanova, 121–38. Lanham, MD: Lexington Books, 2011.

Taylor, Charles. *Malaise of Modernity*. Toronto: Anansi, 1991.

Wittgenstein, Ludwig. *Culture and Value*. Translated by Peter Winch. Chicago: University of Chicago Press, 1984.

———. *Philosophical Remarks*. Translated by Rush Rhees. Oxford: Blackwell, 1998.

———. *Tractatus Logico-Philosophicus*. Translated by D.F. Pears and B.F. McGuinness. London: Routledge Classics, 2002.

Wu, Tim. *The Master Switch: The Rise and Fall of Information Empires*. New York: Alfred A. Knopf, 2010.

Žižek, Slavoj. *First as Tragedy, Then as Farce*. London: Verso, 2009.

9

Godard, Schizoanalysis, and the Immaculate Conception of the Frame

David Sterritt

> Since the body–soul pairing means each deforms the other, we must separate
> them to know them properly. The society makes the body seem something more
> than it is and the soul something less. But once separated, when the body returns
> to earth, and the soul is able to return to heaven, we see both in all their purity.
> —Jean-Luc Godard, *De L'Origine du XXIᵉ siècle*

IN AN ARTICLE on montage written in 1956 for *Cahiers du cinéma*, Jean-Luc
Godard made an observation that has been quoted many times in many
contexts: "If direction is a look, montage is a heartbeat ... what one seeks
to foresee in space, the other seeks in time.... Cutting on a look is ... to
bring out the soul under the spirit, the passion behind the intrigue, to make
the heart prevail over the intelligence by destroying the notion of space in
favor of that of time."[1] This passage appeared almost thirty years before
Gilles Deleuze published *Cinema 1: The Movement-Image* and *Cinema 2: The
Time-Image* in 1983 and 1985.[2] Yet the young critic's remark anticipates the
philosopher's film-theoretical stance. The need to displace a traditional
bias toward space with the realization that time is a concrete and dynamic
force is the single most vital element in the thinking of Henri Bergson,
whose ideas about this subject—carried into such areas as affect, memory,
perception, language, and the ontology of mind itself—play indispensable
roles in Deleuze's writings on cinema and allied areas of immanence, difference, and multiplicity.

Godard's statement also resonates with Deleuzian theory in its prefer-
ence for the material (heart) over the abstract (intelligence) and in its praise
of filmmaking that breaks what Deleuze calls the "link between man and

the world." When technique detaches a film and its spectator from the "general system of commensurability" that normally orders action and perception in space and time, cinema performs its liberating function of bringing thought "face to face with its own impossibility" and animating the "higher power of birth" that this encounter can catalyze. "The sensory-motor break," Deleuze declares, "makes man a seer who finds himself ... confronted by something unthinkable in thought." Seeking to express precisely this—the unthinkable in thought—Godard works montage and *mise en scène* into volatile folds that reveal, refract, and reflect upon their own rich mysteries. Above all he probes the potential of the irrational cut, which for Deleuze marks a limit or interface between images that are paradoxically joined and disjunctive, "non-linked" and "relinked,"[3] at once. By means of these techniques, Godard evades the classical linearity of arborescent film—rooted in convention like a firmly planted tree—and produces structures more like the branchings of the rhizome, which grows and spreads in every direction it can find.

In this essay I consider ways in which ideas developed by Deleuze and Félix Guattari, particularly in connection with the practice they call schizo-analysis, cast light on the 1985 film *Je vous salue, Marie (Hail Mary)*, which is actually two films in one. The longer portion, the *Hail Mary* written and directed by Godard, presents the myth of the Virgin Mary translated to the present day; this is preceded by Anne-Marie Miéville's short *Le Livre de Marie (The Book of Mary)*, about an adolescent girl coping psychologically and spiritually with her parents' divorce. The movies are connected by a splendid irrational cut: the Mary of Miéville's film is sitting at a table with a soft-boiled egg before her; a tight close-up shows her cracking off the egg's top with a knife; the severed portion falls onto the table; and an intertitle reading *En ce temps-là* (At that time) instantly appears, followed by a shot of light rain falling across windswept reeds on a country slope. Godard's film slides into existence so softly and subtly that at first one isn't sure it has begun.

I focus on Godard's *Hail Mary* because its complex blend of narrative drama, theological speculation, Catholic iconography, and Protestant music are well suited to the themes I want to explore, starting with the connection between Godard's highly intuitive cinema and the transcendental or "non-metaphysical" unconscious that Deleuze and Guattari speak of as they seek to rediscover the unconscious as a machinic assemblage geared to the production of desire and "libidinal investments of the social field."[4] Remembering that Godard was influenced by the work of Françoise Dolto, one of France's most celebrated psychologists, I wish to show that *Je vous salue, Marie* is best illuminated not by her theologically informed psychoanalysis but by the schizoanalytically informed atheology developed by Deleuze and Guattari in their *Capitalism and Schizophrenia* books, *Anti-Oedipus* and *A Thousand Plateaus*.[5] More specifically, I want to explore how key schizoanalytical tropes—deterritorialization, non-human becoming, lines of flight, and the body without organs—apply to *Je vous salue, Marie*, which deterritorializes being in ways that are physical, metaphysical, astrophysical, and sometimes all three. Throughout this I'll be considering the notion of *soul* as it winds through Godardian film and Deleuzian theory, often under such aliases as *virtuality* and *élan vital* and *spiritual automaton*.

Rather than arriving at a particular destination, I want to emulate the strolling schizo imagined by Deleuze and Guattari, scanning the horizon for intriguing desiring-machines, spiritual automata, flows of becoming, and breaths of fresh film-philosophical air. My guide for the excursion is Godard, who tries in *Je vous salue, Marie* to achieve "an 'Immaculate Conception' of the frame"[6]—an improvisational cinema that avoids preconceived organization in order to open new frontiers of intuitive perception. The most powerful way to experience his work is to follow its flows toward a non-place that Deleuze and Guattari describe: "a world created in the process of its ... coming undone, its deterritorialization."[7] In other words: find the body without organs in Mary's enigmatic egg; apply a "schizoanalytic flick of the finger"[8] as decisively as she cracks the shell; then watch as one story closes and another, surpassingly schizoid tale begins.

GOD/ARD

Godard was interested in psychoanalysis when he started conceptualizing *Je vous salue, Marie*; more precisely, he was interested in a particular kind of Freudian thought that he found in a book by Françoise Dolto, a French physician and psychoanalyst who specialized in child psychology, working alongside Jacques Lacan for many years. By the late 1970s she was "the best known and most beloved psychoanalyst in France," according to psychologist Sherry Turkle, who summarizes her core contribution thus: *"Where other psychoanalytic thinkers stressed childhood sexuality, Dolto insists on childhood lucidity."*[9]

Most important for our purposes, Dolto was also a practising Roman Catholic who injected large doses of Christianity into her psychoanalytic theories. As historian Élisabeth Roudinesco puts it, Dolto believed that the Incarnation and the Resurrection, through the Crucifixion, "pulled Christ out of a 'placenta' and a uterine world to accede to eternal life," allowing him to become the "metaphor of desire that leads humankind ... on a great identity quest."[10] One of Dolto's projects was a series of radio dialogues with Gérard Séverin, another Freudian School psychoanalyst. These were published in book form as *L'Évangile au risque de la psychoanalyse*, the text that captured Godard's interest.[11]

According to biographer Richard Brody, the roots of *Je vous salue, Marie* lie in a project Godard never completed; provisionally called "Fathers and Daughters," it was to be a film "about incest" that would feature Godard playing the role of God, an "invisible and ubiquitous" presence, opposite the young actress Myriem Roussel, on whom Godard had a major crush. When Roussel became anxious over the ticklish material he was cooking up, he looked for a more sensitive way of approaching the subject of forbidden desire. For a while he considered a story about Sigmund Freud and the early patient known as Dora, and then, he said later, "I looked at it with regard to God the Father. And I came upon the story of Mary."[12] He also came upon Dolto's work, or at least one corner of it.

The typical Godard film is liberally strewn with literary allusions and quotations, but there is often a certain murkiness about them, since he doesn't hesitate to cite a work on the basis of fleeting acquaintance rather than serious engagement. No matter what appears within a movie, biographer Colin MacCabe warns, "it would always be a mistake to assume that Godard had read a particular book."[13] This uncertainty extends to Dolto's work. "In her introduction—I didn't really read the rest of the book—she spoke of Mary and Joseph in a way that I never heard before," Godard recalled later. "It seemed very cinematic: the story of a couple. And I'm very traditional. I've always made love stories and stories of couples. So that's how I got to the story of 'God and his Daughter.'"[14] This theme—a couple in love—sounds too conventional for Godard in the 1980s, and his account of its origin sounds too neat, painting him as an uninhibited thinker who considers all kinds of audacious ideas—incest and taboo, father Freud and daughter Dora, God and Godard himself—and then settles on a "traditional ... story of a couple." Something is wrong with this picture, since not even Godard could have set out to make a traditional story of a couple and somehow ended up with the rhizomatic schizo-film that *Hail Mary* turned out to be. Here as elsewhere, Godard's statement of intent is a creative semi-fiction—a deliberately inchoate *supplement* to a cinematic experience whose singularities are irreducible to language. Although his films usually tell stories of a sort, his real business is forging what Deleuze calls a cinema of *between* and a cinema of *and*, which "does away with all the cinema of Being = is" and makes "the indiscernible" visible.[15] Godard was interested enough in *L'Évangile au risque de la psychoanalyse*, or at least the introduction, to mention it in interviews about the movie, and a few of its phrases appear in the dialogue. But the finished film reflects little of Dolto's thought, so on this score the anti-psychoanalytic authors of *Anti-Oedipus* can rest easy. (And so can I, since I find Dolto's book to be a naive and superficial stew of essentialism, nebulous language, and biblical hermeneutics that quickly turn into flights of self-indulgent fantasy.)

... AND ... AND ... AND ...

Deleuze and Guattari say that the infinite series "... and ... and ... and ..." is "the very fabric of the rhizome."[16] It is also a concept long embraced by Godard, whose work strives to erase boundaries and celebrate paradox: an endless "... and ... and ... and ..." would be the perfect subtitle for his entire oeuvre.[17] One of Godard's closest affinities with Deleuze lies in his insistence on a radically intuitive cinema that opens lines of escape *from* linearity and rationality and *toward* the open-ended multiplicities of the non-metaphysical unconscious—the spiritual automaton within thought that radiates desire, operating *on* and *through* the individual subject, which has "no fixed identity" but is "forever decentered, *defined* by the states through which it passes."[18] Although he doesn't use schizoanalytic language, Godard approaches the unconscious in a schizoanalytic manner, not as a site for archeology (à la psychoanalysis) but as a plane that pulsates with positive desire, which can either be diverted into static *being* or liberated into boundless *becoming* free of entrenched habits and beliefs. Released two years after schizoanalysis made its anti-oedipal debut, *Je vous salue, Marie* envisions a virtual, intensive realm, showing Mary's becomings as lines of flight toward the non-human sexualities of impregnation by spirit and merging of Word and flesh, while Joseph wrestles with social stratifications that are ultimately nullified by his intimacy with Mary's deterritorializing flows.

At the end of the film both characters are again enmeshed in everyday reality, and the addition of their child to the household (... and ... and ... and ...) indicates that they are newly defined by the states through which their decentred becoming-souls have passed. "The big error, the only error," Deleuze said in *Dialogues II*, "would be to believe that a line of flight consists of fleeing life; a flight into the imaginary, or into art. But to flee ... on the contrary, is to produce the real, to create life, to find a weapon."[19] This is what Mary and Joseph have done, and what their child will keep on doing. As the boy's biblical counterpart says in the book of Matthew, "Think not that I am come to send peace on earth: I came not to send peace, but a sword."[20] A weapon.

A EUCLIDEAN POSTULATE

I now wish to put two statements into dialogue with each other. The first is Godard's remark, prominently echoed in *Hail Mary*, that it isn't the body that has a soul but the other way around. As a youth he said, "I found that line in Artaud, in which, by a simple play on words, he posits, like a theorem, a Euclidean postulate: 'I want the soul to be body, so they won't be able to say that the body is soul, because it will be the soul which is body.'"[21] The second statement is from Deleuze, who writes in *Cinema II* that subjectivity "is never ours, it is time, that is, the soul or the spirit, the virtual."[22]

Bearing in mind Deleuze's high regard for Godard, we may ask whether the two film-philosophers have the same sort of thing in mind when "soul" comes into the picture. Clearly neither is referring to conventional beliefs of traditional religions. "I'm not a religious person, but I'm a faithful person," Godard has said. "I believe in images."[23] Deleuze and Guattari write in *What Is Philosophy?* that atheism "is not a drama but the philosopher's serenity and philosophy's achievement."[24] Still, all three of these thinkers bring soul, spirit, and related words into play when it suits their purposes, and I don't think this is merely a case of careless terminology. Godard has said that while he doesn't practise the Protestant religiosity he was brought up on, he is "very interested" in aspects of Roman Catholic thought.[25] And no philosopher exercised a stronger influence on Deleuze than Henri Bergson, whose metaphysics of body, mind, and soul—of *corps*, *esprit*, and *âme*—leads him to say that "giving the name of Idea to a certain *settling down into easy intelligibility*, and that of Soul to a certain *longing after the restlessness of life* … an invisible current causes modern philosophy to place the Soul above the Idea."[26] Some thirty years later he declared that if we are able to get beyond the brain's restrictive focus on the instrumental and extensive, "there enters in something of a 'without' which may be a 'beyond.'… Suppose that a gleam from this unknown world reaches us…. Joy indeed would be that simplicity of life diffused through the world by an ever-spreading mystic intuition."[27]

These are not theistic statements, and it would make no sense to tie Deleuze or Guattari to them. What does make sense, I think, is to detect a connection between Bergson's conception of soul and the notion of the body without organs (BwO). Deleuze and Guattari discovered the BwO in Antonin Artaud's extraordinary 1947 radio play *To Have Done with the Judgment of God*, which concludes thus:

> Man is sick because he is badly constructed.
> We must make up our minds to strip him bare in order to scrape off that animalcule that itches him mortally,

god,
and with god
his organs.
For you can tie me up if you wish,
but there is nothing more useless than an organ.
When you will have made him a body without organs,
then you will have delivered him from all his automatic reactions
and restored him to his true freedom.
Then you will teach him again to dance wrong side out
as in the frenzy of dance halls
and this wrong side out will be his real place.[28]

Deleuze and Guattari proffer the body without organs as the antithesis of the theological body whose unyielding organ-ization, imposed by God, is a nexus of "accumulation, coagulation, and sedimentation"[29] devoted to stopping up fluxes, draining off flows, squashing intensities, and blocking becomings at every pass. The body without organs, free, fluid, and ungraspable, is a deterritorialized flux with strong links to schizo-cinema. Films that connect us to the BwO can engulf us with mystery and affect, subverting stability and unravelling symbolic order.

The body without organs inhabits the *chaosmos*, a portmanteau word (borrowed from James Joyce by various writers) conjoining *cosmos* and *chaos*, order and disorder.[30] As a chaosmic being, the BwO is "that which one desires and by which one desires." It is "nonstratified, unformed, intense matter, the matrix of intensity, intensity = 0; but there is nothing negative about that zero."[31] It is "the body without an image," on which "attraction and repulsion ... produce, starting from zero, a series of states in the celibate machine; and the subject is born of each state in the series ... consuming-consummating all these states that cause him to be born and reborn."[32] And it is the "tantric egg."[33]

The BwO is also a barely glimpsed presence in *Je vous salue, Marie*, evoked in subtle ways that are all the more striking by virtue of the fortuitous nature of their congruity with schizoanalytic discourse. Deleuze and Guattari write that there is "a fundamental convergence between ... the biological egg and the psychic or cosmic egg," so perhaps it is the tantric egg, "the full egg before ... the organization of the organs,"[34] that closes *Le Livre de Marie* and opens the chaosmos of Godard's film, in which Mary's indiscernible ovum plays a pivotal role. Maybe the non-negative zero is what we see in the 10 on Mary's basketball jersey, or maybe it's what we hear when Gabriel asks Joseph, "What's the common denominator between zero and Mary? Mary's body!" or maybe it's what we sense when he calls Joseph an "asshole." More substantially, it is surely the body without organs

149

that pulses within the deterritorialized flows of soul-body-becoming when Mary endures a night of solitary schizo-orison before the birth of her child, wracked with delirium as her soul and body pass through the molecular deaths and births of dis-organized parturition. For schizoanalysts the body without organs is a destratified pulse of desires and intensities that escape the judgment of God on the transcendental plane of immanence. For Godard it crystallizes a cinema of frameless images, immaculate signs, and what he once called the "process of making nature possible."[35]

"Reason is always a region carved out of the irrational," Deleuze has declared. "Underneath all reason lies delirium, and drift."[36] Like him, Godard sees delirium and drift as emphatically positive qualities that offer the best hope for freeing our machinic flows from stifling cultural categories and liberating them into torrents of untrammelled love and productive desire.

CONCEPTUAL PERSONAE

Particularities of style in *Je vous salue, Marie* are crucial in conveying what Godard has on his mind. A starting point for the film was his wish to juxtapose "Catholic images and Protestant music,"[37] not as harmonious consorts but as contrapuntal elements in steady dialogue. The sound and spirit of J.S. Bach serve as what Deleuze and Guattari call *conceptual personae*, the "something else, somewhat mysterious, that ... seems to have a hazy existence halfway between concept and preconceptual plane, passing from one to the other."[38] As such they are "fluctuating figures who," in theorist D.N. Rodowick's words, "express qualities or perspectives that want to become-other, to deterritorialize towards another plane by constructing its concepts."[39]

Similar observations can be made about the film's painterly impulses. Filmmaking is "like painting," Godard told me in 1994, "but it's also different from painting, because you use not just space but time."[40] His love of painting mirrors his respect for Renaissance Catholicism, which responded to Martin Luther's faith in words (and Bach's music) by reaffirming the power of images. God has long been an alter ego for Godard, who imagines himself a "distant as well as omniscient and omnipotent creator"; hence the special vitality of light in his aesthetic, serving not only as the material ground of cinema but also as a symbol of and metaphor for the divine.[41]

Turning to montage, *Je vous salue, Marie* may be Godard's most far-reaching essay in the irrational cut. Destabilizing edits occur constantly, and their effects are often intensified by camera placements that blur conventional notions of foreground and background. The primary narrative, centring on Mary and Joseph, is intercut with subplots so jaggedly that first-time viewers often have trouble sorting out what's going on, much less fathoming its deeper dimensions. With these devices Godard turns narrative thrust, linear montage, figural representation, and naturalized *mise en scène* into a rhizomatic assemblage of ontological conundrums and epistemological ruckuses.

SUBLIMITY

Now for a central question: Can we claim that *soul* has connotations for Godard and Deleuze that go beyond the negative, skeptical, or metaphorical meanings often encountered in materialist philosophy and art? I think the answer is yes, with the obvious caveat that the soul I'm speaking of is not the one of religious orthodoxy. Deleuze made a fascinating remark in his 1980 seminar on Spinoza, saying that "if philosophers have spoken to us so much of God—and they could well be Christians or believers—this hasn't been lacking an intense sense of jest. It wasn't an incredulous jesting, but a joy arising from the labour they were involved with.... God and the theme of God offered the irreplaceable opportunity for philosophy to free ... concepts ... from the constraints that had been imposed on them."[42] Deleuze may be jesting too, but if that's so, the jest has the richly positive aura to which he alludes. Godard jests a good deal in *Hail Mary* as well—at times Gabriel is almost a slapstick character—and he does so in the same affirmative spirit. He too knows the joy of freeing concepts from the pre-conceptions and prejudices that block their infinite becoming-flows.

The supreme act of philosophy, Deleuze and Guattari write, is "not so much to think THE plane of immanence as to show that it is there, unthought in every plane, and to think it in this way as the outside and inside of thought, as ... that which cannot be thought and yet must be thought."[43] Accordingly, the challenge for each of us is to discover, in Rodowick's words, the "thinker within me that is the unthought of my thought [and] is ... the power to transform life by revealing new lines of variation in our current ways of ·thinking and modes of existence."[44] Godard comes amazingly close to visualizing this insight at the end of *Je vous salue, Marie*, when Mary hears Gabriel's last greeting ("Nothing. Hail, Mary!") and then gets into her car and lights a cigarette. She is simply having a smoke, like countless characters in countless New Wave movies; but sometimes a cigarette is not just a cigarette. Its smoke blurs the border-lines between inner and outer—body and world—as it transubstantiates an ordinary herb into a vaporous essence, subliminally dis-organizing Mary's self in an act of *inspiration* that is both literal and metaphorical. Then she draws a lipstick toward her lips, and the film ends on an extreme close-up of her open mouth, so large that parts of it don't fit within the frame, dominated by the dark emptiness at its centre.

One Deleuzian interpretation of this shot would lead in negative directions: we are looking at a black hole, the part of the white-wall–black-hole facial system wherein the latter element, modelled after light-trapping singularities in space, is a territorializing blockage, the upshot of a failed line of flight.[45] But we can also interpret it positively—as an instance of what Deleuze calls the "gaseous image, beyond the solid and the liquid," which seeks (like drugs) to "*stop the world*" and "*make one see the molecular intervals*, the holes in sound, in forms, and even in water" and to "*make lines of speed pass through* these holes in the world."[46]

I incline toward the positive option, but I think a more liberating way of fathoming this image leads beyond the realm of mystery to that of mysticism. Cultural critic Michael Goddard links Deleuzian theory with mysticism by understanding the mystical as an ecstatic pathway to and through the crystalline regime of signs, whereby "the 'spiritual' or 'spirits' ... can be conceived of as virtually inhering in the material world in the form of temporalities, or conversely the material world can be conceived of as existing in the spiritual or in God in the same way that it exists in time. The spiritual and the material are simply two distinct yet indiscernible sides of the same fold."[47]

Godard, the faithful filmmaker who believes in images, might well agree; and so might Mary, who conceives a singularity—a child, a soul, a thought, a virtuality, an unprecedented upsurge of the élan vital—that promises to deterritorialize the actual in literally inconceivable ways. "At the limit," Deleuze observed, "it is the mystic who plays with the whole of creation."[48] In this play there arises the intense sense of jest—of joy—that brave philosophers have found by pursuing thinking toward the becomings-flows of the infinite. If we share this delight it's because, as Deleuze tells us, "the essence of art is a kind of joy, and this is the very point of art. There ... is a necessary joy in creation: art is necessarily a liberation that explodes everything."[49] Mary too feels the gladness of creating, and never more so than at the end of her tormented night, when she climbs out from under the impenetrable judgment of an inexplicable God and says, softly and simply, "I am joy. I am she who is joy." At such a moment the unthought in thought, for Mary and Godard and perhaps us as well, is tremblingly close to being thought.

NOTES

A longer version of this essay appeared as "Schizoanalyzing Souls: Godard, Deleuze, and the Mystical Line of Flight," in *Journal of French and Francophone Philosophy—Revue de la philosophie française et de langue française* 18, no. 2 (2010): 9–27.

1   Jean-Luc Godard, "Montage, My Fine Care," in *Godard on Godard*, ed. Jean Narboni and Tom Milne, trans. Tom Milne (New York: Da Capo Press, 1986), 39. (Originally published as "Montage, mon beau souci," in *Cahiers du cinéma* 65 [1956].)

2   Gilles Deleuze, *Cinema 1: The Movement-Image*, trans. Hugh Tomlinson and Barbara Habberjam (Minneapolis: University of Minnesota Press, 1986); and Gilles Deleuze, *Cinema 2: The Time-Image*, trans. Hugh Tomlinson and Robert Galeta (Minneapolis: University of Minnesota Press, 1989).

3   Deleuze, *Cinema 2*, 168–69, 277–78 passim.

4   Gilles Deleuze and Félix Guattari, *Anti-Oedipus: Capitalism and Schizophrenia*, trans. Robert Hurley, Mark Seem, and Helen R. Lane (Minneapolis: University of Minnesota Press, 1983), 350.

5   See *Anti-Oedipus* in previous note; and Gilles Deleuze and Félix Guattari, *A Thousand Plateaus: Capitalism and Schizophrenia*, trans. Brian Massumi (Minneapolis: University of Minnesota Press, 1987).

6   "Godard/Sollers: The Interview (Extracts)," trans. Pasquale G. Tatò, in *Jean-Luc Godard's Hail Mary: Women and the Sacred in Film*, ed. Maryel Locke and Charles Warren (Carbondale: Southern Illinois University Press, 1993), 124.

7   Deleuze and Guattari, *Anti-Oedipus*, 322.

8   Ibid., 321.

9   Sherry Turkle, "Tough Love: An Introduction to Françoise Dolto's *When Parents Separate*," *PsicoMundo* (1995), http://psiconet.org/dolto/textos/turkle.htm (emphasis in original).

10 Élisabeth Roudinesco, "Françoise Marette Dolto," in *The Columbia History of Twentieth-Century French Thought*, ed. Lawrence D. Kritzman (New York: Columbia University Press, 2005), 508.

11 Françoise Dolto and Gérard Sévérin, *L'Évangile au risque de la psychoanalyse* (Paris: Éditions universitaires, Jean-Pierre Delarge, 1977). Published in English as *The Jesus of Psychoanalysis: A Freudian Interpretation of the Gospel*, trans. Helen R. Lane (Garden City, NY: Doubleday, 1979).

12 Quoted in Richard Brody, *Everything Is Cinema: The Working Life of Jean-Luc Godard* (New York: Metropolitan Books, 2008), 457–58.

13 Colin MacCabe, *Godard: A Portrait of the Artist at Seventy* (New York: Farrar, Straus and Giroux, 2003), 207.

14 Brody, *Everything Is Cinema*, 457.

15 Deleuze, *Cinema 2*, 180.

16 Deleuze and Guattari, *Thousand Plateaus*, 25.

17 For more discussion see David Sterritt, *The Films of Jean-Luc Godard: Seeing the Invisible* (Cambridge: Cambridge University Press, 1999), 14, 141, 262.

18 Deleuze and Guattari, *Anti-Oedipus*, 20 (emphasis in original).

19 Gilles Deleuze and Claire Parnet, *Dialogues II*, trans. Hugh Tomlinson and Barbara Habberjam with Eliot Ross Albert, 2nd ed. (New York: Columbia University Press, 2002), 49.

20 Matthew 10:34 (Authorized [King James] Version).

21 "Godard/Sollers," 124.

22 Deleuze, *Cinema 2*, 82–83.

23 Quoted in Sally Shafto, program note for Religion and Cinema: A Conference, Princeton University, 2001.

24 Gilles Deleuze and Félix Guattari, *What Is Philosophy?* trans. Hugh Tomlinson and Graham Burchell (New York: Columbia University Press, 1994), 92.

25 Shafto, program note for Religion and Cinema, n.p.

26 Henri Bergson, *An Introduction to Metaphysics*, trans. T.E. Hulme (Basingstoke, UK: Palgrave-Macmillan, 2007), 46–47 (emphases in original).

27 Henri Bergson, *The Two Sources of Morality and Religion*, trans. R. Ashley Audra and Cloudesley Brereton with W. Horsfall Carter (Notre Dame, IN: University of Notre Dame Press, 1977), 315–17.

28 Antonin Artaud, *To Have Done with the Judgment of God*, in *Antonin Artaud: Selected Writings*, ed. Susan Sontag, trans. Helen Weaver (Berkeley: University of California Press, 1976), 571.

29 Deleuze and Guattari, *Thousand Plateaus*, 158–59.

30 James Joyce, *Finnegans Wake* (New York: Viking Press, 1958), 118.

31 Deleuze and Guattari, *Thousand Plateaus*, 165, 153.

32 Deleuze and Guattari, *Anti-Oedipus*, 8, 20.

33 Deleuze and Guattari, *Thousand Plateaus*, 153.

34 Ibid., 181–82, 153.

35 Katherine Dieckmann, "Godard in His Fifth Period," in *Jean-Luc Godard: Interviews*, ed. David Sterritt (Jackson: University Press of Mississippi, 1998), 170–71.

36 "On Capitalism and Desire," in Gilles Deleuze, *Desert Islands and Other Texts: 1953–1974*, ed. David Lapoujade, trans. Michael Taormina (Los Angeles: Semiotext[e], 2004), 262.

37 Jean-Luc Godard, interview with Giuseppina Marin, in *Corriere della Sera* (April 25, 1985), quoted in David Sterritt, "Miéville and Godard: From Psychology to Spirit," in *Jean-Luc Godard's Hail Mary: Women and the Sacred in Film*, ed. Maryel Locke and Charles Warren (Carbondale: Southern Illinois University Press, 1993), 55.

38 Deleuze and Guattari, *What Is Philosophy?* 61.

39 D.N. Rodowick, "Unthinkable Sex: Conceptual Personae and the Time-Image," *Invisible Culture* 3 (2000), http://www.rochester.edu/in_visible_culture/issue3/rodowick.htm.

40 David Sterritt, "Ideas, Not Plots, Inspire Jean-Luc Godard," in *Jean-Luc Godard: Interviews*, ed. David Sterritt (Jackson: University Press of Mississippi, 1998), 177.

41 Sally Shafto, "Artist as Christ/Artist as God-the-Father: Religion in the Cinema of Philippe Garrel and Jean-Luc Godard," *Film History* 14 (2002): 144, 145.

42 Gilles Deleuze (seminar on Spinoza, November 25, 1980, trans. Timothy S. Murphy), quoted in Philip Goodchild, "Why Is Philosophy So Compromised with God?" in *Deleuze and Religion*, ed. Mary Bryden (London: Routledge, 2001), 156.

43 Deleuze and Guattari, *What Is Philosophy?* 59–60 (emphasis in original).

44 D.N. Rodowick, *Gilles Deleuze's Time Machine* (Durham, NC: Duke University Press, 1997), 200–1.

45 Ronald Bogue, *Deleuze on Music, Painting, and the Arts* (London: Routledge, 2003), 89.

46 Deleuze, *Cinema 1*, 64, 85 (emphases in original).

47 Michael Goddard, "The Scattering of Time Crystals: Deleuze, Mysticism and Cinema," in *Deleuze and Religion*, ed. Mary Bryden (London: Routledge, 2001), 62.

48 Gilles Deleuze, *Bergsonism*, trans. Hugh Tomlinson and Barbara Habberjam (New York: Zone Books, 1988), 112.

49 "Mysticism and Masochism," in Gilles Deleuze, *Desert Islands and Other Texts: 1953–1974*, ed. David Lapoujade, trans. Michael Taormina (Los Angeles: Semiotext[e], 2004), 134.

BIBLIOGRAPHY

Artaud, Antonin. *To Have Done with the Judgment of God*. In *Antonin Artaud: Selected Writings*, edited by Susan Sontag, translated by Helen Weaver, 553–71. Berkeley: University of California Press, 1976.

Bergson, Henri. *An Introduction to Metaphysics*. Translated by T.E. Hulme. Basingstoke, UK: Palgrave Macmillan, 2007.

———. *The Two Sources of Morality and Religion*. Translated by R. Ashley Audra and Cloudesley Brereton with W. Horsfall Carter. Notre Dame, IN: University of Notre Dame Press, 1977.

Bogue, Ronald. *Deleuze on Music, Painting, and the Arts*. London: Routledge, 2003.

Brody, Richard. *Everything Is Cinema: The Working Life of Jean-Luc Godard*. New York: Metropolitan Books, 2008.

Deleuze, Gilles. *Bergsonism*. Translated by Hugh Tomlinson and Barbara Habberjam. New York: Zone Books, 1988.

———. *Cinema 1: The Movement-Image*. Translated by Hugh Tomlinson and Barbara Habberjam. Minneapolis: University of Minnesota Press, 1986.

———. *Cinema 2: The Time-Image*. Translated by Hugh Tomlinson and Robert Galeta. Minneapolis: University of Minnesota Press, 1989.

———. *Desert Islands and Other Texts: 1953–1974*. Edited by David Lapoujade. Translated by Michael Taormina. Los Angeles: Semiotext(e), 2004.

Deleuze, Gilles, and Félix Guattari. *Anti-Oedipus: Capitalism and Schizophrenia*. Translated by Robert Hurley, Mark Seem, and Helen R. Lane. Minneapolis: University of Minnesota Press, 1983.

———. *A Thousand Plateaus: Capitalism and Schizophrenia*. Translated by Brian Massumi. Minneapolis: University of Minnesota Press, 1987.

———. *What Is Philosophy?* Translated by Hugh Tomlinson and Graham Burchell. New York: Columbia University Press, 1994.

Deleuze, Gilles, and Claire Parnet. *Dialogues II*. Translated by Hugh Tomlinson and Barbara Habberjam with Eliot Ross Albert. 2nd ed. New York: Columbia University Press, 2002.

Dieckmann, Katherine. "Godard in His Fifth Period." In *Jean-Luc Godard: Interviews*, edited by David Sterritt, 167–74. Jackson: University Press of Mississippi, 1998.

Dolto, Françoise, and Gérard Sévérin. *L'Évangile au risque de la psychanalyse*. Paris: Éditions universitaires, Jean-Pierre Delarge, 1977.

Godard, Jean-Luc. "Montage, My Fine Care." In *Godard on Godard*, edited by Jean Narboni and Tom Milne, translated by Tom Milne, 39–41. New York: Da Capo, 1986.

Godard, Jean-Luc, and Philippe Sollers. "Godard/Sollers: The Interview (Extracts)." Translated by Pasquale G. Tatò. In *Jean-Luc Godard's Hail Mary: Women and the Sacred in Film*, edited by Maryel Locke and Charles Warren, 123–24. Carbondale: Southern Illinois University Press, 1993.

Goddard, Michael. "The Scattering of Time Crystals: Deleuze, Mysticism and Cinema." In *Deleuze and Religion*, edited by Mary Bryden, 53–64. London: Routledge, 2001.

Goodchild, Philip. "Why Is Philosophy So Compromised with God?" In *Deleuze and Religion*, edited by Mary Bryden, 156–66. London: Routledge, 2001.

Joyce, James. *Finnegans Wake*. New York: Viking Press, 1958.

MacCabe, Colin. *Godard: A Portrait of the Artist at Seventy*. New York: Farrar, Straus and Giroux, 2003.

Rodowick, D.N. *Gilles Deleuze's Time Machine*. Durham, NC: Duke University Press, 1997.

———. "Unthinkable Sex: Conceptual Personae and the Time-Image." *Invisible Culture* 3 (2000). http://www.rochester.edu/in_visible_culture/issue3/rodowick.htm.

Roudinesco, Élisabeth. "Françoise Marette Dolto." In *The Columbia History of Twentieth-Century French Thought*, edited by Lawrence D. Kritzman, 506–9. New York: Columbia University Press, 2005.

Shafto, Sally. "Artist as Christ/Artist as God-the-Father: Religion in the Cinema of Philippe Garrel and Jean-Luc Godard." *Film History* 14 (2002): 142–57.

———. Program note for Religion and Cinema: A Conference, Princeton University, 2001.

Sterritt, David. *The Films of Jean-Luc Godard: Seeing the Invisible*. Cambridge: Cambridge University Press, 1999.

———. "Ideas, Not Plots, Inspire Jean-Luc Godard." In *Jean-Luc Godard: Interviews*, edited by David Sterritt, 175–78. Jackson: University Press of Mississippi, 1998.

———. "Miéville and Godard: From Psychology to Spirit." In *Jean-Luc Godard's Hail Mary: Women and the Sacred in Film*, edited by Maryel Locke and Charles Warren, 54–60. Carbondale: Southern Illinois University Press, 1993.

Turkle, Sherry. "Tough Love: An Introduction to Françoise Dolto's *When Parents Separate*." *PsicoMundo* (1995). http://psiconet.org/dolto/textos/turkle.htm.

10

The "Hidden Fire" of Inwardness: Cavell, Godard, and Modernism

Glen W. Norton

THE FOLLOWING IS a consideration of Jean-Luc Godard's contribution to modernist cinematic practice in the early 1960s. My concern is not only with Godard's reinvention of cinematic possibilities via reflexivity and intertextuality but more especially with his modernist skepticism regarding the cinematic depiction of inwardness. In short, inwardness connotes not the psychological but the ontological depth of a person, that mysterious and perhaps even unfathomable depth we nonetheless acknowledge in the eyes of those we meet every day. Cinematic inwardness, then, challenges us to acknowledge the embodied, lived aspect of those who inhabit the world depicted on the screen. In *À bout de souffle* (1960), Godard utilizes certain elements of what Stanley Cavell sees as cinema's natural relationship with cinematic inwardness, namely its affinity for presenting characters as types. Because of this, Cavell believes it to be Godard's masterpiece.[1] Cavell claims that those who populate Godard's later work have, for the most part, an "inability to feel," and therefore by extension that they lack inwardness.[2] Cavell intuits this depersonalization as an abandonment of artistic responsibility leading to a debased modernism. Using a salient moment from *Vivre sa vie* (1962) as an example, I argue instead that Godard's early cinema consistently examines the modernist conditions under which an acknowledgement of inwardness is cinematically possible.

Although Cavell's rather hostile appraisal of Godard's work following *À bout de souffle* precipitates my inquiry, my intention is not to "refute" him but, as Rothman and Keane advise, "to check his words against one's own experience—to allow Cavell's words to prompt one's own thoughts."[3] Cavell's assessment is therefore justified only to the extent to which it helps us clarify Godard's modernist skepticism regarding cinema's ability to depict inwardness. Before tracing this assessment we must first understand Cavell's characterization of modernist cinema, for his argument depends upon a particular judgment about Godard's inclination toward reflexivity.

Cavell understands Godard's modernism to explore, as all modernist cinema does to an individual extent, "the conditions of [cinema's] possibility."[4] Yet it is true that cinema has always, to a certain degree, existed in this mode—thus cinema has always been modern. Cavell's point, however, is that cinema could not make a *modernist* turn because it had no tradition to reflect upon until Hollywood began to standardize its output.[5] Our ability to be convinced by the world Hollywood presented was predicated upon this standardization, which in time naturalized conventions to the point where they seemed intrinsic to Hollywood's ontological status as cinema. As Cavell notes, throughout its classical period Hollywood cinema remained at "ease within its assumptions and achievements—its conventions remaining convenient for so much of its life, remaining convincing and fertile without self-questioning."[6] The modernist turn of the 1960s was not an attempt to break away from but to *maintain* this conviction in the cinematic world when the conventions used to present this world no longer seemed natural. In this sense, modernism demarcates "the work of an artist whose discoveries and declarations of his medium are to be understood as embodying his effort to maintain the continuity of his art with the past of his art, and to invite and bear comparisons with the achievements of his past."[7] For Cavell, then, modernist cinema is reflexive or self-questioning only to the extent to which it attempts a continuation with its past. Understanding this notion is crucial lest he be charged with ignoring—or worse, being ignorant of—the waves of so-called modernisms which cinema has undergone since its inception. Indeed, Cavell acknowledges at least two of these waves, namely the early Soviet example of the 1920s and the experimental cinema which was flourishing during the late 1960s when he was writing *The World Viewed.*[8] Yet for Cavell these are avant-garde—that is, forward-looking—movements rather than modernist ones.

Thus the modernist inception of cinema in the 1960s skeptically questions the naturalization of Hollywood's conventions, attempting to maintain a similar conviction in the world it presents via other means. Therefore Cavell can claim, and rightly so, that "the allusions to Hollywood films in the films of French New Wave directors are not simple acts of piety toward a tradition they admire, but claims to be a continuation of that tradition."[9] We can see this in Godard's first feature, *À bout de souffle*, which, in its attempt to maintain our conviction in the conventions of the crime noir drama, ends up reflexively interrogating them as well. Godard is well aware of these conventions, and he lets us know this by giving his hero, Michel Poiccard (Jean-Paul Belmondo), a hero of his own: "Bogie." There could be no better choice for Poiccard's idol than the iconic Humphrey Bogart, a staple of Hollywood's crime noir genre. As *À bout de souffle* is both a genre film and a reflection upon this genre, Poiccard is not only based upon but bases *himself* upon Bogart as a type—that is to say, not only is Godard aware of tradition, but his characters are as well. Bogart, as this certain type, has (or at least had) a certain natural affinity with cinema which stems precisely from the sense that he is the real embodiment of an ideal, a mythic figure personified. To accomplish this, he draws upon what Cavell (borrowing from Baudelaire) labels as "hidden fire"—that is, this type is defined by a capacity to embody inwardness as a certain self-assuredness, a depth which springs from a seemingly unlimited capacity for self-knowledge: "The feature of the 'hidden fire' is essential. Our conviction in the strength of the hero depends upon our conviction in the strength and purity of character he has formed to keep his fires banked.... He does not *know* he will succeed; what he knows is himself."[10] Self-assuredness sets this type apart from society at large. As Cavell tells us, such heroes "are not outside society because they have been pushed out ... they have stayed out."[11] Hence Poiccard's vast capacity for embodying inwardness comes across as an imperviousness to emotion resulting in his incarnation of freedom and, by extension, "coolness." Cavell's notion that *À bout de souffle* is Godard's masterpiece hinges on this articulation of its hero as this type.[12] The question becomes why this mode of individualization is held in such esteem.

Before the onset of 1960s modernism, cinema's reliance on the use of type to reveal a character's inwardness was taken as a given. Cavell points to this fact, remarking that "types are exactly what carry the forms movies have relied upon.... What [this] means is that [the use of type] is the movies' way of creating individuals: they create *individualities*."[13] We knew all we needed to know to acknowledge a character's inwardness—their capacity for self-awareness, their tendency toward self-doubt—through their embodiment of type. Hence for Cavell, cinema's method of creating individuals capable of manifesting inwardness is not opposed to but is precisely the *result* of its natural reliance upon types. The type *is* the individual—there need be no separation, no movement from one to the other. To make the distinction between, say, type and "well-rounded character," or type and "person," is to mistake the notion of type from the outset. For Cavell, the label of "type" is not pejorative but is instead a necessary element in the manifestation of inwardness. This manifestation occurs not at the moment when the individual escapes or transcends the type but at the moment when the type is fully realized as an individual.

Though he does represent this fully realized type, Poiccard's embodiment of inwardness is denaturalized by the ironic distance between any concrete, fully realized, self-aware sentiment he might act out and the film's presentation of it as such. Any and all moods and sentiments Poiccard portrays reflexively connote "acting" and are thus "acts" in a dual sense: the ironic actions of a man who bases himself upon the Bogart type and the ironic actions of a character based upon this Bogart type. Each refers to an extratextual culture, specifically a past film culture whose naturalized embodiment of persons as types is now subject to modernist skepticism from within. Almost every action Poiccard makes is one which is to be expected of such a type—we know it, Godard knows it, and most importantly, Poiccard knows it. Early in the film he speaks directly to us, acknowledging us as his audience, making sure we do not miss this reflexive aspect of his character. Ironic distance from any and all expression therefore becomes simply that which is expected, hence our skepticism about his embodiment of inwardness. Godard seeks to maintain our belief, and perhaps his own as well, in this type as the embodiment of an individual, a person, by allowing us to experience a shared sense of ironic distance with the film and its main character. But the die was already cast; there was no going back. It only took a few short years for Godard to abandon this attempt to sustain a faith which was already waning, if not lost altogether.

In *À bout de souffle* Godard relies on the convergence of type and individual in order to grant Poiccard his depth and acknowledge his lived inwardness. The film, as we have seen, is already aware that this convergence is no longer accepted as a cinematic given, and therefore its reflexive stance is already an attempt to measure the possibility of depicting inwardness and not simply its natural presentation. Cavell's appreciation of the film seems to miss this point; his argument that in later works Godard moves away from type, removing these human "somethings" from their humanity only to try and return it to them through more conceptual means, ignores the fact that *À bout de souffle* already begins this process.[14] Cavell reproaches Godard for forcing his characters to *demonstrate* their inwardness, but even with *À bout de souffle* Godard was never interested in depicting inwardness in and of itself so much as examining various cinematic conditions under which its manifestation might still be possible after the modernist turn.

What disturbs Cavell about Godard's work after *À bout de souffle*, then, is an apparent abandonment of artistic responsibility toward his cinematic antecedents and thus toward his audience. Gone is the "hidden fire" which

Cavell deems essential to our acknowledgement of character inwardness, replaced by a critique of consumer culture which treats people as if they were soulless automatons while offering no alternative notion of what a "humanizing" culture, or indeed any notion of what the "human," entails. Cavell therefore notes a certain ambivalence in Godard's cinema: "The sort of depersonalization [Godard] requires depends both upon our responding to these characters as persons and upon our continuously failing to read their motions within the stresses of ordinary human emotion and motivation."[15] As a result of this depersonalization, Cavell finds that

> [Godard's] claims to serious criticisms of the world are empty. If you believe that people speak slogans to one another, or that women are turned by bourgeois society into marketable objects, or that human pleasures are now figments and products of advertising accounts and that these are directions of dehumanization—then what is the value of pouring further slogans into that world (e.g., "People speak in slogans" or "Women have become objects" or "Bourgeois society is dehumanizing" or "Love is impossible")? And how do you distinguish the world's dehumanizing of its inhabitants from your depersonalizing of them?[16]

Cavell's critique is similar to the Situationist condemnation of Godard, which contends that he merely apes cultural norms, and that his work therefore remains part and parcel of the dominant culture it attempts to critique.[17] In other words, the argument is that this period of Godard's oeuvre constitutes "a beautiful consumer good which denounces consumerism."[18] In fact, one of Godard's more simplistic methods for presenting or invoking thought in this early period takes the form of Situationist *détournement* by appropriating cultural artifacts and placing them in new contexts. Often Godard will quote the words of others as quick primers aiming at the heart of the matter all at once; they act as place-holders demonstrating a character's (or more importantly Godard's) point of view in relation to the world. Hence one can argue that Godard's sometimes contrasting and opaque references to outside texts are surface gestures which treat words as mere currency to be spent, that no real relation to thought is created, and, as Cavell suggests, that what is created tends more toward sloganism rather than thoughtful engagement. In this sense, Godard's insertion of thought into his films is indicative of a postmodern reduction of ideas to their sign value, one which implies an equivalence of exchange value. For a certain sentiment, a range of words will suffice, and in some cases it is only the images or partial images of the words themselves, without reference to the ideas they aim at, that Godard is interested in.

Yet if Godard's position toward inwardness in fact explores the conditions for its possibility, can this critique remain tenable? Though Cavell claims Godard's cinema lacks a position from which to question the world and our place in it with any legitimacy, my claim is that it amounts to a continual questioning of the place from which cinema is presupposed legitimately to speak. Take, for example, Godard's fourth feature film, *Vivre sa vie*. Though Cavell deems Godard's film strips its protagonist, Nana (Anna Karina), of personhood, and therefore of inwardness, it is ironic that Godard is in fact seeking something essential, namely her soul. We discover this quite early on, as Nana is framed playing pinball with her lover Paul (André S. Labarthe) in a two-shot. Paul recounts hearing an anecdote about a child's description of her favourite animal: "A chicken is an animal with an inside and an outside. Remove the outside, there's the inside. Remove the inside, you see the soul." These words are marked with a specific and deliberate pan which reframes Nana by herself. We therefore cannot help but understand this story to be about her. Godard's film is an exploration of the cinematic possibilities that might remove Nana's layers, allowing us to see her soul.

One such possibility for revealing inwardness comes via what Cavell calls "the sound of philosophy, in those longish dialogues his women illicit from actual philosophers."[19] This method of inquiry sees its inception within Godard's oeuvre during *Vivre sa vie*'s eleventh episode ("Nana fait de la philosophie sans le savoir"),[20] in which Godard sets up a dialogue between Nana and the very real philosopher Brice Parain.[21] Cavell's complaint here is that the women who inspire philosophical discourse in Godard's films do not care about what is said, and that this position mirrors not only Godard's but our own as well. In this manner, cinematic philosophical discourse is reduced to sophistry: "[Godard] does not care whether what the philosopher says is valid or not—that is, he listens to it the way his girls do, or the way a bourgeois audience does, somewhere within embarrassment, envy, contempt, and titillation."[22] Two assumptions are made here. The first is that, by deferring to an actual philosopher, Godard wishes to invoke actual philosophical statements or discussion. It is more accurate to say that he wishes to explore the cinematic conditions necessary for statement and discussion, how and if these are possible in cinema. The second is that, in order for it to be philosophical—or, more to the point, because this human "something" on the screen is an actual professional philosopher—this cinematic discourse must in some sense be *valid*. In order for it to be valid it must be validated, and since we are absent from the world screened, the only ones who can do this are Nana and Godard himself. But why Cavell's need for validation? Does this not succumb to an a priori attitude about what discourse on film should be, and moreover, of what a philosopher on film should say? This would seem to violate Cavell's principle that "the question what becomes of particular people, and specific locales, and subjects and motifs when they are filmed by individual makers of film ... has only one source of data for its answer, namely the appearance and significance of just those objects and people that are in fact to be found in the succession of films, or passages of films, that matter to us."[23] Cavell's need for "valid discourse" implies that conceptual reasoning has a greater capacity for evoking lived inwardness than the phenomenal immediacy of the person who speaks it. On the contrary, Siegfried Kracauer claims conceptual reasoning has little to do with what is cinematic. For it to be cinematic, conceptual thinking must first "divest the spoken word of its leading role."[24] Toward this end, Kracauer invokes the existential thought of Gabriel Marcel, which answers precisely to the topic at hand. When a philosophy professor speaks on film, says Marcel, what is important is not the content of the speech but bodily attitude, comportment, intonation, facial expression, and the like.[25] Only this grants the speech legitimacy, by granting the speaker lived inwardness from which to speak.

Giving Cavell the benefit of doubt, perhaps what he disapproves of more than its loss of validity is the assumption that a base form of seduction begets this discourse, one which displaces the ideas themselves: "While [Godard's] talent and wit lead him to remark that philosophy is now stimulated by pretty girls, either he fails to recognize the humor and sadness of this, or else he sees nothing further."[26] Cavell concludes from this that "philosophy ought either to be a nobler seduction or else its acceptance of separateness ought to be acknowledged as its power."[27] Yet a nobler seduction, perhaps in the manner of Johannes the Seducer, Kierkegaard's reflective aesthete, is a conceptually based method which transforms seduction into continual fascination. True seduction cannot be enacted via concepts; no one is seduced by the bare factual content of words spoken but by the voice which speaks them. Whom then does Cavell insist is being seduced here? Godard in fact makes sure that these characters and their discourse remain separate, which is surely the condition of their mutual fascination and, as Cavell inadvertently intimates, the source of this moment's power. For if, at bottom, *Vivre sa vie* is an attempt to reveal Nana's inwardness, her soul, and if this moment is no exception, then its importance, its "power" if you will, lies not in reaching its goal but precisely in the way it acknowledges its own inability to do so.

This scene begins with a long continuous tracking shot which eventually catches Nana sauntering down the sidewalk. But, as is typical with this film, we see from the outside looking in. Whether in a car (as in this shot), or in a record shop, or from a great distance above, or from a long way away, our view of the flow of life does not place us within it as *À bout de souffle* does. This implies not the "cool" self-awareness of a Poiccard type but the isolation of the self from society at large, and, as suggested in Nana and Parain's dialogue, of the self from oneself. The depiction of a soul must first acknowledge the difficulty of plumbing its own depths.

As the scene continues, this aspect of separation becomes more pronounced. Nana enters a café and looks off-camera, asking an unseen man what he is doing. He is reading. She asks if he will buy her a drink. He will. Nana gets up to join him and there is a cut to a close-up of Parain. For an instant we see Nana flash by the camera as she sits down across from him. This will be the only instant in which the two are seen together in the same shot. My discomfort and anxiety when viewing this moment (and perhaps Cavell's sense of its invalidity as well) is based primarily upon the lack of a shot establishing these two as actually sitting together. Spatiotemporal unity remains quite tenuous throughout this moment—but this is not a weakness or an error but a deliberate ploy on Godard's part. Error plays no part in the film experience; I can attend only to what is, not to what I determine should be. Godard is asking a question here: what are the cinematic conditions necessary for revealing dialogical inwardness? To maintain primary focus on what is being said, the participants are kept at a distance via shot/reverse-shot editing, and in doing this Godard shows us precisely what Kracauer and Marcel discovered before him: depicting pure conceptual discourse deters the cinematic depiction of lived inwardness.

Objectively speaking, the conversation revolves around the possibility of authentic speech. This involves skepticism not only of knowing other minds, other selves, but of knowing oneself, of one's ability to mean what one says and say what one means. Godard's method of depicting this skepticism does not involve these characters' acknowledgement of each other but instead suspends them within themselves; this comes across as a certain mutual yet distanced fascination. Early on in the conversation Nana will remark that she suddenly does not know what to say, that her words betray what she means to say. In response, Parain tells the famous story of Porthos from *The Three Musketeers*, who, the first time he pondered how it is that he could place one foot in front of the other to walk, stopped dead in his tracks. This sets up a particular intuitive/cognitive dichotomy in their conversation: Nana will attempt to speak from experience, from her heart, and Parain will respond and correct her with examples from the history of philosophy. As such, the conversation becomes more and more one-sided. Nana offers a few thoughts of her own, which Parain either confirms or denies according to how they conform to historical thought.

There are attempts to construct overlapping dialogue, but for the most part Nana's questions are isolated, non sequitur responses to theoretical ideas. Cinematic form adds to this affect: the shots of Nana asking questions are followed by short pauses in which her comportment is meant to denote "thinking." She looks this way, now that, as if struggling with herself. At a certain point in this struggle she looks directly into the camera at us. Unlike the moment in *À bout de souffle*, when Poiccard directly addresses us in order to denote a reflexive self-awareness of himself as a certain type, Cavell deems this instance works in the opposite manner:

> Godard has found a way to stage an eyes-on interview with his sub-
> jects (in particular, with Anna Karina). But he has not done this by
> justifying a subject's acceptance of the camera—that is, by establishing
> a character capable in a given context of accepting her own self-aware-
> ness, knowing the effect she has on others (as, say, in Manet's
> *Olympia*)—but by taking a subject with no character, from whose
> person he has removed personhood, a subject incapable of accepting
> or rejecting anything.[28]

Cavell's claim is that Nana remains only a sounding board for Parain, and therefore that she is stripped of inwardness. Certainly her reactions can at times be read, as Cavell notes above, as disinterest, and because of this, as Cavell also notes, Nana's rote questions force us into reading them as issuing instead from the mouth of Godard: "One reads the distance from and between his characters as one does in reality, as the inability to feel; and we attribute our distance from the filmed events, because of their force upon us, to Godard's position toward them."[29] But can we conclude from this, as Cavell does, that "because the events of the films do not themselves justify or clarify his position, it remains arbitrary?"[30] Cavell's critique maintains that, because Godard lacks a "position" toward his own work, we are forced into filling this gap for him. But my experience of this moment has no such gap. Godard does not take a stance only to renounce it, does not grant Nana personhood only to take it away from her, but instead remains at a constant distance throughout, and this distance *is* his stance. Godard's position is precisely that of exploring the possibilities and impossibilities of embodying inwardness—in this case of noting the impos-sibility of embodying lived inwardness via conceptual means. This *is* the meaning of Nana's direct address—it does not mark her disinterest in what Parain says but her inability to contend with the way he says it. We come to suspect that this is Godard's position as well; whereas Cavell wants these thoughts to acknowledge a "noble seduction" and thus avoid skepti-cism, Godard cannot help but be skeptical because this is his position from the start. Thus when Nana asks Parain "What do you think of love?" the soundtrack marks the difference between her question and his response via the sudden insertion of elegiac music. This music marks Parain's response ("The body had to come into it") as inappropriate—not only because of his now absolute deferral to a theoretical response (Leibniz and the contingent; the history of German vs. French philosophy), but because this is the exact opposite of the spirit of Nana's question. The insertion of elegiac music underscores the sad fact that Parain the philosopher can only understand the question of love cognitively and that he can only respond with words pertaining to his knowledge about it. Nana's spiritual question about love has not been acknowledged but reduced to the mechanics of the body. There is no longer any authentic dialogue, nor any seduction, noble or otherwise, only a certain and growing distance between the two which hampers them, and us as well, from acknowledging any inwardness their words might convey. By inserting this music Godard shows how conceptual thinking impedes the depiction of cinematic inwardness.

Contrary to Cavell's notion that Godard's position toward his art remains arbitrary or, worse, absent, I have shown his attitude or position to be self-questioning about the cinematic conditions necessary for revealing inwardness. This skepticism is by no means limited to the two films analyzed here but pertains to Godard's oeuvre as a whole, one which continually puts cinema's possibilities under scrutiny. Thus in Godard's work it is not the world per se but a specific and individual skepticism regarding the abilities of cinema, of what cinema has been and is and can be, which we are shown. The world which does appear, filtered through this specific subjectivity, is not the one we live in nor the one we know but the one which cinema can or cannot become. In this manner Godard looks to the past, but also maintains an open attitude toward possibilities for future filmmaking. It is in this fuller sense that we can truly understand Godard's early work as heralding the arrival of cinematic modernism.

NOTES

1 Stanley Cavell, *The World Viewed: Reflections on the Ontology of Film*, enlarged edition (Cambridge, MA: Harvard University Press, 1979), 84.

2 Ibid., 97

3 William Rothman and Marian Keane, *Reading Cavell's "The World Viewed": A Philosophical Perspective on Film* (Detroit: Wayne State University Press, 2000), 136.

4   Stanley Cavell, *"Prénom: Marie,"* in *Cavell on Film*, ed. William Rothman (Albany: State University of New York Press, 2005), 177.

5   This difference between "modern" and "modernist" in Cavell's thought is clarified in William Rothman, "Film, Modernity, Cavell," in *Cinema and Modernity*, ed. Murray Pomerance (New Brunswick, NJ: Rutgers University Press, 2006), 316–32.

6   Cavell, *The World Viewed*, 15.

7   Ibid., 216.

8   Ibid., 216–17.

9   Ibid., 124.

10 Ibid., 56.

11 Ibid.

12 It is interesting in this context to note that the only other Godard film Cavell values to any extent in *The World Viewed* is *Alphaville* (1965), which is also entirely dependent upon the use of type, in this case the hard-boiled detective. Accordingly, Cavell remarks that it is "as underrated a film as most of the rest of Godard is overrated" (84).

13 Cavell, *The World Viewed*, 33.

14 The human "something" is a term Cavell uses to highlight the difficulty of ontologically defining those who inhabit the cinematic screen. See *The World Viewed*, 26.

15 Cavell, *The World Viewed*, 97.

16 Ibid., 99.

17 The core Situationist attack on Godard can be found in "Le rôle de Godard," *Internationale situationiste* 10 (1966): 58–59. Accounts of this attack, as well as explorations of the parallels between Godard's work and Situationist *détournement*, are explored in Brian Price, "Plagiarizing the Plagiarist: Godard Meets the Situationists," *Film Comment* 33, no. 6 (1997): 66–69; as well as in Alan Williams, *"Pierrot* in Context(s)," in *Jean-Luc Godard's "Pierrot le fou,"* ed. David Wills (Cambridge: Cambridge University Press, 2000), 43–63.

18 Williams, *"Pierrot* in Context(s)," 60.

19 Cavell, *The World Viewed*, 100.

20 "Nana the unwitting philosopher."

21 Brice Parain (1897–1971), contemporary of Sartre and Camus, is perhaps best known for his work on the philosophy of language.

22 Cavell, *The World Viewed*, 100.

23 Stanley Cavell, "What Becomes of Things on Film?" in *Cavell on Film*, ed. William Rothman (Albany: State University of New York Press, 2005), 9.

24 Siegfried Kracauer, *Theory of Film: The Redemption of Physical Reality* (Princeton, NJ: Princeton University Press, 1997), 264.

25 See ibid., 264–65.

26 Cavell, *The World Viewed*, 100.

27 Ibid., 100–1.

28 Ibid., 99.

29 Ibid., 97.

30 Ibid.

BIBLIOGRAPHY

Cavell, Stanley. *"Prénom*: Marie." In *Cavell on Film*, edited by William Rothman, 175–81. Albany: State University of New York Press, 2005.

———. "What Becomes of Things on Film?" In *Cavell on Film*, edited by William Rothman, 1–9. Albany: State University of New York Press, 2005.

———. *The World Viewed: Reflections on the Ontology of Film*. Enlarged edition. Cambridge, MA: Harvard University Press, 1979.

Kracauer, Siegfried. *Theory of Film: The Redemption of Physical Reality*. Introduction by Miriam Bratu Hansen. Princeton, NJ: Princeton University Press, 1997.

Price, Brian. "Plagiarizing the Plagiarist: Godard Meets the Situationists." *Film Comment* 33, no. 6 (November–December 1997): 66–69.

"Le rôle de Godard." *Internationale situationiste* 10 (1966): 58–59.

Rothman, William. "Film, Modernity, Cavell." In *Cinema and Modernity*, edited by Murray Pomerance, 316–32. New Brunswick, NJ: Rutgers University Press, 2006.

Rothman, William, and Marian Keane. *Reading Cavell's "The World Viewed": A Philosophical Perspective on Film*. Detroit: Wayne State University Press, 2000.

Williams, Alan. *"Pierrot* in Context(s)." In *Jean-Luc Godard's "Pierrot le fou,"* edited by David Wills, 43–63. Cambridge: Cambridge University Press, 2000.

11

The Romance of the Intellectual in Godard: A Love–Hate Relationship

Tyson Stewart

INTELLECTUALS IN THEORY

Godard's signature method of blending documentary and fiction has yielded many fascinating results, including a cinematic deconstruction of the figure of the intellectual and his or her vocation. This Nouvelle Vague filmmaker repeatedly used real-life public intellectuals to interact with fictional characters in some of his most politicized films, like Brice Parain in *Vivre sa vie* (1962), Francis Jeanson in *La Chinoise* (1967), Jane Fonda in *Tout va bien* (1972), and Godard himself in *Notre Musique* (2004). It is significant perhaps that the public intellectual is already an icon of representation (in the political sense) when he or she enters the terrain of the fictional. In this respect, political and fictional representations intertwine at a similar level of cultural importance. By featuring public intellectuals in his films, Godard achieves a cinematic realism unique in film history at the time of their creation. I argue that performance and the will to image are essential components of the role of the intellectual in late modernity, as suggested by the likes of Sartre and Said. This essay surveys the films of the 1960s period, and highlights the most significant appearances of the intellectual in turn.

Few histories of intellectuals or educators on film actually exist. Yveline Baticle's small but useful 1971 study *Le professeur à l'écran* lays out two types of intellectuals in film history and notices a clear shift in the way students and teachers are depicted after the events of May 1968 in France. Before the mid-1960s, teachers and professors are represented as angry, strict authority figures. They are also roundly mediocre at what they do and the reason why they have become teachers is because they are failures in the "real world."[1] *Zéro de conduite* (1933), *Les Diaboliques* (1955), and *Who's Afraid of Virginia Woolf?* (1966) feature the old type of professor. The new type that emerged during the late 1960s is characterized by hipness with a propensity for experimentation in the classroom. Godard's intellectuals occupy neither Baticle's old or new model. His intellectuals belong to a decidedly alternative camp. Students step into the role of professor, and teachers often get schooled.

What is innovative about Godard is that he was ready to engage with prominent public intellectuals and pit his characters, who have their own intellectual arguments, against these forceful individuals. By placing the intellectual in key positions within the films, he has ensured that one legacy of his cinema lies in discovering new possibilities for the intellectual, public or otherwise. In the cameos especially, Godard is showing a certain intellectual labour in progress, one that depends heavily on the spontaneous production of philosophical discourse. Godard recognizes that the ways we communicate are—whether the philosophers like it or not—changing. Debate has become compressed, more superficial, the product of an atomization of knowledge that has taken place within late modernity and that has been partly due to the culture industry as a whole. Godard's films attempt to chart the decline of intellectualism in the West. Yet he has never shied away from highlighting the negative consequences of intellectual inaction. It is optimistic perhaps that, in Godard, being an intellectual is a complex affair and what makes the intellectual's life challenging is not simply brute capitalism but a whole host of travails, including the ability and will to represent a thinking and politicized self in our media environment.

According to Edward Said, the social elements that constitute the "true" intellectual's vocation are as follows: "Intellectual representations are the activity itself, dependent on a kind of consciousness that is sceptical, engaged, unremittingly devoted to rational investigation and moral judgment; and this puts the individual on record and on the line. *Knowing how to use language well and knowing when to intervene in language are two essential features of intellectual action.*"[2] As men of letters, the intellectuals can and must be held accountable for their arguments. They are in no way "cut off" from the wider society. The performative aspect of being an intellectual turns out to be extremely important in modern society. The appeal to documentary truth in the films is a commentary on the performative aspect of the intellectual. By contrasting the actors' performances with the intellectual's, both Brechtian reflexivity and documentary truth become intertwined. Said quotes Sartre's statement on the role of the intellectual: "Whatever game he may want to play, he must play it on the basis of the representation which others have of him. He may want to modify the character that one attributes to the man of letters in a given society; *but in order to change it, he must first slip into it.*"[3]

INTELLECTUAL CAMEOS!

Godard's intellectuals come to the fictional world of the film already as polysemic figures, as both intellectuals (academics or philosophers) and representatives of their nation or community. They are already media-bound and media-defined as well. Godard's oeuvre is rich in part for the endless references and hypertextual strategies that go into his films. Giving real-life intellectuals cameo appearances in the same world as his fictional characters means these scenes take on a documentary appeal. The cameo instantly places the guest within a new cultural debate or context. These strategies are also there in order to challenge preconceived notions of cinematic storytelling, thus expanding the possibilities of the medium. A long conversation with a professor in a movie may not have any narrative consequences but it does tell us something about this social type's place in the world. One of the most enduring legacies of Godard has been just this kind of reflexivity that emphasizes the polysemic nature of his performers.

We can look at the cameo for its politics, what it says about the person being represented and how that person is representing him- or herself.[4] Looking at the mingling of characters of different ontological status in Godard, Robert Stam asks the following: "Does the diegetic universe annex the real or the reverse?"[5] By expanding its meanings and deliberately confusing the fictional with the non-fictional, the cameo plays a game with the concept of representation. The notable cameos in 1960s Godard include Jean-Pierre Melville (*À bout de souffle*, 1960), Brice Parain (*Vivre sa vie*), Roger Leenhardt (*Une femme mariée*, 1964), Philippe Labro (*Made in USA*, 1966), and Francis Jeanson (*La Chinoise*). The cameo will be self-reflexive in any film, but how far does the cameo in Godard differ from how it is employed in, say, Hitchcock? This essay argues that the cameo in Godard is of a special kind that has not been discussed fully yet, especially when it comes to the sociological dimension and attributions of the social type that is in the cameo. The cameo does not call attention to the author's presence, as it does in Hitchcock. Rather, it invites a shared social experience by embracing the medium's deictic properties. In what follows, the cameo's relation to the overall narrative will be investigated.

ROGER LEENHARDT IN *UNE FEMME MARIÉE* (1964)

Roger Leenhardt (1903–1985) was a highly regarded French filmmaker and critic whom Godard once called "the most subtle film theoretician in France."[6] Leenhardt also provided a model for critics who wanted to write about cinema intelligently for a mass public.[7] Between 1935 and 1936, he contributed to a series of columns in *Esprit* dedicated to the idea of cinema as art and popular entertainment. His influence was solidified when, in "A Certain Tendency of the French Cinema" (1954), Truffaut listed Leenhardt as one of the eight directors of the previous generation of French film-makers that was an auteur and was thus a source of inspiration. As a fellow film *auteur*, Leenhardt's presence in the film surely serves as a kind of stand-in for Godard himself.

The editing style of *Une femme mariée* is an important part of the film's overall argument—it consists of assembling many brief shots that focus on parts of things, as in the opening moments where jarring shots of a couple's naked limbs are put into a montage. Godard's editing style makes fragments out of daily life, puts everything in packages, and reminds us how everything is potentially ready for consumption. The montage of ads of women's products near the end is ahead of its time in terms of media analysis found within a film. Leenhardt's monologue is also fragmented like the rest of the film. His monologue is placed between the husband's and wife's monologues in order to show how the married woman's opinions are just as significant as his own—she can argue for frivolity and the bourgeois life *just as well* as he can argue for comprehension before action and the importance of compromise. His monologue is also packaged under the heading "L'intelligence"—his philosophical discussion is presented as a commodity, much like the protagonist's new brassiere.

In the first thirty minutes of the film, we see the married woman leave her lover at a hotel room and meet her pilot husband after he has flown in from Germany. In a long and somewhat moving passage, Leenhardt distills the attitude that Godard has toward the intellectual. The following passage comes around the thirty-minute mark. The monologue done in long take and close-up on Leenhardt is in fact the last time we see his character and it is his comments that give the film its moralistic edge. With his expressive facial movements and emphatic delivery, Leenhardt comes across as incredibly real, authentic. As always with Godard's monologues or interviews, it is a nuanced and somewhat conflicted philosophy. Leenhardt says:

> Intelligence is to comprehend before acting. It's the idea of seeking, seeking the limits, seeking one's opposite. To reach an understanding of others, a bridge between oneself and others. We then find, bit by bit, a part of the path. I'm aware that not everyone cares for [this] intellectual approach. Most men want brilliant colors or things that are either black or white without nuances or shades. But to me, the fanatics, the dogmatics are the boring ones. To begin with, you know what they are going to say in advance. But those who embrace paradox are more amusing and engaging.

The moralism of the monologue is directed at the actions of the married woman, who throughout does not seem to think things through. Rather, she lets the modern city and its possibilities dictate her actions. Eloquent and serious, the intellectual offers her something to think about, yet cannot add to her existence meaningfully. The scene reminds us that this woman is free but still operates within a dream world of consumerism where higher, more intellectual pursuits are not likely.

The ideas that Leenhardt discusses in the monologue are present in many of the cameos, where an appeal to thinking and comprehension prevails. Thinking, in distinction to action, is a theme in the films and gets vocalized within this strategy. Tying these themes to the intellectual character and his politics is a convenient and quick way of framing the entire narrative around them. The intellectual is a thinker, while the protagonists are often doers that are alienated but are not necessarily aware of their alienation. No doubt, there is something appealing about this kind of intellectual stance for Godard. After all, he is a filmmaker who makes films about ways of thinking that aim to change the ways audiences think. The onscreen intellectuals have been the most vocal about this disposition.

BRICE PARAIN IN *VIVRE SA VIE* (1962)

In many of Godard's 1960s films, the intellectuals seem to be freer than the characters because their alienation is never depicted. Godard's female protagonists are nearly always alienated. Locked into narrative, they reside within their characters' types: prostitutes, wives, labourers, disenfranchised youth. Nicole Brenez touches on a few of the ways Godard structures the work of intellectuals. She notes that the character of the journalist as detective (or detective as journalist) features strongly throughout Godard's films, perhaps most prominently in *Made in USA*. Lessons, interviews, interrogation (or conversation) sequences allow intellectuals to represent themselves and the intellectual vocation in general. She briefly describes a running strategy in the films that often also contains a cameo appearance: "A random character, who is not in any way a professional in the art of questioning, meets another character, by chance, who is invested with knowledge and authority, and asks him to explain a number of phenomena. The sequence consists therefore of offering to the master the opportunity to put forth his world view. We might thus call this device the heuristic offering."[8] The heuristic offering, as Brenez defines it, suggests that the intellectual who is talking in the cameo is discovering things as he speaks and is being filmed. Godard's intellectual cameo slot gives his guest a media forum wherein he may test out ideas, where learning can be somewhat spontaneous. In these cameos, everyone learns—the intellectual, the character, Godard, and, finally, the audience.

The Nana-Parain conversation in *Vivre sa vie* brings up the theme of thinking versus action once again. Brice Parain (1897–1971) talks about the balance needed between talking and thinking, or silence and action. Their discussion begins with Nana's declaration that she sometimes does not know what to say. She asks him why it is necessary to always talk. He talks about the importance of thinking as opposed to, for example, loving something for the wrong reasons. Through a largely reciprocal exchange of ideas, Parain and Nana debate the proper use of language. Parain makes clear that language is the very stuff of living in a society, but also suggests it can betray us. "It is not a question of speaking or not speaking, but of speaking well," as Sontag notes. "Speaking well demands an ascetic discipline (*une ascèse*), detachment."[9]

This scene demonstrates the work of the intellectual as he himself describes it: there is the thinking part and the doing part: if ideas are going to take shape they must first be communicated. To ensure that thinking doesn't go to waste, there must be communication, one of the intellectual's most fundamental responsibilities. The communication part is the responsibility of the intellectual. The great irony of this scene is that Nana, as the chapter heading suggests, participates in this intellectual work. Chapter Eleven's title card describes it thus, "Nana fait de la philosophie sans le savoir" (Nana does philosophy without knowing it). Her character goes through various, mostly unsuccessful roles. First, she is a girlfriend (and possibly a mother) and service worker, then a prostitute, and finally a philosopher. The description recalls Gramsci's famous dictum, "All men are intellectuals but not all men have in society the function of intellectuals."[10] Moreover, the openness of the exchange, unlike her relations with others throughout the film, stands out for its sense of freedom of thought and even emancipatory aspiration.

Nana is killed in the chapter following Parain's cameo, but it is arguable that this brief encounter with a philosopher is the climax of the film: the most exploited social type, the prostitute, turns into the most autonomous of social types, the intellectual. The reason why this is not merely a last ditch effort to signal the importance of the life of ideas is in part due to Parain's very natural delivery and complex explanation of language. It implies that if there had been more thinking than action for Nana perhaps she wouldn't have met this end. Parain stresses that to talk well means to look at life with detachment. "Speech is like a resurrection," he states. The metaphor of Porthos can be applied to Nana. Porthos sets a bomb, runs away, and then stops to think about how it is possible for him to walk. The bomb explodes and he dies under the rubble days later. He dies because he thought for the first time in his life. Parain suggests we can talk well only when we have renounced life for a certain time. That is the price. Nana suggests that thinking, and a life devoted to thought, is in fact not living. "I think life should be easy," exclaims Nana. Karina's character starts thinking too late but she is also aware of it. It is an anti-climactic ending and Parain allows Nana to participate in intellectual exchange tragically too late.[11]

A certain detachment is felt specifically because Nana talks to a real-life intellectual, which makes us far more aware of Karina's acting: "Godard uses the apparent objectivity of the camera as a way to create cinematic 'doubles,' deliberately blurring the lines between reality and fiction, internal and external, personal and impersonal."[12] The cameos suggest there is an intellectual performance going on beneath (or beside) the construction of the character. Perhaps more than any other filmmaker, Godard's cinematic universe is populated by a multitude of intellectuals and intellectual dispositions. In order to instruct, the actor has to be an intellectual with certain critical insights on a host of societal issues. And the cameos are mostly shot as documentaries—it is interesting to note that Parain did not expect to receive monetary compensation for his role in the film. He told the producer Pierre Braunberger that there would be no charge. Braunberger, however, insisted that there be one.[13] In any case, the cameos are very much performances characterized above all by a sense of experimentation and play.

Stanley Cavell suggests that one of the motivations these philosophers have for always talking to young women is that they desire them.[14] But I see these cameos as much more substantive than that. Cavell writes, "[Godard] does not care whether what the philosopher says is valid or not—that is, he listens to it the way his girls do, or the way a bourgeois audience does, somewhere within embarrassment, envy, contempt, and titillation."[15] Godard's depiction of the philosophers is somewhat ambiva-lent, but Cavell may be going too far when he argues Godard is not inter-ested in "the sound of philosophy," or the sound of sense in a world of chaos and cynicism. Godard does not make these cameo appearances "easy." This could explain why there are such divergent responses to them. One thing they do accomplish, however, is to challenge the notion that philosophers are not doing anything. Indeed, their performances are mate-rial and thus highly social. Cavell continues, "The love that philosophy can teach is the power to accept intimacy without taking it personally.... Godard's girls walk away intact from these confrontations. Is this sup-posed to show that they are unseducible? So are prostitutes. Anyway, they are seduced—by slogans, advertisements, and illicitness."[16] The philosophers may seduce us but they fail to seduce the women (because they disagree with them and say as much)—which suggests that the depiction of the intellectual is never innocent and therefore can be productive.

Thus far, in the representations of intellectuals in Godard, we get thoughtful people who open up new ways of thinking and hint at an autonomy that, in the main, is not reflected in the protagonists' lives. Yet, although the intellectuals are peripheral to the narratives, they offer a moral centre to the films. The intellectual has been romanticized in Godard's oeuvre since its early days (i.e., the heuristic offering), but gradually the director put the limitations of the intellectual vocation under the microscope in the next (Maoist) chapter of his career, and this skepticism continues to inform his recent films. Our discussion of *La Chinoise* will provide more insights into this general transition and will offer reasons why Godard might have felt it necessary to reassess the importance of the intellectual vocation for contemporary French society, head-on.

FRANCIS JEANSON IN *LA CHINOISE* (1967)

As previously stated, the appeal to transparency and documentary truth within fiction is an important factor in how Godard thinks about cinema. He shows how the idea of a binary opposition between fiction and documentary is untenable. Francis Jeanson (1922–2009) effectively slips in and out of *La Chinoise* narrative constraints as well—mostly, he is seen as a socially constructed individual, promulgating a trait that is tied to the French intellectual, namely, fending off accusations of cowardice. The documentary aspect of Jeanson's cameo and role was very much on Godard's mind—he was conscious of Jeanson's history of revolutionary action and how that would imbue meaning in this scene. Godard says, "I was really relying on the allusion to Algeria. I was afraid I'd hear people say what they said when they saw Brice Parain in *Vivre sa vie*, that 'they wished that old shit would shut up,' or even that I'd meant to make him look a fool. Because of the allusion to Algeria, they can't."[17] We would have to look hard to find similar devices where the confluence of fiction and non-fiction in French film has had similar effects.[18]

When *Cahiers du cinéma* asked Godard, in 1967, why he included Jeanson in *La Chinoise*'s key scene (another intellectual in the film's climax), the filmmaker explained that he was aware of Jeanson's role as an intellectual and how that would serve his cinematic ends: "[Anne Wiazemsky had] studied philosophy with him. That meant they'd be able to talk. Anyway, Jeanson's the kind of man who really likes talking to people. He'd even talk to a wall ... I needed him, Francis Jeanson, not someone else, for a TECHNICAL reason: the man Anne talked to would have to be a man who understood her, who'd be able to fit his speed to hers."[19] Philippe Sollers opted out of appearing in the film because he thought Godard was trying to trick him. Godard's games are cinematic and highly intellectual. The way the scene was executed involved many takes and required Wiazemsky to wear an earpiece so that Godard could dictate to her the questions for Jeanson. When the close-up of Jeanson was shot he did not know the questions so he had to answer them spontaneously. Jeanson answered spontaneously, but his personality and convictions, his vocation as an intellectual, were completely intact. According to Alain Bergala's excellent historical account of Godard's 1960s productions *Godard au travail*, seven camera setups were needed to create the scene.[20] One angle was a close-up of Wiazemsky and Jeanson's hands. One was Jeanson smoking while listening to the Maoist student. Two were reaction shots of Jeanson and Wiazemsky. And the three main shots were filmed with a Mitchell camera that could do sync sound recording: a close-up on Wiazemsky, a close-up on Jeanson, and finally, a two-shot. Jeanson had to answer many of the questions up to four different times and they both repeated all the dialogue for the close-up for the two-shot, yet their spontaneity meets the needs of performance. The title cards are meant to elicit ideas as well as to smooth out the transitions. Is this a mere trick, a game on Godard's part, or has he created a space within his approach to the cameo where political debate and art coexist perfectly?

Jeanson advocates a position similar to Gramsci's organic intellectual. That is, when he says a revolution needs support, he is appealing to a form of representative democracy: "You can participate in a revolution, but you can't invent one.... Your actions will lead to nothing if they aren't upheld by a community, a class," Jeanson says to Véronique (Wiazemsky). Jeanson is the organic intellectual par excellence—he studied under Sartre in Paris and is on his way to rural France to instruct his fellow Frenchmen under a state-sponsored program to bring culture to the people.[21] Véronique wants to skip over the need to get people on board and start the revolution immediately, an attitude that is telling of the events of 1968, which included a little bit of both—a little violence here, a little collective action there. Véronique and her peers are taking a different route than Jeanson's and this gestures to a shift in politics from the deliberation that typifies intellectual life to any-means-necessary anarchist action. The idea of the intellectual has lost some of its organic weight, and politics is speaking with the rhetoric of urgency more than ever.

Jeanson, the leader of a clandestine National Liberation Front support group in France during the Algerian war, is put in the somewhat ironic position of debating the merits of a more direct approach to revolutionary action. As Jeanson's biographer Marie-Pierre Ulloa shows, Jeanson is traditionally a man who has been accused of espousing a contradictory position in light of his actions in the past. In the Algerian war, when Jeanson had formed a pro-FLN group called the Jeanson Network, he was one of the only members of the group who refused to make comparisons between the Algerian conflict and the French Resistance movement during the Second World War.[22] Thus, he tried to see each new conflict and resistance as unique and did not want to draw overarching parallels between historical moments that would cover up the complexities and different nature of individual conflicts. By invoking the memory of past resistances as a parallel for current ones, *La Chinoise* draws on Jeanson's and many French intellectuals' difficult choices in determining how to conduct contemporary revolutionary endeavours.

The dialogue, coupled with the actors' body language and the *mise en scène*—a train compartment, where Wiazemsky and Jeanson are sitting across of each other—makes this scene one of the most useful for understanding the politics of engaged intellectuals in 1967 French society. Jeanson argues that any kind of change must come with the support of a *peuple* or collective. He tells Véronique any sort of terrorist action will most certainly lead to a political dead end. "But during the Algerian war when Djamila Bouhired blew up cafés, you defended her while all the press was against her," Véronique throws his way. Godard is very much willing to point out the perceived hypocrisy of Jeanson's statements. In doing so, he demonstrates the difficulty in undertaking organic political projects in a country and for a country with a history of colonization. Now the lighting has changed slightly. The two are silhouetted, and the top of the frame is filled with the *paysage* fleeting by in the background. In the end, the structure of the film may indeed indicate that Jeanson comes out as the winner here, which would make Godard's strategy much more complex than is traditionally noted. Jeanson argues collective action and Véronique turns around and assassinates the wrong man, creating a real mess.

Public intellectuals, such as Parain, and Jeanson, are quite aware of their social role as intellectuals. These cameos demonstrate a resistance to the idea that we can innocently live outside of representation and discourse. It works for them to be smoothly integrated into films that examine in practice what they have been discussing in their real lives. Godard contends it is a matter of technique but acknowledges the more relevant social dimensions too: "Because [Jeanson] had taught Anne philosophy, I thought at first that I'd film a lesson in philosophy—a mind giving birth to an idea, prompted by Spinoza or Husserl."[23] The intellectuals' incorporation into Godard's films is a smooth transition because they seem more able to offer insight and moral direction. The fact that they can do this spontaneously would suggest that, for Godard, the intellectual has a responsibility to offer answers to difficult questions. Simply put, the films draw on the philosophers' experience.

For Godard, these specific cameos represent moments when he is open to debate. The knowledge these intellectuals bring to his films may correct, challenge, or accentuate Godard's own worldview, that is, his own ideological outlook—Jeanson's call for collective action challenges Godard's Maoism at the time. Thus, it is quite probable that Jeanson opposes Godard's own views on violence, while Leenhardt's monologue supplements Godard's critique of consumerism. Notice, too, the change from Leenhardt to Jeanson: the monologue has been replaced with a more open interview format. Debate is emphasized over closed-off forms of communication. The cameos might be criticized for being stylistically uninteresting. Godard does not want to distract from the ideas with his own legendary stylistic flourishes: the use of primary colours, dynamic camera work, charged movement choreography, etc., so he creates discussion fora that are much more reminiscent of television talk show interviews on a public TV network than cinematic spectacles.[24]

NEW INTELLECTUAL ITINERARIES

In *Letter to Jane* (1972), Godard and Gorin ask squarely, "What is the role of the intellectual today?" But the more satisfying answer can be found in *Tout va bien*, a film that diagnoses the alienation that not only the workers feel but the intellectuals feel as well. For it is Susan Dewitt's (Jane Fonda) "prostitution" as a bourgeois journalist that makes her blithely unaware of what happens in the Salumi factory and indeed how her marriage has become routine. A shot like the one where Fonda is among workers, stuffing sausages, comments not only on her character (a bourgeois intellectual), but enters into a discussion with Fonda's star status as well, upsetting her Hollywood image. The re-education of intellectuals goes hand-in-hand with the re-education of stars (and the re-education of the audience too). Thinking of themselves historically—understanding their place in class structure—also means alienating intellectuals from their autonomous position. The heuristic offering is a missing trope now—Dewitt importantly does not speak at the moment when she interviews the workers. The intellectuals need to listen to the workers instead of lecturing them. Even though the intellectual is the star of this film, she is placed to the side in order to learn more about the limits and pressures that other social actors face.

Godard has persistently made the partial uselessness of intellectuals explicit within many of his narratives: recall that Leenhardt's moralism goes without notice; Parain can't save Nana from death (nor does he even ask her what she does); Fonda's self-exile from the bourgeoisie leads her ironically to a merely private existence; the professor in *Je vous salue, Marie* (1985) has no effect on pretty much anything; and the philosophy professor in *For Ever Mozart* (1996) waxes philosophical as she is forced to dig her own grave. What is interesting in the later films is how they show that the winds of history have been increasingly blowing against the politicized Western intellectual for many years now. The alienation of intellectuals is a topic that characterizes many of Godard's the post-1960s films, such as *Passion* (1982), *For Ever Mozart*, *Éloge de l'amour* (2001), and *Notre musique*. Godard's films mourn a certain intellectually communicative, active, and moral temperament. In many of his 1960s films, the intellectual is always on the wayside, in a brief cameo sequence, and thus coming through as disposable. It is within the cameos that we find the roots of some of his most deep-seated concerns. But, his politics of mourning are actually constructive and even hopeful. In the cameos, the performavity of the intellectual is at its most playful and memorable.

NOTES

1   Yveline Baticle, *Le professeur à l'écran* (Paris: Édition du Cerf, 1971), 110.
2   Edward Said, *Representations of the Intellectual: The 1993 Reith Lectures* (New York: Pantheon Books, 1994), 20 (my emphasis).
3   Ibid., 74–75 (my emphasis).
4   Notably, Woody Allen has given intellectuals cameo appearances in his films as well—Marshall McLuhan in *Annie Hall* (1977) and Susan Sontag in *Zelig* (1983). Not only do they afford the films a documentary dimension, but they also pose broader questions about the intellectual star system within and beyond academia and the world of literature.
5   Robert Stam, *Reflexivity in Film and Literature: From Don Quixote to Jean-Luc Godard* (New York: Columbia University Press, 1992), 136.
6   Jean-Luc Godard, *Godard on Godard: Critical Writings by Jean-Luc Godard*, ed. Jean Narboni and Tom Milne (New York: Da Capo Press, 1972), 47.
7   Emilie Bickerton, *A Short History of Cahiers du cinéma* (London: Verso, 2009), 7.
8   Nicole Brenez, "The Forms of the Question," in *For Ever Godard*, ed. Michael Temple, James S. Williams, and Michael Witt (London: Black Dog, 2004), 165.
9   Susan Sontag, "Godard's *Vivre sa vie*," in *Against Interpretation and Other Essays* (New York: Picador, 1966), 204.

10 Antonio Gramsci, *The Antonio Gramsci Reader: Selected Writings 1916–1935*, ed. David Forgacs (New York: New York University Press, 2000), 304.

11 In Steven Soderbergh's *The Girlfriend Experience* (2009), basically an updated *Vivre sa vie*, the high-class call girl played by Sasha Grey sits down with an older man—his grey hair and sports jacket immediately conjure up Parain—in a posh restaurant to discuss a prospective book project about her work experiences. In the Soderbergh film, economic exchange is the logic behind every relationship.

12 Peter Mathews, "The Mandatory Proxy," *Biography* 29, no. 1 (Winter 2006): 48.

13 Alain Bergala, *Godard au travail: Les années 60* (Paris: Cahiers du cinéma, 2006), 115.

14 Stanley Cavell, *The World Viewed: Reflections on the Ontology of Film* (Cambridge, MA: Harvard University Press, 1979), 101.

15 Ibid., 100.

16 Ibid.

17 Jacques Bontemps et al., "A Struggle on Two Fronts: A Conversation with Jean-Luc Godard," *Film Quarterly* 22, no. 2 (Winter 1968–69): 20.

18 Recently, Claire Denis' *Vers Nancy* (2002) pays homage to the train sequence in *La Chinoise*. This time, the philosopher is Jean-Luc Nancy who talks to a young woman about foreigners in France.

19 Bontemps et al., "A Struggle on Two Fronts," 20.

20 Bergala, *Godard au travail*, 356–60.

21 Marie-Pierre Ulloa, *Francis Jeanson: A Dissident Intellectual from the French Resistance to the Algerian War*, trans. Jane Marie Todd (Stanford, CA: Stanford University Press, 2007), 258.

22 Marie-Pierre Ulloa, "Memory and Continuity: The Resistance, the Algerian War, and the Jeanson Network," in *Memory, Empire and Postcolonialism: Legacies of French Colonialism*, ed. Alec G. Hargreaves (Lanham, MD: Lexington Books, 2005), 120.

23 Bontemps et al., "A Struggle on Two Fronts," 20.

24 As Tamara Chaplin notes, the television book show genre was invented in France. *Lectures pour tous*, which aired from 1953 to 1968, was an instant success and featured France's most prominent intellectuals, such as Sartre, Camus, Bachelard, Jeanson, and Foucault. What characterized *Lectures pour tous*, besides its obvious attempt at creating intellectual celebrities and making philosophy reach the masses, was its style. The use of long static takes and a two-shot editing style forced the audience to watch television differently. The show allowed (perhaps for the first time) philosophers an opportunity to perform philosophy on television. See Tamara Chaplin, *Turning on the Mind: French Philosophers on Television* (Chicago: University of Chicago Press, 2007), 82.

BIBLIOGRAPHY

Baticle, Yveline. *Le professeur à l'écran*. Paris: Édition du Cerf, 1971.

Bergala, Alain. *Godard au travail: Les années 60*. Paris: Cahiers du cinéma, 2006.

Bickerton, Emilie. *A Short History of Cahiers du cinéma*. London: Verso, 2009.

Bontemps, Jacques, Jean Louis Comolli, Michel Delahaye, and Jean Narboni. "A Struggle on Two Fronts: A Conversation with Jean-Luc Godard." *Film Quarterly* 22, no. 2 (Winter 1968–69): 20–35.

Brenez, Nicole. "The Forms of the Question." In *For Ever Godard*, edited by Michael Temple, James S. Williams, and Michael Witt, 160–77. London: Black Dog, 2004.

Cavell, Stanley. *The World Viewed: Reflections on the Ontology of Film*. Cambridge, MA: Harvard University Press, 1979.

Chaplin, Tamara. *Turning on the Mind: French Philosophers on Television*. Chicago: University of Chicago Press, 2007.

Godard, Jean-Luc. *Godard on Godard: Critical Writings by Jean-Luc Godard*, edited by Jean Narboni and Tom Milne. New York: Da Capo Press, 1972.

Gramsci, Antonio. *The Antonio Gramsci Reader: Selected Writings 1916–1935*, edited by David Forgacs. New York: New York University Press, 2000.

Mathews, Peter. "The Mandatory Proxy." *Biography* 29, no. 1 (Winter 2006): 43–53.

Said, Edward. *Representations of the Intellectual: The 1993 Reith Lectures*. New York: Pantheon Books, 1994.

Sontag, Susan. "Godard's *Vivre sa vie*." In *Against Interpretation and Other Essays*, 196–208. New York: Picador, 1966.

Stam, Robert. *Reflexivity in Film and Literature: From Don Quixote to Jean-Luc Godard*. New York: Columbia University Press, 1992.

Ulloa, Marie-Pierre. *Francis Jeanson: A Dissident Intellectual from the French Resistance to the Algerian War*. Translated by Jane Marie Todd. Stanford, CA: Stanford University Press, 2007.

———. "Memory and Continuity: The Resistance, the Algerian War, and the Jeanson Network." In *Memory, Empire and Postcolonialism: Legacies of French Colonialism*, edited by Alec G. Hargreaves, 112–24. Lanham, MD: Lexington Books, 2005.

Part IV
Formalist Legacies:
Narratives and Exhibitions

12

Principles of Parametric Construction in Jean-Luc Godard's *Passion*

Julien Lapointe

IN THE PENULTIMATE chapter to *Narration in the Fiction Film*, David Bordwell undertakes to analyze a set of films whose stylistic constructions adhere to a delimited mode of film narration, termed "parametric narration." He defines parametric films as those in which the "stylistic system creates patterns *distinct from the demands of the syuzhet system* [or plot]."[1] Such a film may present two or more consecutive shots that are nearly identical in framing, composition, and content. Likewise, a director might structure their ostensible narrative as a series of discrete episodes or sequences, each one "characterized by one or more variants on possible camera/subject relations."[2] Episode one might comprise only one shot framing the lead characters from behind; episode two presents only lateral tracking camera movements; episode three arranges its characters "perpendicular to the lens axis";[3] etc. In all the above examples, however, no thematic rationale is forthcoming to account for the director's stylistic idiosyncrasies. The purpose, rather, is a kind of felicitous art for art's sake—in the words of E.H. Gombrich, "the joyful exuberance of a craftsman who display[s] both his control and his inventiveness"[4]—albeit studiously applied during the course of an entire film.

Such enthusiasm notwithstanding, "parametric narration" poses unique challenges to any film scholar. It is not tied to any national tradition, mode of production, or historical era, such that parametric films share little else other than exemplifying a certain approach to style. In the previous paragraph, the first referenced film is Yasujiro Ozu's *What Did the Lady Forget?* (1937), while the second is Jean-Luc Godard's *Vivre sa vie* (1962)—a gulf of some three decades and an entire continent separate these works. Moreover, the assumptions the film theorist or critic brings to bear in identifying a film or group of films as parametric include the conviction that style, in narrative cinema, can operate independently of plot or other forms of content—that narrative cinema, in short, can be style-centred.[5]

Parametric films, to a qualified extent, are therefore resistant to interpretation as no clear ascription of meaning is likely when confronting their overt
stylistic constructions. They are necessarily of limited interest to film
scholars practising what Bordwell has termed "interpretation-centered
criticism."[6] Conversely, parametric cinema seems most ideally suited to,
and possibly stands as the most eminent justification for formalist film
theory or what has alternately been termed "neo-formalism," or a "poetics
of cinema."[7] This includes affording the historian of film style an indispensable conceptual category in grasping how certain individual directors
cultivated signature approaches. Unfortunately, privileging the study of
such films returns us to the first challenge in that parametric films are not
exactly plentiful in the history of cinema, nor are they, excepting the rare
instances of Ozu, Godard, and others, easy to find. The film scholar is
beholden to defining parametric narration, and also to citing instances of
this curious atypical mode.

The aim of this chapter is to discuss the parametric construction of
Jean-Luc Godard's 1982 feature film *Passion*, analyzing the shot selection,
editing, and occasionally the use of sounds employed in select passages of
his film. In doing so, I hope first to elucidate the use of a stylistic procedure
(i.e., "parametric construction") in the work of a filmmaker who as
Bordwell has argued, has not tended to align himself consistently or exclusively with any narrational mode or stylistic system,[8] yet who nonetheless,
as I show with *Passion*, makes use of parametric constructions of various
kinds. Second, whereas Bordwell distinguishes between two types of parametric construction—termed "ascetic" and "replete"—I point to another
set of subcategories: production-centred vs. post-production-centred.
While such a distinction may already have been gleaned in several of
Bordwell's own examples, I argue that *Passion* is a more significant (or
central) instance of post-production-centred parametric cinema. Studying
this film enhances our understanding of parametric narration and its
diverse strategies. It can also elucidate, as I note in the conclusion, Godard's
artistic legacy to modern cinema.

As noted above, Bordwell distinguishes between two types of parametric narration: the "ascetic" (or "sparse") approach, and the "replete"
option. In the first case, the filmmaker restricts his/her range of stylistic
devices "to a narrower range ... than are codified in other [filmmaking
traditions]."[9] Bordwell cites a few examples: "The Mizoguchi of the mid-
and later 1930s selects the long take in long shot or medium long shot;
Bresson confines himself to the straight-on medium shot, often of body
parts; Tati utilizes long shots with decentered framing in deep space; and
so on."[10] In the "replete" approach, the filmmaker avails him/herself of a

varied range of stylistic procedures: for example, *Vivre sa vie*, which encompasses a seemingly infinite range of camera set-ups and occasional editing patterns. Stylistic consistency is achieved not so much through the visual likeness of one shot to the next, as through the shared purpose of each of the sequences, described by Bordwell as "variants on 'how to shoot and cut character interaction.'"[11]

I prefer to introduce another distinction—one more fundamental to the *poetics* of cinema. In the above example from *Vivre sa vie*, the parameters are largely operative upon the placement of the camera in relation to a subject, while the editing is comparably less prominent. In contrast, Bordwell discusses another Ozu film, *An Autumn Afternoon* (1962), whose parametric constructions consist of sets of recurring establishing shots whose order changes unexpectedly. The first series of establishing shots shows a row of bar signs, followed by a shot of the street, and then a shot of the sign for the bar where the action is to take place. Subsequent scenes set at the bar alter this sequence, by omitting a shot that had appeared in a prior sequence (e.g., the bar sign) or rearranging the order of shots altogether.[12] By sequencing its shots in a certain order, the film privileges editing as a means of achieving its parametric construction—such that, *contra* the Godard film, it is the *mise en scène* and camera work that are comparably less prominent.

The point is not to create a rigid opposition between shooting and editing. As Godard hastened to note in a 1956 article, "montage [i.e., editing] is above all an integral part of *mise en scène* [...] the two are interdependent. To direct means to scheme, and one says of a scheme that it is well or badly mounted."[13] By designating one type of parametric construction "production-centred" (e.g., *Vivre sa vie*) and the other "post-production-centred" (e.g., *An Autumn Afternoon*), I frame the argument differently. "Centred" suggests a degree of prioritizing, as opposed to exclusion: every circle (or other such shape) has its centre, but also its margins, just as some films (parametric and otherwise) subordinate their editing to effects of *mise en scène* or vice versa. These two types of parametric cinema are not mutually exclusive categories, but delimited boundaries. A film may be more thoroughly production-centred or not, or mix elements of the two poles. As revealed by Bordwell, the parametric devices in *What Did the Lady Forget?* are a series of near-identical graphic matches, which results both from the composition and framing of the images (production-centred) and the fact that these images are edited together (post-production-centred). Michael Snow's *Wavelength* (1967), in turn, achieves a degree of stylistic prominence by being comprised only of an extended take—a clearer instance of production-centred parameters.

Passion is partly about the travails of a Polish émigré filmmaker, Jerzy (Jerzy Radziwilowicz), whose current project consists of filming *tableaux vivants* modelled after famous European paintings in a munificently funded studio. However, the plot also includes multiple characters whose respective arcs repeatedly intersect or converge with Jerzy's. The three other main characters are Hanna (Hanna Schygulla), whom it is suggested is a former flame of Jerzy's and who owns the motel where his production team is lodged; Michel (Michel Piccoli), Hanna's spouse and the owner of a nearby factory from where Jerzy draws some of his extras; and Isabelle (Isabelle Huppert), both a former flame of Jerzy's and an employee of Michel's, who spends a good portion of the film attempting to rally Michel's other employees in protest at her having been fired and to enlist Jerzy to her cause. The film begins with each of the main characters, and ends with Hanna, having broken off her relationship with Michel, departing for Poland with Isabelle while Jerzy, having abandoned his film project, follows suit.

While this sounds straightforward, *Passion* presents obstacles to the viewer's comprehension. Its manipulations of the soundtrack and image-track (most likely attained in post-production) are so brazen as to call attention to themselves, while also serving frequently to impede the spectator's grasp of the story. Consider the soundtrack. Kristin Thompson has noted in her essay on *Sauve qui peut (la vie)* that several scenes in the film "[play] on uncertainties about sound sources and temporal consistency between sound and image."[14] A similar principle is enhanced or even exacerbated in *Passion*. Classical music continually starts, only to stop abruptly, during scenes, sometimes carrying over a succession of shots in various locations. At the same time, whether the music is diegetic or not is far from clear. In one shot set in the studio, Jerzy orders that the music be turned on, as if to indicate that the classical music we will then hear is diegetic. But other scenes have already had classical music in other settings than the studio. Mozart's *Requiem* plays during Isabelle's labour meeting. As this scene is later followed by action set at the studio (during which the *Requiem* continues), it is impossible to ascertain if Jerzy is playing the *Requiem* at the studio and one hears it first during Isabelle's meeting in anticipation of the eventual transition to the new setting, or if the music comes from another (diegetic or non-diegetic) source.

The editing of the image-track proves equally vexing. Several transitions from shot-to-shot within a sequence or from one sequence to the next, involve matches on action, either executed by the same or different characters. Rather than aid the flow of the narrative, however, they serve more as visual associations that exist for their own sake. For example, Hanna is shown at the end of one sequence crossing a parking lot. This is followed by a cut to her walking up the stairs outside her motel. The second shot does not necessarily present a continuation of the same action: there is no way of gauging whether Hanna has walked to the stairs from the parking lot, or if this is another moment later on in the day. Rather, what links the two shots is their rhyming effect—the one ending and the other beginning by depicting similar actions in different locations. Another cut, later in the film, exemplifies the same process. As Isabelle begins ascending the stairs in her home, the action shifts to a nude model accomplishing a similar movement in a studio. The extent to which the edit juxtaposes otherwise disparate shots simply by virtue of the fact that they respectively end and begin with similar movements is even more emphasized. The location has changed, as have the characters: all that unites the two shots is the act of climbing stairs.

Other transitions are less literal, and appear to be more deliberately associative. Godard cuts from a shot of Jerzy lifting Isabelle's skirt to an assortment of feathers in the studio. The association involves colour, movement, and shape. The skirt and the feathers are similarly dark-coloured. Jerzy lifts Isabelle's skirt by thrusting his hand in between her legs and jerking it upwards so that the skirt seems to rise from the back, outwards to the right. The feathers in the next shot, part of an extra's costume, are outstretched to the right, and placed more or less in the same position in the frame as Isabelle's skirt. Finally, while the feathers are immobile, the camera here rotates, to suggest some continuity with the motion in the previous shot. An even bolder, and less evidently perceptible association, occurs several shots later. Godard cuts from a panning shot over a forest to an airplane. While a verbal account of these images makes them sound disparate, seeing them together reveals that they are complementary. In the shot of the forest, the camera is panning to the left, which gives the impression that the trees are circulating to the right. The plane in the next shot is on the runway, moving in a semi-circle to the right.

Beyond these edits, Godard creates even more intricate configurations of shot sequencing during the film's opening fifteen minutes. Here, one can divide the successive shots into groups, which are all edited according to distinct patterns. The first two groups are edited, as we shall see, according to a similar ABAB pattern. As such, the first two groups *share* an editing pattern and therefore can be said to form a paired set. Moreover, the same may be said of the third and fourth groups, although these shots are edited according to different modalities from the first two groups (i.e., the ABAB structure is discarded). Finally, a fifth group of shots exhibits a unique construction all its own, and is arguably among the most jarring moments in the movie—I therefore reserve it for the close of my analysis.

Perhaps a few words are in order on what is my basis for demarcating, when I do, the beginning and end of a certain group of shots—especially given the frequent ambiguities at play within *Passion*. In each of the groups of shots, the divisions I perceive are operative upon: (a) recurring locations and/or characters, and (b) the attributable function of the shot within the overall plot. For example, the first group alternates between recurring shots of the sky (criterion a) and shots introducing the lead characters (criterion b). The second group, as we shall see, follows an identical pattern of recurring shots of a given character in her workplace (criterion a) and shots conveying, among other salient details, a central dramatic conflict that will prove pertinent to the rest of the plot (criterion b). Comparable principles are maintained in the other groups I consider.

No doubt another set of characteristics could be invoked to group the various images and sounds in the film differently, obtaining an alternative set of relations among the constitutive images and/or sounds, but this does not entail that my criteria have been selected arbitrarily. When confronted with the relative challenge (or not) of comprehending a narrative film, one typically scans the said film for salient cues or prominent details: recurring locations and characters (or changes of locations and characters); a given action or line of dialogue that serves to further the plot. In other words, if a character is shown exiting a locale and, in the next shot, arriving at a new locale, one will reasonably expect some continuity in the narrative action; conversely, a sudden change from one location and character to another (as is so frequently the case in "network narratives") should signal the plot is now moving into hitherto unexpected terrains. The act of comprehending narrative films, even those as unorthodox as the cinema of Jean-Luc Godard, involves being able to divide and/or group various shots and/or scenes according to the principles outlined above.

I now turn to the first two groups of shots. After the opening credits, the film begins with alternating shots of the sky (and a jet) and the four principal characters: Isabelle, Hanna, Michel, and Jerzy. In the first shot, the camera pans diagonally up to the left, as the plane flies in the same direction. The music begins in this shot, and carries over into the next shot of Isabelle at the factory. In the third shot, the camera continues panning around the sky, as if searching for the plane, which is no longer in view. After, there is a cut back to one of the main characters: Jerzy is driving in his car (with a woman on a bicycle, by his side). There is a cut back to the sky, with the camera still panning, as if searching for the plane: this time, however, the plane enters the frame. A cut back to the main characters shows Hanna and Michel finishing getting dressed as they leave their room, after which there is a return to a shot of the sky: this time, the plane is absent, but one can see the exhaust trail left behind by its jet.

To begin with, one notes that the shots of the sky display variations akin to those observed by David Bordwell in his aforementioned analysis of Ozu's films. In *An Autumn Afternoon*, Bordwell has characterized the continually unpredictable ordering and reordering of establishing shots as "playful [and] constantly self-correcting."[15] A similar insight applies to the shots of the sky and the plane: first the plane is present in the shot, then absent, then present, and then again absent, albeit with a visible exhaust trail left behind. A kind of amusing suspense is created in the second and third shots of the sky, as to whether or not the panning camera will "find" the plane: in the second shot, it does; in the third, it does not. Moreover, just when it seems a *predictable* pattern can be attributed to the sequencing of these shots (presence, absence, presence, etc.), there is a twist: in the fourth shot, the plane is absent as expected, but an indication of its passage is still visible—that is, the exhaust trail.

One need also consider, moreover, the alternations between the shots of the sky and those introducing the major characters. Commenting on these opening images, Kaja Silverman opines that they "[introduce] us to two of the antitheses which *Passion* will most insistently dismantle: heaven and earth, and truth and fiction."[16] But it seems hardly plausible that images of a plane can be made to stand in for some celestial signification—much less for "truth." It is more fruitful to observe how these shots function with regards to the incipient storyline, and to note that Godard is juxtaposing images which have, alternately, putative narrative and non-narrative functions: the shots of the characters help establish the plot, by introducing us to the dramatis personae; in contrast, the shots of the plane and the sky, while perhaps part of the diegesis, do not.

Another reason for moving beyond Silverman's interpretation is that the juxtaposition of narrative and non-narrative shots adheres to an editing pattern—one may dub it ABAB, with A standing in for the non-narrative, and B for the narrative—which is pursued during the next group of shots. For this second group, we return to a shot of Isabelle at the factory, going about her work. Images of her working are then intercut, over an alternating series of six shots, with scenes from the studio. The studio scenes reveal the various extras posing for a *tableau vivant* and an off-screen dialogue between the producer and the various members of the crew. During the first of these scenes, he asks the script girl (Sophie Loucachensky) to tell him about the story of the film being made. The two subsequent scenes in the studio have the producer asking the same question to Patrick Bonnel and Raoul Coutard. This series of shots ends with a heated argument between the producer and Jerzy.

Here, the same ABAB pattern prevails, such that the "A" (non-narrative) shots are the recurring shots of Isabelle, while the "B" (narrative) shots consist of the images (and soundtrack) set at the studio. In the latter case, one sees images of the production (the *tableau vivant*) and can begin to gauge, through the dialogue, the tempestuous nature of this production: Jerzy (with the consent of his crew) is set on making a film which is plotless, while the producer adamantly reminds them that this procession of *tableaux vivants* must ultimately tell a story. In contrast, the "A" shots of Isabelle at the factory, not unlike the opening shots of the sky, are superfluous to the narrative: once she has been shown at work, there is little need (in terms of advancing the plot) to belabour the point.

A third and a fourth group of shots also lend themselves to comparative analysis. The third group is an abortive conversation between Isabelle and Jerzy, which follows shortly after the aforementioned argument between Jerzy and his producer. The conversation is divided into two shots. In the first shot, Isabelle is running alongside Jerzy's car, while he remains out of the frame. Midway through the conversation, there is a cut to Jerzy, and this time it is Isabelle who is out of the frame. In both shots, the soundtrack is out of sync (Isabelle's and Jerzy's lips are shut, but their voices can be heard; they move their lips, but it does not correspond to the words on the soundtrack; etc.), although the dialogue revolves around Isabelle's pursuit to recruit Jerzy for her protests, and his uneasy refusal.

The fourth group is an equally abortive conversation between Isabelle and one of her (former) colleagues, Magali. Again, there is overt manipulation of the soundtrack: both Isabelle's and Magali's voices are out of sync; hence, when their lips move, either they emit no sound, or the words they appear to be mouthing do not match those on the soundtrack. Again, the conversation is divided into two shots: one of Magali, then one of Isabelle. As well, the shot selection in both this conversation and the above encounter between Jerzy and Isabelle eschew establishing shots and the timing of the cut from one character to the other is arbitrary. In each case, Isabelle and Jerzy, and then later Magali and Isabelle, have already exchanged several words before Godard cuts from one to the other, such that the editing is ultimately autonomous of the recorded dialogue. Finally, dramatically both scenes are similar. In the third group, Isabelle is speaking to Jerzy with regards to her protest faction, and in the fourth group, when Isabelle speaks to Magali, the latter informs her that she is quitting Isabelle's faction. In short, just as the first two groups of shots form a paired set by virtue of their similar stylistic construction, so too do these groups of shots complement one another stylistically and dramatically.

Finally, a fifth group alternates between shots of Isabelle, her co-workers, and a medium two-shot of Isabelle and one of the co-workers.

While each of them talks, as with earlier scenes in the film, the sound is out of sync, such that it is impossible to determine who is saying exactly what, and when (with the possible exception, of course, of Isabelle Huppert). It therefore becomes important to consider the shot selection as adhering to other requirements than the development of the plot. One can identify the shots by letters to arrive at the following scheme: ABBBBC ABB ABC. In this instance, A stands for the shots of Isabelle alone; B, of her co-workers; and C, for the two-shots of Isabelle with her colleague. One can then group the shots into three series which, with one exception, all begin with an "A" shot, are followed by one or more "B" shots, and end with a "C" shot. Moreover, from one series to the next, the number of "B" shots decreases by half: from four, to two, to one.

There is an exception to this pattern in the second series, in which the "C" shot is absent. Its absence can be understood by other proportional requirements that regulate the distribution of shots. If one looks more closely at the "B" shots, one can subdivide them as follows: B1, B2, B3, B4. In this scheme, each number stands for a different co-worker, present in the shot. The above three series can be demarcated as such: A B1–B2–B3–B4 C; A B3–B4; A B3 C. Here, the number of shots in each series is first cut by half, and then repeated: six shots in the first series, and then three, plus three more. Moreover, if one notes the recurrence of shot "B3" in the second and third series, its centrality becomes prominent: in each series, it is preceded and followed by another shot. The absence of the "C" shot can therefore be understood with regards to two potentially conflicting requirements: (a) that series two and three mirror each other, as far as where "B3" is positioned; and (b) that from the first to the third series, the number of "B" shots is continually reduced by half.

Skeptics may balk at the above analysis, but this is to overlook the frequent role counting and arithmetic designs have played in Godard's filmmaking—an aspect of his work subject to prior study.[17] However one cares to interpret this filmmaker's numerical inclinations, what remains indisputable throughout his oeuvre is his seeming mystifying faith in the safety of numbers: that patterning of various kinds, such as those detailed in *Passion*, will provide a semblance of stability to an otherwise a chaotic flux of sounds, images, facts, and figures.

Admittedly, the argumentative thrust of this essay may seem somewhat contrary to that of the other chapters in this volume. To address the parametric cinema of Godard is not so much to commemorate this filmmaker's legacy to modern cinema, as to adumbrate his antecedents. As Bordwell establishes, parametric cinema can be seen as an outgrowth of the formal and stylistic tendencies of, among other artistic currents, mid-twentieth-century serial music and the *nouveau roman*. This strengthens the likelihood that the various precursors of parametric cinema exercised a decisive influence on Godard, who, as per Bordwell's reasonable conjecture, "could not have been unaware of combinatory theories of serial music and the *nouveau roman* when he made *Vivre sa vie*."[18]

This still leaves unanswered the question as to what impact Godard's forays into parametric cinema have had on film. If parametric cinema is something of a minority practice, and is overlooked moreover by most film scholars, the fact remains that it has engaged among the most seminal auteurs of cinematic modernism: Ozu, Tati, Bresson, etc. My contention throughout has been that studying *Passion* not only augments one's understanding of parametric cinema, but also encourages one to take interest in this neglected avenue of research. One need at least consider the possibility that other Godard films might be seen to adhere to the parametric mode. From the elliptical editing in *Breathless* (1960) to the extended tracking shots in *Week-end* (1967) and *Tout va bien* (1972), to, more recently, the video-edited image transitions in the various chapters of *Histoire(s) du cinéma* (1988–1998), it is no secret that Godard's films have long contained stylistic constructions that seek to challenge the viewer's comprehension. Yet it is this aspect of Godard's oeuvre that academics have tended to subordinate to a more philosophically derived hermeneutics of the different ideas, ideologies, and theories as conveyed and/or alluded to in his frequently aphoristic and occasionally fragmentary body of work.[19] Reading the scholarly commentary on this director, the sum impression seems to be that Godard is only ostensibly a *film*maker, using the medium (and art form) of motion pictures in pursuit of loftier intellectual aims.

At the risk of inviting contention, it is time to shift tracks and take a renewed interest in Godard's cinema as cinema—from the standpoint of form and style. After all, Isabelle's plea to her colleagues, in *Passion*, is expressed in the merest of visual terms: "*il faut voir*." To learn to look at the cinema anew: ultimately, this may be the most enduring of all Godard's legacies to the seventh art.

NOTES

1 David Bordwell, *Narration in the Fiction Film* (Madison: University of Wisconsin Press, 1985), 275.

2 Ibid., 281.

3 Ibid.

4 Cited in Bordwell, *Narration in the Fiction Film*, 281.

5 Ibid., 275. The term comes from Tynianov, which Bordwell cites as "style-centered."

6 David Bordwell, *Making Meaning: Inference and Rhetoric in the Interpretation of Cinema* (Cambridge, MA: Harvard University Press, 1989), xiii.

7 See Kristin Thompson, *Breaking the Glass Armor: Neoformalist Film Analysis* (Princeton, NJ: Princeton University Press, 1988), and David Bordwell, *Poetics of Cinema* (New York: Routledge, 2008), 11–55, for their respective explications of these scholarly approaches.

8 In Bordwell's words: "Godard ... raises as does no other director the possibility of a sheerly capricious or arbitrary use of technique." *Narration in the Fiction Film*, 312. Kristin Thompson has also examined the parametric constructions in Godard's *Sauve qui peut (la vie)* (1979), in *Breaking the Glass Armor*, 263–88.

9 Bordwell, *Narration in the Fiction Film*, 285.

10 Ibid.

11 Ibid., 286.

12 Ibid., 287.

13 Jean-Luc Godard, *Godard on Godard: Critical Writings by Jean-Luc Godard*, ed. Jean Narboni and Tom Milne (New York: Viking, 1972), 39–40.

14 Thompson, *Breaking the Glass Armor*, 283.

15 Bordwell, *Narration in the Fiction Film*, 287.

16 Kaja Silverman and Harun Farocki, *Speaking about Godard* (New York: New York University Press, 1998), 172.

17 See Richard Neer, "Godard Counts," *Critical Inquiry* 34, no. 1 (September 2007): 135–73. Among other examples, Neer lists the titles of Godard's films (e.g., *One Plus One*, 1968; *Numéro deux*, 1975), as well as passages from his articles (in "My Approach in Four Movements," Godard states: "1 + 2 + 3 = 4"). See particularly Neer, "Godard Counts," 141–42.

18 Bordwell, *Narration in the Fiction Film*, 281.

19 For instances of this, especially in connection to *Passion*, see Silverman and Farocki, *Speaking about Godard*, 170–96, and Jean-Louis Leutrat, *Des traces qui nous ressemblent: "Passion" de Jean-Luc Godard* (Paris: Éditions Comp'Act, 1990).

BIBLIOGRAPHY

Bordwell, David. *Making Meaning: Inference and Rhetoric in the Interpretation of Cinema*. Cambridge, MA: Harvard University Press, 1989.

———. *Narration in the Fiction Film*. Madison: University of Wisconsin Press, 1985.

———. *Poetics of Cinema*. New York: Routledge, 2008.

Godard, Jean-Luc. *Godard on Godard: Critical Writings by Jean-Luc Godard*. Edited by Jean Narboni and Tom Milne. New York: Viking, 1972.

Leutrat, Jean-Louis. *Des traces qui nous ressemblent: "Passion" de Jean-Luc Godard*. Paris: Éditions Comp'Act, 1990.

Neer, Richard. "Godard Counts." *Critical Inquiry* 34, no. 1 (September 2007): 135–73.

Silverman, Kaja, and Harun Farocki. *Speaking about Godard*. New York: New York University Press, 1998.

Thompson, Kristin. *Breaking the Glass Armor: Neoformalist Film Analysis*. Princeton, NJ: Princeton University Press, 1988.

13

"A Place of Active Judgment": Parametric Narration in the Work of Jean-Luc Godard and Ian Wallace

Timothy Long

IN A RECENT interview, Ian Wallace concisely identified the goal of his photo-collage paintings: "they are a place of active judgment."[1] An internationally recognized member of the "Vancouver School" of photo-based art, Wallace has developed a practice over the past three decades that combines monochrome painting and documentary photography. While the inspirations for his practice are multiple, one source of particular interest is the filmmaking of Jean-Luc Godard.[2] Wallace has followed Godard's cinema since the early 1960s and in recent years he has incorporated stills from selected films into the paintings of his *Masculin/Féminin* series (see Fig. 13.1), which derives its title from the Godard film of the same name. While these cinematic quotations readily connect Wallace to Godard on a thematic plane, they also participate in a pictorial strategy that is aligned with the filmmaker's structural approach. The concept of "parametric narration," despite its specific application to film theory, offers a productive way to discuss the generic and formal practices that are shared by artist and filmmaker.[3] First elaborated by David Bordwell in his 1985 publication *Narration in the Fiction Film*, parametric narration defines a category of hybrid filmmakers who combine the narrative conventions of the European art film with the formal experimentation of the avant-garde filmmaking tradition.[4] Both artist and auteur use "parametric" devices to break the frames of painting and cinema respectively to create for the viewer "a place of active judgment." The focus for this discussion will be Jean-Luc Godard's films *Masculin féminin* (1966) and *Le Mépris* (1963) and a new series of paintings by Wallace based on these two films—paintings that situate the question of judgment in relation to the cinematic and social construction of gender binaries.[5] Though not referenced specifically in Wallace's paintings, the 1986 video *Soft and Hard (A Soft Conversation on Hard Subjects)* by Godard and fellow filmmaker Anne-Marie Miéville offers

Fig. 13.1 *Installation view of* Ian Wallace: Masculin/Féminin, *MacKenzie Art Gallery, Regina, Canada, September 4, 2010, to January 23, 2011. (Photo by Don Hall, courtesy of the MacKenzie Art Gallery)*

further points of comparison that take into account Godard's evolving approach to modes of image production and reception and the thematic of gender relationships.[6]

One of the striking features of the films of Jean-Luc Godard is the frequency of their allusions to the work of painters, from Rembrandt to Yves Klein, and Velasquez to Andy Warhol. The references are repeated and insistent and demonstrate the extent to which Godard identifies with the medium. As film historian Sally Shafto has pointed out, before turning to cinema Godard wanted to become a painter, an interest that carried through to his filmmaking career; indeed, at the time of the release of *À bout de souffle* (1960) he commented in an interview: "I work like a painter."[7] In summarizing Godard's creative process, Jacques Aumont declares: "Painting is the paradigm for solitary art making, and the painter thus a paradigm for creation."[8] Not surprisingly, the reception of his films has been particularly strong in the visual arts, as witnessed by his 1992 retrospective *Jean-Luc Godard: Son + Image 1974–1991* at the Museum of Modern Art in New York and, more recently, the controversial *Voyage(s) en Utopie, Jean-Luc Godard, 1946–2006* at the Centre Georges Pompidou in 2006.

However, of even greater interest to this investigation is how critical discussions of Godard's technique have resorted to analogies from the language of painting to articulate key ideas. David Bordwell is exemplary in this regard. In developing his concept of parametric narration, he points to the model of Cubist still life to explain how stylistic interventions have the effect of subordinating perceptual and cognitive coherence of the narration to the "spatial organization of the whole."[9] This comparison is further developed in his discussion of Godard's collage aesthetic, an approach manifest in a variety of unorthodox techniques, such as the use of repeated sound or image elements or the insertion of temporal discontinuities. Collage results in a "spatialization" of narration, although the incredible variety and frequent arbitrariness of Godard's technique leads Bordwell to wonder whether any organizational principle is discernible to the spectator. Where collage falters as an explanatory key, Bordwell is able to find one in yet another analogy drawn from visual art: the palimpsest, or artistic practice of leaving in the finished artwork signs of earlier stages of the act of creation. "Godard is like a painter who leaves a pencil grid or a patch of underpainting visible in the finished picture, not only as a compositional element but also as a fastidiously preserved sign of process."[10] This analogy offers, for Bordwell, an answer to the charge of arbitrariness, because, as in a painting, "each inscription bears witness to one identifiable hand."[11]

In the other direction, the connections of painter to filmmaker are equally abundant. Wallace is among the many artists to be inspired directly or indirectly by Godard. One need only think of the recent proliferation of video installations that respond to Godard's 1968 portrait of the Rolling Stones, *One Plus One (Sympathy for the Devil).*[12] But Wallace's interest is not a recent phenomenon. As a high school student, he saw *À bout de souffle* in its initial release, starting a lifelong fascination with Godard and other New Wave filmmakers. And, just as Godard at one time wanted to be a painter, so Wallace wanted to be a filmmaker, to the extent of applying, if unsuccessfully, to the American Film Institute in 1970.

Wallace's early interest in cinema has never dissipated and, over the course of his development, he has made frequent reference to the language of film. A quick survey of his career reveals the breadth of this engagement. In one of his earliest photo-based conceptual works, *Pan Am Scan* (1970), Wallace structures his photo-montage to mirror the viewpoint of a slowly panning camera. A filmic arrangement of a sequence of images reappears in *An Attack on Literature* (1975) with its implication of a narrative fiction. Later works, such as *In the Museum (the Musée d'Orsay series)* (1988), take up a filmic sequence of shots that progressively zoom in from a panoramic cityscape to a tight close-up of a painting. *The Cinema Museum, Lodz, Poland* (1990–91) engages the material history of film itself, both in its double reverse-shot format and in its content: the props, posters, and equipment that are the production apparatus of the film industry. However, nowhere

Fig. 13.2 *Ian Wallace, I Remember You, 2010, photolaminate with acrylic on canvas, 243 x 183 cm. (Courtesy of the artist and Catriona Jeffries Gallery, Vancouver. Photo by Scott Massey)*

is Wallace's engagement with cinema more obvious than in his *Masculin/Féminin* series which he began in 1987 with paintings incorporating stills from the New Wave cinema of Godard, Roberto Rossellini, and Michelangelo Antonioni, and which he has continued most recently with paintings based exclusively on two early films by Godard.

In his *Masculin/Féminin* series, Wallace employs a range of parametric strategies that are analogous to those used by the filmmaker. A close analysis of the paintings reveals connections to Godard on a number of levels. Although earlier works in the *Masculin/Féminin* series at times feature a

Fig. 13.3 *Ian Wallace, I Know the Way, 2010, photolaminate with acrylic on canvas, 243 x 183 cm. (Courtesy of the artist and Catriona Jeffries Gallery, Vancouver. Photo by Scott Massey)*

single still, Wallace's standard practice has been to incorporate two stills in an offset vertical arrangement, as in the paintings *I Remember You* and *I Know the Way* (see Figs. 13.2 and 13.3). The appearance of the two frames together suggests a temporal and spatial relationship; however, they are frequently unrelated in time or setting, although the upper frame is usually from a point earlier in the film. These disjunctions echo the spatial disruptions created by Godard's interspersing of unrelated street scenes in *Masculin féminin* and the temporal disorderings introduced by the jump-cut technique in general. In the inkjet studies for the paintings, a different technique is employed, according to which the same frame is cut in two and reversed (see Fig. 13.4). This technique replicates, at least on the surface, the effect of a conventional shot/reverse shot editing sequence, a filmic technique generally eschewed by Godard. However, by presenting both frames simultaneously, an effect is created that runs counter to its cinematic counterpart. Instead of creating the impression of two gazes converging, the painting presents characters whose sight lines ultimately diverge, emphasizing the subtext of the scenes, which is the disconnection between male and female points of view. This strategy makes manifest

Fig. 13.4 *Ian Wallace,* Enlarged Inkjet Study for Masculin/Féminin VI, *2010, inkjet on paper, edition of 3, 119 x 89 cm. (Courtesy of the artist and Catriona Jeffries Gallery, Vancouver)*

Fig. 13.5 *Ian Wallace,* Enlarged Inkjet Study for Masculin/Féminin I, *2010, inkjet on paper, edition of 3, 119 x 89 cm. (Courtesy of the artist and Catriona Jeffries Gallery, Vancouver)*

what is often implied in Godard's cinematography, such as the placement of characters at the extreme edges of the frame in the opening scenes of *Masculin féminin* (see Fig. 13.5), or the use of back-and-forth pans across an intervening object, as in the famous lamp scene in *Le Mépris* (see Fig. 13.6).

The use of subtitles offers a further point of contact. In Wallace's paintings based on *Masculin féminin*, the subtitles incorporated into the stills are not from the film at all, but were invented by the artist. In adopting this approach, Wallace consciously references Godard's practice of adding dialogue to scenes after the fact, as in the opening scenes of *Vivre sa vie* (1962). The effect of Wallace's assigned subtitles is disorienting, inviting the viewer to engage in a double game of creating relations between image and text,

Fig. 13.6 *Ian Wallace,* Enlarged Inkjet Study for Le Mépris VI, *2010, inkjet on paper, edition of 3, 119 x 89 cm. (Courtesy of the artist and Catriona Jeffries Gallery, Vancouver)*

and between film and painting. Take, for instance, the canvas *Who Will I Become?* (see Fig. 13.7). Wallace's subtitle for the upper image, "Who will I become?" may be read as a summary of Paul's (Jean-Pierre Léaud) existential poem of ennui and alienation, while the subtitle for the lower image, "You forgot me," may be taken as Madeleine's (Chantal Goya) recognition that, despite Paul's interest in her, he is essentially self-absorbed in his angst-filled ruminations. However, it is equally possible to read the subtitles as the voice of the person outside the frame. "Who will I become?" thus becomes

Fig. 13.7 *Ian Wallace,* Who Will I Become? *2010, photolaminate with acrylic on canvas, 243 x 183 cm. (Courtesy of the artist and Catriona Jeffries Gallery, Vancouver. Photo by Scott Massey)*

Madeleine's question about her career, while "You forgot me" now reads as a statement of Paul's self-doubt regarding her interest in him. Each of the three paintings based on *Masculin féminin* shares this structure: one subtitle a question, the other a declaration. In each case, the subtitles remain propositions of indefinite origins, thus upsetting the conventional association of passivity with a female perspective and assertiveness with a male perspective.

Fig. 13.8 *Ian Wallace,* Le Mépris (Divisions In Space), *2010, photolaminate with acrylic on canvas, 243 x 183 cm. (Courtesy of the artist and Catriona Jeffries Gallery, Vancouver. Photo by Scott Massey)*

In the paintings based on *Le Mépris*, by contrast, the subtitles are original to the film (or at least as it was distributed on VHS tape in North America). However, in this case it is not the subtitles, but another introduced element that disorients the viewer. Instead of capturing stills from DVD, Wallace has chosen to photograph the film as it appeared on the screen of a conventional (4:3 ratio) CRT monitor. Through this choice, Wallace introduces three elements: the curvature of the screen, the uncropped black edges of the monitor, and the interference bands of the video frame caught in mid-scan. These last elements obscure the image and divide the screen horizontally. As the

Fig. 13.9 *Ian Wallace,* Le Mépris (Use Your Own Ideas), *2010, photolaminate with acrylic on canvas, 243 x 183 cm. (Courtesy of the artist and Catriona Jeffries Gallery, Vancouver. Photo by Scott Massey)*

title of the painting *Le Mépris (Divisions in Space)* declares, these bands are related to the other techniques used by Wallace to emphasize spatial divisions between the images and characters (see Fig. 13.8). But the bands are also analogous to the wide array of devices used by Godard to interrupt vision and make the viewer aware of the mediated nature of the filmic image. The effect is to reinscribe the distancing that permeates *Le Mépris*. Wallace's *Le Mépris (Use Your Own Ideas)* focuses on Paul's (Michel Piccoli) passivity—how he borrows ideas, how he mirrors his wife's desires, how he does both in bad faith (Fig. 13.9). *Le Mépris (Divisions in Space)* shows the

Fig. 13.10 *Ian Wallace,* Le Mépris (The Contempt Scene), *2010, photolaminate with acrylic on canvas, 243 x 183 cm. (Courtesy of the artist and Catriona Jeffries Gallery, Vancouver. Photo by Scott Massey)*

characters absorbed in thought: Camille (Brigitte Bardot) deep in reflection on the toilet, Paul brooding at his typewriter, and both thinking about how the other thinks about them. *Le Mépris (The Contempt Scene)* features medium distance shots of figures looking or moving off screen (Fig. 13.10). These are conversations at a distance, of desires moving apart.

Looking beyond the incorporation of filmic elements, Wallace's distinctive method of combining photographic images with monochrome abstraction shows close affinities with Godard's structural strategies. In the place of a Godardian union of art-film narration and avant-garde technique, Wallace brings together the representational conventions of photography with the formal experimentation of the modernist avant-garde. Interestingly, as Sally Shafto has demonstrated, Godard's own negotiation between abstraction and figuration owes much to his interest in painting, particularly the work of Nicolas de Staël.[13] Shafto's analysis, however, falls short when it comes to addressing the larger question: what is produced by Godard's parametric approach beyond a novel aesthetic form? This is a criticism which might be levelled equally at Bordwell. By contrast, the broader intention behind Wallace's combination of monochrome abstraction and photography, a combination which has marked his work since the 1980s, is well defined and points to an answer to this question of purpose. For Wallace, the monochrome represents a pictorial "ground zero," replete with the utopian possibilities of transcendence. Photography, on the other hand, offers narrative possibilities that derive from its indexical relation to reality. As Wallace puts it, photography allows the viewer to "think the world through an image of the world."[14] Combined, the two modes have a critical relationship to one another. The rhetorical power of photography critiques the limits of aesthetic judgment and what is possible as a work of art. At the same time, abstraction confronts the dominance of photography, film, and media, its symbolic negation bringing into question the authoritative model of reality. "The recuperation of the monochrome," Wallace asserts, "is not so much a desire to return to the emblem of an unachievable ideality as to reground photography within the problematic of painting and return it to a question of limits."[15] This statement is analogous to Godard's project, which Bordwell characterizes as the conflict between style and narration. Narrative fiction is regrounded within this problematic of filmmaking and returns filmmaking to a question of its limits, even as the basis for the authority of narrative fiction is brought into question. Just as Wallace asks, "What is possible as a painting," Godard asks, "What is possible as a film?" And, just as Wallace asks, "What is possible to think through art," Godard asks, "What is possible to think through cinema?"

These are fundamental issues and they point to a questioning of the primary set of relationships that govern the reception of images: the relationship of the content to the frame and of the frame to the audience which is assembled before it. In this regard, it is important to affirm the essential continuity of the history of the frame as shared by both painting and film. From the religious icon, to the Renaissance picture window, to the Cubist breakdown of one-point perspective, to the modernist monochrome, the frame has been essential for producing presence. Jacques Derrida, in an essay on the nature of frames notes that "the *parergon* [or frame] is a form which has as its traditional determination not that it stands out but that it disappears, buries itself, effaces itself, melts away at the moment when it deploys its greatest energy."[16] Following the cultural anthropology of René

Girard, one could argue that the frame is essentially a sacrificial mechanism; the presence it produces derives from the same violent exclusionary logic that drives other religious and cultural forms.[17] Just as scapegoating yields a sacred presence through the forcible expulsion of a single victim from the collective, so the frame yields aesthetic presence through the exclusion of the image from the mundane world around it. This is most readily apparent in the iconic images of antiquity—deific, imperial, mortuary—where the linkage between the image and the sacrificial victim is only at one remove. It is the era of art which transmutes this image, secularizes it, trading sacred presence for the aura of art. In the process, the role of the image as a controller of collective behaviour is transformed. The ritualized redirection of the rivalrous desires of the collective through sacrificial expulsion is subsumed under the sign of the aesthetic, through which potential sources of conflicting desire—sexual, political, or economic—are now are mediated by the auratic function of the frame.

As an inheritor of the Western image tradition, film also participates in the auratic regime, despite Walter Benjamin's argument claiming a new, non-auratic relation to the collective gaze.[18] Film's participation in this lineage is epitomized by the projection-identification mechanism of classical cinema, which, far from resulting in an emancipated collective of free individuals, as Benjamin hoped, has more often resulted in the dream-like passivity of consumers of mass entertainment. This is the problem of "dark spectatorship," of the screen that must darken in order to bear the image. The perspectival system represented by cinema's architecture and technical apparatus has remained concealed with only a few exceptions, such as the architectural cinema projects of Erwin Piscator, Johannes Duiker, and Dan Graham.[19]

To return to Godard, his films address the frame of cinema on a number of levels. Most noticeable is the device of the *mise en abyme* of characters attending a film, as in *Masculin féminin,* or making a film, as in *Le Mépris.* In both cases, the reconciling frame of cinema is shown to be a house divided, an ineffective mediator between the sexes. More profoundly, Godard's collage aesthetic accomplishes what Cubism did a half-century earlier—to open up the frame to multiple points of view. Just as Picasso and Braque shattered the dream of a single, omnipotent viewer, so Godard's films, with their constantly shifting points of reference, are subject to multiple, non-cohesive readings. Similarly, Godard's aesthetic of the palimpsest achieves what Pop art did—to show art as a mediated object, pre-processed desire that already incorporates the collective as an object of mass consumption. Thus, Godard's films render impossible the dream of a unified, collective audience, even as they use the format and conventions designed for this form of spectatorship.

The insights of Godard's early films regarding the place of the viewer continue to resonate, not only in Wallace's paintings, which look back to a moment in the 1960s when traditional roles and forms of masculinity were being brought into question, but also in Godard's more recent video essays. Of particular interest is Godard's 1986 video, *Soft and Hard (A Soft Conversation on Hard Subjects)*, which he co-directed with his partner and fellow filmmaker, Anne-Marie Miéville. The video begins with a deconstruction of the basic elements of narrative film: image versus sound, title versus voice-over, male narrator versus female narrator, voice-over versus music. The purpose of this parametric prologue is made clear by the narration when the question of "objects versus subjects" is introduced. This is a very personal question for Godard and Miéville and one that is framed as an interrogation of their relationship: "all belonging to him" versus "whom did he belong to." At the same time, it is a world-historical question, as the narrators intone: "It was still the time of massacres in Beirut, flights to Mars and Venus, television, the dollar's rise, the Black Forest burning, McEnroe's defeat, fifth-generation computers, famine in Africa, and the last cinema show." The events in this list are touched upon later in the conversation between Godard and Miéville, a dialogue in which they compare their individual histories of filmmaking. Despite humorous interludes, including a telling scene in which Miéville irons the laundry while a tennis-racket-swinging Godard quips, "I'm making films instead of children," the tone is reflective (Fig. 13.11). By the end of their conversation, which echoes in its setting the famous dialogue between Michel Piccoli

Fig. 13.11 *Still from* Soft and Hard, *a film by Jean-Luc Godard. (Photo © 1986 Gaumont)*

Fig. 13.12 *Still from* Soft and Hard, *a film by Jean-Luc Godard. (Photo © 1986 Gaumont)*

and Brigitte Bardot in *Le Mépris* (note the intervening lamp) (Fig. 13.12), it becomes clear what the problem is. "All belonging to him" refers to Godard's male privilege and authoritative voice, while "whom did he belong to" refers to Miéville's need for validation and the space to explore her own perspective.

In a striking final image, their dialogue is restated in visual terms, again with a direct reference to *Le Mépris*, a film about the problems of making a film. Miéville and Godard together cast a shadow on a wall overtop of a projection of the opening scene of *Le Mépris*—a scene that resonates with the question of point of view and the mechanics of film-making (Fig. 13.13). Both inside and outside the frame, an indexical trace of the body and a figure of symbolic transcendence (a camera eye or the angel Gabriel!), their shadows unite, for a brief moment, abstraction and figuration, and thus perform the very tasks that Wallace sets for his paintings. Just as the shadows cast by Godard and Miéville superimpose their positions onto the screen, so the stills and subtitles selected by Wallace project male and female perspectives onto the space of the canvas, united, but held separate, by the solidus of the monochrome field in which they float. Most significantly, the space before the cinematic frame is opened up as a place of questioning, with the possibility of projections other than that of the camera-projector apparatus. In this gesture, which is both physical

Fig. 13.13 *Still from* Soft and Hard, *a film by Jean-Luc Godard. (Photo © 1986 Gaumont)*

and cinematic, we have a confirmation that the task of parametric narration is never complete, and that the approach must be renewed continually. Only this way will it be possible to create for viewers of both cinema and painting that elusive space: "a place of active judgment."

NOTES

1   Ian Wallace, interview with the author, Vancouver, January 25, 2010. Subsequent quotations from the artist, as well as biographical details, are taken from this interview. I wish to thank the artist for his insights and comments during the preparation of this essay.

2   For an informative discussion of Wallace's response to Godard's treatment of gender themes, see Cindy Richmond, *Ian Wallace: Masculin/Féminin*, exhibition catalogue (Montreal: Leonard and Bina Ellen Art Gallery, Concordia University, 1997).

3   I would like to thank to Dr. Philippe Mather of Campion College, University of Regina, who introduced me to this concept.

4   David Bordwell, *Narration in Fiction Film* (Madison: University of Wisconsin Press, 1985).

5   The paintings were the subject of the exhibition *Ian Wallace: Masculin/Féminin* (September 4, 2010–January 23, 2011), curated by the author for the MacKenzie Art Gallery and presented in conjunction with the symposium *Sonimage: The Legacies of Jean-Luc Godard* (September 16–18, 2010). I wish to thank Jeannie Mah and Heather Hodgson for suggesting the idea for the exhibition and for their initial invitation to participate in the symposium.

6   Screenings of *Soft and Hard* were presented at the MacKenzie Art Gallery in conjunction with the *Sonimage* symposium and the exhibition *Ian Wallace: Masculin/Féminin*.

7   See Sally Shafto, "Leap into the Void: Godard and the Painter," *Senses of Cinema*, 39 (2006), http://www.sensesofcinema.com/2006/39/godard_de_stael; and "Filmmakers Painting: The Case of Jean-Luc Godard," *Art Papers* 22, no. 5 (September–October 1998): 24.

8   Jacques Aumont, cited in Sally Shafto, "Artist as Christ/Artist as God-the-Father: Religion in the Cinema of Philippe Garrel and Jean-Luc Godard," *Film History*, 14, no. 2 (2002): 145.

9   Bordwell, *Narration in the Fiction Film*, 283.

10 Ibid., 332.

11 Ibid.

12 Recent examples of works inspired by Godard's *One Plus One (Sympathy for the Devil)* include video installations by Adam Pendleton, Hadley + Maxwell, and Aïda Ruilova.

13 Shafto, "Leap into the Void."

14 Ian Wallace, "Photography and the Monochrome (Short Revised Version)," in *Ian Wallace: A Literature of Images*, ed. Monika Szewczyk, exhibition catalogue (Berlin: Sternberg Press, 2008), 170.

15 Ibid., 171.

16 Jacques Derrida, *The Truth in Painting*, trans. Geoff Bennington and Ian McLeod (Chicago: University of Chicago Press, 1987), 61.

17 For an extended version of this argument, see the author's essay (entitled "Theatroclasm") in *Theatroclasm: Mirrors, Mimesis and the Place of the Viewer*, ed. Timothy Long, exhibition catalogue (Regina, SK: MacKenzie Art Gallery, 2009), 9–27.

18 Walter Benjamin, "The Work of Art in the Age of Mechanical Reproduction," in *Illuminations*, ed. Hannah Arendt, trans. Harry Zohn (New York: Schocken Books, 2007), 217–51.

19 For a discussion of Graham's projects in relation to the work of Duiker, see Dan Graham, "Cinema 1981," in *Dan Graham Works 1965–2000*, ed. Marianne Brouwer, exhibition catalogue (Düsseldorf: Richter Verlag, 2001), 199–201.

BIBLIOGRAPHY

Benjamin, Walter. "The Work of Art in the Age of Mechanical Reproduction." In *Illuminations*, edited by Hannah Arendt, translated by Harry Zohn, 217–51. New York: Schocken Books, 2007.

Bordwell, David. *Narration in the Fiction Film*. Madison: University of Wisconsin Press, 1985.

Derrida, Jacques. *The Truth in Painting*. Translated by Geoff Bennington and Ian McLeod. Chicago: University of Chicago Press, 1987.

Graham, Dan. "Cinema 1981." In *Dan Graham Works 1965–2000*, edited by Marianne Brouwer, exhibition catalogue, 199–201. Düsseldorf: Richter Verlag, 2001.

Long, Timothy, ed. *Theatroclasm: Mirrors, Mimesis and the Place of the Viewer*, exhibition catalogue. Regina, SK: MacKenzie Art Gallery, 2009.

Richmond, Cindy. *Ian Wallace: Masculin/Féminin*, exhibition catalogue. Montreal: Leonard and Bina Ellen Art Gallery, Concordia University, 1997.

Shafto, Sally. "Artist as Christ/Artist as God-the-Father: Religion in the Cinema of Philippe Garrel and Jean-Luc Godard." *Film History* 14, no. 2 (2002): 142–57.

———. "Filmmakers Painting: The Case of Jean-Luc Godard." *Art Papers* 22, no. 5 (September–October 1998): 24.

———. "Leap into the Void: Godard and the Painter." *Senses of Cinema* 39 (2006). http://www.sensesofcinema.com/2006/39/godard_de_stael.

Wallace, Ian. "Photography and the Monochrome (Short Revised Version)." In *Ian Wallace: A Literature of Images*, edited by Monika Szewczk, exhibition catalogue. Berlin: Sternberg Press, 2008.

14

Godard's Utopia(s) or the Performance of Failure

André Habib

AFTER FOUR YEARS of intensive labour, after much talk and many post-ponements, Jean-Luc Godard's long-awaited Pompidou exhibition *Voyage(s) en utopie, JLG, 1946–2006, À la recherche d'un théorème perdu* opened on May 11, 2006, and was met with skepticism and dismay even among his friends in the milieu. Antoine de Baecque would write in *Libération*: "*Godard est une catastrophe et il en est fier.*"[1] Crowds gathered to witness what a great majority of critics and the press too quickly labelled an utter failure.[2]

Fig. 14.1 "Ce qui peut être montré ne peut être dit" *(What can be shown cannot be said), Ludwig Wittgenstein. (Courtesy Jean-Luc Godard,* Voyage[s] en utopie *[2006], Centre Georges-Pompidou [view of the exhibit]. Photo by Michael Witt)*

The visitor was welcomed by two olive trees (bought at great cost apparently) and a Wittgensteinian sentence written by hand directly on the wall: "*Ce qui peut être montré ne peut être dit*" (What can be shown cannot be said) (see Fig. 14.1). Side by side, there were two reproductions of the same Fragonard painting (*Le verrou* [1774–78], in which a young man is putting the lock on a door in order to prevent the young women he is with from escaping)[3] and a black and white image taken from the 1939 version of *The Cat and the Canary*[4] with—appropriately—Paulette Goddard entering a room (through the back) where a horrifying character is hiding (in the front). As very often in Godard's work (*Histoire[s] du cinéma* for instance), one simply needs to enumerate and describe the elements that come into play in his composition in order to set in motion the web of their possible interpretations. He sets up here an elaborate interspace of reflection on the confrontation between showing and saying, revealing and hiding (*The Secret Behind the Door* could have been the subtitle of the montage); a young girl enters a room as another tries to escape (shot/counter-shot)—as we are about to enter a room (Godard seems to say "abandon all hope, ye who enter here").[5] There was another door (in red metal), placed against the wall, set alongside wood panels, with four details from famous portraits of female subjects (Vermeer's *Girl with a Pearl Earring* [c. 1665], da Vinci's *Madonna* [c. 1490], his *Portrait of Cecilia Galleran* [1489–90], and La Tour's *The Cheat* [1620s], in a Warburgian visual montage. Before entering the gallery proper, pinned on the wall, one could also read this warning sign (next to a crossed-out image of the initial exhibition project) (see Fig. 14.2):

> *Le centre Pompidou a décidé de ne pas réaliser le projet d'exposition* Collage(s) de France, archéologie du cinéma, *d'après JLG, en raison de difficultés* ~~financières, techniques et~~ *artistiques qu'il présentait, et de la remplacer par un autre projet antérieurement envisagé par Jean-Luc Godard et intitulé* Voyage(s) en utopie—Jean-Luc Godard 1946–2006. *Ce second projet inclut la présentation partielle ou complète de la maquette de* Collage(s) de France. *JLG et Péripheria ont agréé la décision du Centre Pompidou*[6].

The baffled visitor who then entered the 1,100 square metres of the Galerie Sud, divided into three distinct spaces—*Avant-hier (avoir été) (salle 2), Hier (avoir) (salle 3), Aujourd'hui (être) (salle 1)*—(see Fig. 14.3)—was engulfed in a noisy, multi-layered, maze-like accumulation of quotidian objects (chairs, beds, tables, desks); writing on the walls and on the floor (an unattributed quote by Bergson, a verse by Cuban poet José Lezama Lima);[7] film excerpts presented on television sets, iPods (a clip from *The Searchers*, inside one of the scale models), or plasma screens (in the room *Hier*, some of Godard's mainly late-1960s and '70s films [*Vent d'Est, One Parellel Movie* (with

Fig. 14.2 *"The exhibition* Collage(s) de France, archéologie du cinéma, d'après JLG has been replaced by Voyage(s) en utopie—Jean-Luc Godard 1946–2006." *(Courtesy Jean-Luc Godard,* Voyage[s] en utopie *[2006], Centre Georges-Pompidou [view of the exhibit]. Photo by Michael Witt)*

Fig. 14.3 *General view of* salle 2, Avant-hier. *(Courtesy Jean-Luc Godard,* Voyage[s] en utopie *[2006], Centre Georges-Pompidou [view of the exhibit]. Photo by Michael Witt)*

Pennebaker), *Week-end, One + One*], as well as *JLG/JLG*, Miéville's *Après la réconciliation* and *Nous sommes tous encore ici*; in *Avant-hier*, in a corner of the room, one could find *Vrai faux passeport*, made especially for the exhibit and, on tiny screens, other films, hung like paintings: *Une bonne à tout faire, Je vous salue Sarajevo, Ecce Homo*, clips from *The Old Place*, etc.); and in *Hier* one could also find clips from fellow filmmakers such as Welles (*Don Quixote*), Dovjenko (*Arsenal*) Rossellini (*The Messiah*), Paradjanov (*The Colour of Pomegranates*).

There was also a group of French directors amidst a forest of plants: Guitry (*Faisons un rêve*), Bresson (*Au hasard Balthazar*), Cocteau (*Le Sang d'un poète*), Leenhardt (*Les Dernières Vacances*), Renoir (*Éléna et les hommes*), Miéville (*Bob le flambeur*); side by side, one found Ray (*Johnny Guitar*) and Donen (*On the Town*), and, at the opposite side of the room, Lang's *Testament of Dr. Mabuse*, Wilder, Ulmer, and Siodmak's *Menschen am Sonntag*, etc. (Fig. 14.4).

On the other side, in the *Aujourd'hui* room, was Ridley Scott's *Black Hawk Down*, Téchiné's *Barocco*, Borderie's *La Môme vert-de-gris*, gay pornography, cable TV (two screens lying flat on a table hooked up to Eurosport and TF1); along with scaffolds (flipped on their sides), potted plants (with

Fig. 14.4 *A group of French directors amidst plants in* salle 3, Hier. *(Courtesy Jean-Luc Godard,* Voyage[s] en utopie *[2006], Centre Georges-Pompidou [view of the exhibit]. Photo by Michael Witt)*

the price tags still hanging), bags of soil, books (Bazin's *Qu'est-ce que le cinéma?*, Schopenhauer's *The World as Will and Representation*, Chandler's *The Long Goodbye*), wires hanging from the ceiling, a broom, and various types of debris, unfinished flooring, a barbed-wire fence, a cheap reproduction of an Egyptian sculpture, an homage to Duchamp (*readymades*, a "totem" composed of a tall speaker, a bottle opener, a bicycle wheel, and a book on Freud entitled *Lieux, visages, objets*), an electric train carrying tennis balls, bananas, oranges, and cigars (in Godardian idiolect, this is the train that leads from la Ciotat to Auschwitz [Fig. 14.5], and, appropriately, connects in the exhibit the rooms *Hier* and *Avant-hier*, but doesn't reach *Aujourd'hui*), original paintings by Matisse (*La Blouse roumaine* [1940]), De Staël (*Les Musiciens* [1952]) and Hans Hartung (*P.1960–112*), etchings by Goya (*The Disasters of War* [1810–20], *Aun aprendo* ["I am still learning," 1824–28]), equations ($x+3=1$), a wall of crosses (croix de Lorraine, a David's cross, Symbols of the Crusades, the Croix de Malte, nazi swastikas), a dialogue between Degas and Manet concerning the telephone ("Je ne marche pas," says Degas, next to a reproduction of a Giacometti sculpture showing a man in motion), a typewriter, envelopes on which one could read "plus

Fig. 14.5 *The train from la Ciotat to Auschwitz in salle 3, Hier. (Courtesy Jean-Luc Godard,* Voyage[s] en utopie *[2006], Centre Georges-Pompidou [view of the exhibit]. Photo by Michael Witt)*

jamais ça," "les lendemains qui chantent," "l'appel de Stockholm"[8] on a scale (appeals that were never sent, never received, promises that bear little weight), as well as, throughout the three rooms, the nine scale models (often in different versions and formats) of what this exhibition was supposed to be and of which only this incredibly complex and vertiginous array of ruins remains.

The idea for the Paris exhibition was initiated in 2002 under the patronage of Dominique Païni, curator of the Hitchcock (2002) as well as the Cocteau (2003) exhibits (that Godard admired), ex-director of the Cinemathèque française and of the film department at the Louvre. What had been initially announced in late 2002 as a twelve- and then nine-episode ("*la preuve par neuf*") video-essay (in the spirit of Godard's long-time desire to run a TV channel, as Païni suggests)[9] that was to unfold over a period of nine months in a museum (importantly, not in a cinema space), *Collage(s) de France* (often accompanied by the subtitle *Archéologie du cinéma d'après JLG*) had been transformed very quickly in 2003–2004 into a nine-room exhibition (accompanied by seven films, still the "*preuve par neuf*"), as a "*mise en espace*" (or spatialized version) of the "lessons." In November 2005, Godard and Miéville completed what was to be a companion piece

Fig. 14.6 *General view of* salle 1, Aujourd'hui. *(Courtesy Jean-Luc Godard,* Voyage[s] en utopie *[2006], Centre Georges-Pompidou [view of the exhibit]. Photo by Michael Witt)*

to *Collage(s) de France*, a video piece called *Reportage amateur*. This superb video work—that was never shown in the end and has never been officially released—was a guided visit of the scale model of the exhibition, in which Godard very carefully described the content of each of the nine rooms that he had carefully conceived and constructed (with glue and scissors, which explains the literal dimension of *collage* for the exhibit).[10]

Somehow, at this point, when all that was left was to "build" what was projected, Godard felt that, as Païni writes, "the exhibition, as it appeared in the scale model, should not, could not become a reality."[11] The saga that would then lead from *Collage(s) de France: Archéologie du cinéma selon Jean-Luc Godard* to *Voyage(s) en utopie: JLG, 1946–2006, À la recherche d'un théorème perdu* is a "chronicle of disaster," a succession of various versions, revisions, rewritings, reworkings, requests, frustrations, dismissals, that have produced nonetheless thousands of pages of correspondence, layouts, blueprints, documents, a vast archive that testifies to the incredible labour Godard (as well as Païni and all the staff at Pompidou)—contrary to what was rumoured—undertook (hopefully these documents will, someday, be made public and thoroughly analyzed.)[12]

At different stages of the production of this exhibition, Jean-Luc Godard made requests that were denied by the institution or abandoned by Godard himself (some of which were echoed in the final version of the exhibition). Among those requests there was: an installation of an actual large-size windmill carrying water and operated by homeless people; garbage and debris to be randomly spread out across one of the rooms (*Aujourd'hui*); a henhouse filled with chickens running freely; an electric train circulating not only in the space of the exhibition, but basically throughout the Pompidou museum, including the movie theatres, and the main hall. Païni was able to convince Decaux, one of Paris's most popular advertising agencies, to work on a prototype based on a device of automated ads Godard had seen in Paris (Godard abandoned the idea, after a team at Decaux worked a number of weeks for free to fulfill his request, simply because it didn't correspond to what he had in mind). At a certain point in the discussions, Godard suggested literally having the Peripheria workshop moved into the museum, where, through a maze-like corridor, the visitor would enter the studio to find Anne-Marie Miéville and Godard producing films throughout the time of the exhibition. His requests also included the inclusion of a large painting by Delacroix, that Dominique Païni was to obtain from the Louvre. After an excruciatingly long negotiation, the painting was finally obtained. Godard said, happily, "Very well done, Dominique. We'll include it here, and simply display it on the floor, in the middle of the room." When Païni said it would not be possible, Godard apparently replied: "You see, Dominique, you don't want to do the work."[13] Et cetera. Et cetera. The ultimate refusal of the institution—in these and other cases—seems to have been what paradoxically allowed *an* exhibition to exist, precisely because it could expose itself as a ruin, an unfinished project, or as Anne Marquez would put it, an "impossible exposed."

The Pompidou exhibition is an interesting case of Godardian "utopianism." Like every utopia, it offers a playground of imaginary projections, a rhetorical play with the possibilities of impossibility (a theme dear to Godard since *Passion* at least), a contradictory *jeu d'espace* as Louis Marin would put it.[14] As can be easily deciphered, the failure of the institution to accede to Godard's demands was in many ways programmed—even desired—by Godard himself. As Païni explains, "l'impossibilité *est devenue un thème obsédant pour lui et … le thème de l'utopie est naturellement apparu…. Godard n'est pas masochiste. Je dirais en revanche que pendant ces trois ans, il a eu besoin, pour travailler, d'avoir dressé devant lui une sorte de statute du Commandeur …, une figure à laquelle il puisse se confronter, s'affronter.*"[15]

This confrontation would lead, in the end, to a fantastically dense and complex self-reflexive exhibition, that displayed, through displacements and condensations, held together in its chaotic layout, the many layers of its genealogy.[16] Every scenario, every version of the exhibition seemed to coexist in this inchoate state of flux between promise and ruin. This "catastrophy" very violently self-proclaimed the exhibition's impossibility, the limits of institutional relations, while—and this is the beauty of it all—making a powerful, tragic, melancholic statement about the state of the world, the state of images, the state of the world of images … a world at wits' end.

As one can see, the story behind the exhibition is extremely long and complex—and so is its shifting critical reception (most everyone agrees today that it was an extraordinary "operation"). The exhibition reflects many of the convolutions, communication failures—not because of a lack of communication, but an excess—financial meanderings, and struggles with authorities that Godard has encountered in recent years with producers, actors, distributors, festival organizers, cinematographers, either in the production of his films (for each film made, there are also probably a dozen abandoned versions) or more generally in the many projects he initiated throughout his career.

Many people who saw *Voyage(s) en utopie* considered it an utter failure, a disappointment, a bad joke, etc. I have shown elsewhere, like many others have,[17] the internal logic of the exhibition and the mad precision of its display: piece by piece, room by room, detail by detail, reference by reference, through close analysis, it was possible to explain how, somehow, this big mess *not only* made sense, but was a masterpiece of wit and intelligence, in the line of *Histoire(s) du cinéma* and as a continuation of Aby Warburg's *Mnemosyne*, of Malraux's *Musée imaginaire*, of Henri Langlois's *Musée du cinéma*, etc. I had, by that point, heard all the tales "from the inside" of Pompidou, the four-year saga that led to the "catastrophy," both from people who worked there and from Dominique Païni himself who left his job—or more precisely was fired by Godard—hurt, sick, and destroyed, six months before the show opened. In a way similar to so many of his films, the process became the fiction into which he projected himself (and others). Godard built around it a fantastic mythology in which each person involved became a character (including himself in the very convincing role—since he convinced himself—of the betrayed, humiliated, repressed artist).[18]

Whilst maintaining the validity of the exegesis and the hermeneutic excavation concerning this exhibition, I have also come to believe that it was not a "filmmaker's exhibition" at all—like the ones Kiarostami, Akerman, Varda, Weeresethakul, Marker, and all the other filmmakers who have entered the museum over the past fifteen years, had accustomed us to—but more interestingly or productively considered as a "performance," a "performance in failure." The "display of the exhibition's failure" can then be seen as a record or trace of this four-year performance. Moreover, this "performance of failure" has been deeply tied to a mode of "utopia" that has accompanied most of Godard's projects, from the late 1960s onwards.

The dialectic—and Godard is profoundly a dialectician—between utopia and failure is very clearly the nexus of his creativity, but it can also be read, more generally, as an allegory of *his* (Hi)story of cinema. From its utopian infancy (*l'enfance de l'art*) to its demise, failure, and murder, cinema has many origins and many ends, and these ends have many names: the birth of the scenario, the arrival of sound (that murdered the extraordinary power of silent films), totalitarian regimes, American imperialism, television, etc. This story of *grandeur* and *décadence* is the backbone of *Histoire(s) du cinéma*: cinema's history is a story of a promise and failure, the ultimate failure being—in Godard's historical reading—cinema's incapacity to prevent the Death Camps.[19] Many of Godard's projects have been allegorical replays of this tragic dialectic: and this negativity becomes the condition of possibility of new work. Beckett's leitmotif—"Ever tried. Ever failed. No matter. Try Again. Fail again. Fail better."[20]—seems to apply both to Godard and to his melancholic vision of history. This vision also echoes his conception of the image (which he reworks from Blanchot) that appears at the end of *Histoire(s) du cinéma* (episode 4B) as well as in *Éloge de l'amour*: "*L'image est bonheur, mais près d'elle le néant séjourne et toute la puissance de l'image ne peut s'exprimer qu'en lui faisant appel. Il faut peut-être ajouter encore : l'image,*

225

seule capable de nier le néant, est aussi le regard du néant sur nous."[21] As often in *Histoire(s)*, the *contre-champ* of happiness, or beauty, or infancy, is nothingness, horror, destruction, ruins. But in fact, the power of the image can only be gained by passing through, or through an invocation of, this necessary *néant*.

"EVER TRIED. EVER FAILED." GODARD'S AESTHETIC OF FAILURE

The Godardian archive—probably more than that of any other artist, including Welles, who is notorious for his "failings"—is an accumulation of unfinished, rejected, or unaccomplished projects (scripts, collaborations, associations with institutions, commissioned works). They inhabit a vast *"salon des refusés"* with other great moments of modernism's history. One can probably argue that modern art is the history of refusal, failure, ruin (in all its dimensions). If only in this respect, Godard is probably the most powerful—the last?—continuator of this "incomplete project."

Of course, Godard's "failures" are of different types, and one should consider the term here both literally and metaphorically. A brief enumeration will easily provide an idea of the scope and variety of these failings. There are the abandoned projects: a film project in Abitibi, Québec, in December 1968,[22] titled *Jusqu'à la victoire*, the essay-film financed by the Palestinian Fatah and co-directed with Jean-Pierre Gorin in Palestine, transformed into—and included as a failed project within—*Ici et ailleurs* (co-directed with Anne-Marie Miéville) in 1975; a project to shoot Beckett's *Oh! Les beaux jours / Happy Days* in 1963; a scenario for a Hollywood film with Robert De Niro and Diane Keaton, revolving around a project to shoot a history of Las Vegas; the incredible mass of unshot scripts (*The Ninth Symphony*, *Les Signes parmi nous*, etc.), rejected films (all the Dziga Vertov Group films, rejected by the state televisions who commissioned them), and abandoned ideas that are very much part of the Godardian archive and *body of work*. Alongside these, we could add his failed attempt at helping to develop a national television in Mozambique, in 1978,[23] his failure to obtain a Chair at the Collège de France (one can dwell on the institutional recognition Godard has been seeking since the 1980s); his failure to meet with the Pope, around the time of the *Je vous salue, Marie* scandal, etc. The fact that he went to Mozambique, Abitibi, wrote to the Pope, and to the Collège de France, are all part of what I call his "performances of failure": they perform something of cinema's possible impossibility.

Seen from another angle, many of the films he actually made include, in their narrative, self-reflexively, the production of a film within the film that never seems to amount to much; these include *Le Mépris*, *Passion*,

Prénom Carmen, Grandeur et décadence d'un petit commerce de cinéma, For Ever Mozart, Éloge de l'amour, as well as films such as *King Lear*, which present themselves as abandoned objects (by the producer, the actors, etc.). Others, like *Week-end* are self-proclaimed films "found on the scrapheap" (*"un film trouvé à la ferraille"*). In all these cases, the "performance of the failure" of the film within the film (such as in *Passion*, the hesitation, the search for light, the filmmaker's quest) is more interesting than *what* the film within the film would have been (the same goes for *Collage(s) de France* which is clearly much more interesting as a ruin). In the same way, in *Éloge de l'amour*, Edgar's project on Simone Weil, "opéra, film, roman, théâtre," its genesis, its questions, the movement the "project" creates, obliquely informs, from within, *Éloge de l'amour*. It is as if Godard's film redeems the failure of his protagonist by making a (incredibly beautiful) film out of his creative (unfinished) quest. Many of these films carry within them the weight of a failure, as if it is *out of that failure* that the film we are watching emerged: failure is its horizon, but also its very condition of possibility.

LETTRE À FREDDY BUACHE

And then there is of course the case of the memorable *Lettre à Freddy Buache: À propos d'un film sur Lausanne*. Godard was commissioned by the city of Lausanne to make a film that commemorated the city's 500th birthday. This "film-letter," addressed to Freddy Buache (then director of the Cinémathèque in Lausanne), is a ten-minute essay-film that muses—carried throughout by Ravel's *Boléro*—both on the project of the commissioned film, the "performance" of his idea (we see the shots he had in mind, over and over again, as examples of what the film *could have been if it had been accepted*), and also the reason why the people who commissioned the work believed Godard did not do what he claimed he was going to do. The paradox is that the film talks about its own refusal before the film was "actually" refused, it anticipates the refusal and uses it for the purpose of the film, to show how and why *"ils ont tort de dire qu'on a été malhonnête."*[24] Once the film was shown, people *were* furious, while, at the same time, the film's "success"—it was widely shown—was exactly what the organizers had hoped for.... That is the beauty and paradox of Godardian failure.

LETTER TO AN AMERICAN FRIEND

In 1995, Godard wrote a letter "to an American friend," Armand White of the New York Film Critics Circle, excusing himself for not coming to receive a prize, and explaining why he believed he did not *deserve* this honour.[25] He writes:

> JLG was not able, throughout his career as "movie maker/goer" [*in English*] to: <u>prevent</u> Mr. Spielberg from rebuilding Auschwitz; <u>convince</u> Miss Turner not to paint the dear "Funny Faces" although they had worn out; <u>condemn</u> Mr. Bill Gates for having named his "chip shop" (*usine à puces*) "Rosebud"; <u>force</u> New York critics not to forget Shirley Clarke; <u>force</u> Sony ex-Columbia Pictures to imitate Dan Talbot / New Yorker Films when they send invoices; <u>force</u> the old ladies at the Oscars to vote for Kiarostami instead of Kieslowski; <u>persuade</u> Stanley Kubrick to watch the short films by Santiago Alvarez on the Vietnam War; <u>have</u> Miss Keaton read the biography of the founder of Las Vegas; <u>shoot</u> *Le Mépris* with Sinatra and Novak.[26]

The incredible diversity of "failures" he attributes to himself is of course impressive: it involves critics, filmmakers, distribution practices, archival/restoration issues, filmmaker's regrets, ethics, actors, etc. What is important to insist on, again, is that these "failures" are, somehow, for him, "cinema's failure," while, at the same time, it sheds retroactively a light on the "power" he believes "cinema" (that he somehow embodies) *should have had*.[27] Hence, each one of these "failures" opens an "imagine if," unveiling the utopian potential of cinema (*Faisons un rêve*).

VOYAGE(S) EN UTOPIE TOURS DÉTOURS

The Pompidou exhibition, of course, revealed similar utopian principles, and here, like there, the impossibility unlocked a whole spectre of possibilities: failure operates a declension of ideas. On the ruins of the first exhibit, Godard and his assistants created a combinatory vertigo that encapsulated the different stages of the project, and that the mesmerized visitor was asked to *make sense of*, that is, to piece together, shard by shard, layer by layer, the fragments, debris, etc. Many would agree that Godard, in the words of Rimbaud, is the only one to have "*la clef de cette parade sauvage.*"[28] If not the key, at least the meaning of the multiplicities of locks, appeared on a note, pinned to a wall: "*S'il vient à passer en ces lieux, le visiteur mathématicien saura sans doute percevoir que le nombre de liaisons entre tous les objets et sujets établis dans cette 2ᵉ exposition sur les ruines de la première, que ce nombre est un nombre premier infiniment plus grand que le plus grand premier connu à ce jour.*"[29] Accordingly, *Voyage(s)* was a "chantier," a construction site of infinite possibilities that linked together the many strata of envisioned projects, and many more: one had to move from the scale models to the objects of the museum, move between Yesterday, Today, and The Day before

Yesterday, to understand its historical dialectic, his statement on the world. It was—like *Histoire(s) du cinéma*—an incredibly powerful montage of heterogeneous temporalities, a stratification of anachronisms, a media archaeology, and an intermedial investigation: Godard's "invitation au voyage" incorporated the history of art, philosophy, literature but also explored all the techniques of reproduction (questioning ideas of aura and authenticity within the museum, and, as Païni argues, in dialogue with Benjaminian notions of reproduction).[30] Photography, cinema, television, photocopies, typewriters, reproductions of sculptures, furniture (in *Aujourd'hui* there was a bed and a catalogue page showing the same bed), as well as all the possible formats of moving images: 16/9, 4/3, television sets, plasma screens, miniature screens, 35-mm film (in one of the models), etc. It was a land of Dystopia/Utopia, a thing impossible to "imagine" and "describe" (between amusement park, "cabinet of curiosities," and war zone). It was a place that was made to "exist," above all, in the minds and the bodies of the visitor who was to perform the difficult role of editor, montage-artist or mathematician, lost within an incredibly dense forest of found objects, lost and found footage, images, texts, objects, and sounds. "*Comprenne qui voudra.*"

***

My intention here was not to describe or even analyse *Voyage(s) en utopie*, its montage, its lessons, its depth. I simply wanted to point towards an essential dynamic in Godard's production, which goes beyond the simple "anecdote" or biographical detail: that is, the tension between utopia and failure, a movement that allegorizes both the "grandeur" and the "decadence" of Godard's "petit commerce de cinéma," and the complexities of his museum performance.

Samuel Beckett—the great modern theorist and practitioner of failure—wrote a marvellous statement about the painter Bran van Velde, that seems to encapsulate the internal dynamic of Godard's oeuvre and in particular his Paris exhibition:

> To be an artist is to fail, as no other dare fail, [...] failure is his world and to shrink from it desertion, art and craft, good housekeeping, living. I know that all that is required now, in order to bring this horrible matter to an acceptable conclusion, is to make of this submission, this admission, this fidelity to failure, a new occasion, a new term of relation, and of the act which unable to act, obliged to act, he makes, an expressive act, even if only of itself, of its impossibility, of its obligation.[31]

This quote reveals many of the underlying principles governing Godard's work and *Voyage(s) en utopie* in particular: how a "fidelity to failure" can open a "new occasion, a new term of relation." It is precisely what we witness between the failure of *Collage(s)* and the expressive act that displays *Voyage(s)*, an expressive act of its impossibility, which performs cinema's utopian possibilities. This could be one way of thinking of Godard's utopian legacies, and, possibly, the grandeur of their failures.

NOTES

1 Antoine de Baecque, "A Beaubourg, Jean-Luc Godard en non-chef de chantier(s)," *Libération*, May 11, 2006.

2 Interestingly, Antoine de Baecque's first article on the exhibition, published in *Libération*, was "corrected" two months later when *Libération* published a twelve-page *Cahier spécial*. By that time, many hardened critics had softened, and a certain number of articles had been published that tried to show the value of the exhibition while seeking to go beyond the institutional scandal and slander. Among these articles, which offer diversified and extensive analysis of the exhibit, were: Bernard Eisenschitz, "La Réponse de Godard," *Cinéma* 12 (Fall 2006): 91–101; Bill Krohn, "An Eccentric Exhibition by Jean-Luc Godard Is Worth a Close Look," *The Economist*, June 29, 2006; Alex Munt, "Jean-Luc Godard Exhibition," *Senses of Cinema* 40 (2006), http://www.sensesofcinema.com/2006/40/godard-travels-in-utopia. To which I wish to modestly add my own contributions: André Habib, "Invitation au voyage," *Hors champ* (2006), http://www.horschamp.qc.ca/INVITATION-AU-VOYAGE; and "Un beau souci: Réflexions sur le montage de/dans *Voyage(s) en utopie* de Jean-Luc Godard," *Cinéma et Cie* 10, no. 12 (Spring 2009): 17–25.

3 Interestingly, this painting—to which Daniel Arasse, the famous art historian, devotes a stunning section of his book *Le détail* (1999)—is the one Gus Van Sant decided to put in place of *Suzanne and the Elders* (Tintoretto, 1555–56) in his remake of *Psycho* (1998), in order to reinforce the theme of voyeurism (the spectator's gaze), deceit, and rape, which are all related to Godard's exhibition and his relation to the people at Pompidou.

4 Details of all the films cited in this chapter are given in the Filmography, after the Bibliography.

5 Or, as Dante would say, "*lasciate qui ogne speranza.*"

6 "Financial" and "Technical" were crossed out the morning of the opening by Godard himself. "*The Centre Pompidou has decided not to produce the exhibition entitled* Collage(s) de France, archéologie du cinéma, d'après JLG, *because of the ~~financial, technical and~~ artistic difficulties it represented, and to replace it with another project previously considered by Jean-Luc Godard entitled* Voyage(s) en utopie—Jean-Luc Godard 1946–2006. *This second project includes the complete or partial presentation of the* Collage(s) de France *scale models [maquettes]. JLG and Peripheria have accepted the Centre Pompidou's decision.*"

7 Both excerpts are part of Godard's reservoir of quotations. The phrase by Bergson, which was printed on the floor and runs across the three rooms, was the famous closing statement of his 1896 *Matière et mémoire*: "*L'esprit emprunte à la matière les*

perceptions dont il fait sa nourriture et rend sous forme de mouvement auquel il a imprimé sa liberté" (Spirit borrows from matter the perceptions on which it feeds and restores them to matter in the form of movements which it has stamped with its own freedom). Henri Bergson, *Matière et mémoire* (Paris: Presses Universitaires de France, 1999), 280. The verse by José Lezama Lima, found in a book by Goytisolo, reads in Spanish: *"La luz es el primer animal visible de lo invisible"* (Light is the first visible animal of the invisible). It is taken from a book entitled *La Mémoire matérielle*—see Philippe Lançon, "JLG: 'Ce qu'ils aiment à Pompidou, c'est les morts'," *Libération*, Cahier spécial, July 12, 2006: 2–6. Who but Godard could have brought together these two authors around the idea of *matter* and *memory*?

8   "Never again," "Tomorrow singing" (*Les Lendemains qui chantent* was the title of the autobiography of Communist Gabriel Péri, shot by the Germans in 1941), "the Stockholm Appeal" (which called for an absolute ban on nuclear weapons in 1950).

9   Dominique Païni, "De *Collage(s) de France* à *Voyage(s) en utopie*: Retour(s) d'expositions," *Cinéma et Cie* 10, no. 12 (Spring 2009): 11.

10 *Collage(s) de France* is of course a pun on *Collège de France* and seems to refer to Godard's attempt to be given a Chair at the Collège in the 1990s. See Antoine de Baecque, *Godard: Biographie* (Paris: Grasset, 2010), 720–21.

11 *"L'exposition, telle que présentée dans la maquette, ne devait pas, ne pouvait pas passer dans le réel."* Dominique Païni, De *Collage(s) de France* à *Voyage(s) en utopie*, 12 (my translation).

12 For a more exhaustive description of the production process of the exhibition, as well as examples of the exchanges between Godard, Païni, and the institution, I refer the reader to, among others, de Baecque, *Godard*, 797–809; Dominique Païni, "D'après JLG, ou l'histoire de feu l'exposition Collage(s) de France," in *Jean-Luc Godard Documents*, ed. Nicole Brenez et al. (Paris: Centre Pompidou, 2006); Païni, "De *Collage(s) de France* à *Voyage(s) en utopie*"; and Anne Marquez, "L'Impossible exposé selon JLG: Histoires d'expositions au Centre Pompidou," *May* 1 (June 2009).

13 *"Tu vois Dominique, tu ne veux pas travailler"* (my translation). The information contained here was obtained from Dominique Païni himself, as well as from de Baecque, *Godard*, 797–809, and Marquez, "L'Impossible exposé selon JLG."

14 I refer here to Louis Marin's famous *Utopiques: Jeux d'espace* (1973), as well as to an excellent article by Jennifer Verraes which refers to Marin's theory of utopia in relation to Godard's *Voyage(s) en utopie*: "L'Auto est un avion sans ailes qui rampe sur le sol: L'esprit et la lettre des *Voyage(s) en utopie* de Jean-Luc Godard," *Cinéma et Cie* 10, no. 12 (Spring 2009): 35–42.

15 *"Impossibility* became an obsessive theme for him … and the theme of utopia naturally appeared…. Godard isn't a masochist. But I can say nevertheless that he needed, in order to work, to have standing in front of him a sort of Commander statue …, a figure against which he could confront himself, that would confront him." Païni, "De *Collage(s) de France* à *Voyage(s) en utopie*," 13.

16 Somehow, this reminds me of the fantasy evoked by Freud, in *Civilization and Its Discontents*, where he tries to imagine coexisting, simultaneously on the same spot, all the states of the city of Rome, one on top of the other so to speak. See Sigmund Freud, *Malaise dans la civilisation*, trans. C. and J. Odier (Paris: Presses Universitaires de France, 1992), 13–14.

17 See, for example, Habib, "Invitation au voyage," and "Un beau souci," as well as Eisenschitz, "La Réponse de Godard," and Munt, "Jean-Luc Godard Exhibition," 72.

18 Anne Marquez explains in a footnote how, in their exchanges, Godard very often would refer to the people involved by using mythological names: "Thésée" was Bruno Racine (the president of Pompidou), "Ariane" was JLG himself, the "Minotaur" was the financial controller, etc. Marquez, "L'Impossible exposé selon JLG," 72.

19 In *Histoire(s) du cinéma* 3A, Godard says: "*Que le cinéma soit d'abord fait pour penser, on l'oubliera tout de suite. Mais c'est une autre histoire. La flamme s'éteindra définitivement à Auschwitz*" (That cinema is above all made for thinking, was forgotten very quickly. But that is another story. The flame burnt out definitively in Auschwitz). For a more complete analysis of this delicate question, see Jacques Rancière, *La Fable cinématographique* (Paris: Seuil, 2001), 217–37.

20 Samuel Beckett, *Worstward Ho*, in *Nohow On: Three Novels* (New York: Grove Press, 1996), 89.

21 "Image is happiness. But beside it dwells nothingness. The power of the image is expressed only by invoking nothingness. It is perhaps worth adding: the image, able to negate nothingness, is also the gaze of nothingness on us." Godard, *Histoire(s) du cinéma*, 4B. Blanchot's original quote reads: "*L'image est bonheur, mais, près d'elle, le néant séjourne, à sa limite il apparaît et toute la puissance de l'image tirée de l'abîme en quoi elle se fonde ne peut s'exprimer qu'en lui faisant appel.*" Maurice Blanchot, *L'Amitié* (Paris : Gallimard, 1971), 246–49.

22 This project is the object of a fascinating Québécois film produced by the National Film Board of Canada, *Mai en décembre* (Julie Perron, 1999).

23 There was a project for a film called "Naissance de l'image d'une nation." For a detailed account of this project, see the *Cahiers du cinéma* issue (no. 300) entirely curated by Godard in May 1979.

24 Translation: "they are wrong to say we were dishonest."

25 Very often, Godard's absence—and the reasons he provides—is more interesting and telling than his presence. Among numerous examples: the Lifetime Achievement Award given by the European Film Awards ("I don't have the impression my career is finished"), the 2010 presentation of *Film socialisme* in Cannes ("*suite à des problèmes de type grec …*" [because of a Greek type of problem]), and of course the Oscars Governors Awards in 2010.

26 "*JLG a été incapable, tout au long de sa carrière de 'movie maker/goer' d'empêcher M. Spielberg de reconstruire Auschwitz, de convaincre Mme Turner de ne pas colorier les chères 'Funny Faces' bien que passées, de condamner M. Bill Gates pour avoir nommé 'Rosebud' son usine à puces, de contraindre les critiques new-yorkais de ne pas oublier Shirley Clarke, d'obliger Sony ex-Columbia Pictures à imiter Dan Talbot/New Yorker Films lorsqu'ils envoient un relevé de comptes, d'obliger les mémés de l'Oscar à voter pour Kiarostami et pas pour Kieslowski, de persuader M. Kubrick de visionner les courts métrages de Santiago Alvarez pendant la guerre du Vietnam, de faire lire à Mlle Keaton la biographie du fondateur de Las Vegas, de tourner Le Mépris avec Sinatra et Novak.*" Jean-Luc Godard par Jean-Luc Godard, vol. 2, ed. Alain Bergala (Paris: Cahiers du cinéma, 1998), 344.

27 Among hundreds of statements confirming Godard's belief in cinema's powers, if only we had given cinema a chance, we could quote this one: "*En posant une caméra place de l'Étoile et en filmant ce qui se passe on ferait un film sur le cancer et sur la mort*" (If we placed a camera at Place de l'Étoile and filmed what was going on we could make a film about cancer and death). See Lançon, "JLG," 3.

28 "The key to this savage parade." Arthur Rimbaud, "Parade," in *Oeuvres complètes* (Paris: Gallimard, Bibliothèque de la Pléiade, 1972), 126.
29 "If he is to pass through this place, the visitor-mathematician will without a doubt perceive that the number of connexions between all the objects and subjects established in this 2nd exhibition on the ruins of the first, that this number is a prime number infinitely larger than the largest prime number known to date" (my translation).
30 Païni, "D'après JLG."
31 Samuel Beckett, *Proust and the Three Dialogues with Georges Duthuit* (London: Calder, 1965), 125–26.

BIBLIOGRAPHY

Arasse, Daniel. *Le Détail*. Paris: Flammarion, 1999.
Beckett, Samuel. *Nohow On: Three Novels*. New York: Grove Press, 1996.
———. *Proust and the Three Dialogues with Georges Duthuit*. London: Calder, 1965.
Bergson, Henri. *Matière et mémoire*. Paris: Presses Universitaires de France, 1999.
Blanchot, Maurice. *L'amitié*. Gallimard: Paris, 1971.
De Baecque, Antoine. "À Beaubourg, Jean-Luc Godard en non-chef de chantier(s)." *Libération*, May 11, 2006.
———. *Godard: Biographie*. Paris: Grasset, 2010.
Eisenschitz, Bernard. "La réponse de Godard." *Cinéma* 12 (Fall 2006): 91–101.
Freud, Sigmund. *Malaise dans la civilisation*. Translated by C. and J. Odier. Paris: Presses Universitaires de France, 1992.
Godard, Jean-Luc. *Jean-Luc Godard par Jean-Luc Godard*. Edited by Alain Bergala. Paris: Cahiers du cinéma, 1998.
Habib, André. "Un beau souci: Réflexions sur le montage de/dans *Voyage(s) en utopie* de Jean-Luc Godard." *Cinéma et Cie* 10, no. 12 (Spring 2009): 17–25.
———. "Invitation au voyage." *Hors champ* (2006). http://www.horschamp.qc.ca/INVITATION-AU-VOYAGE.html?var_recherche=Andre%20Habib%20invitation%20au%20voyage.
Krohn, Bill. "An Eccentric Exhibition by Jean-Luc Godard Is Worth a Close Look." *The Economist*, June 29, 2006.
Lançon, Philippe. "JLG : 'Ce qu'ils aiment à Pompidou, c'est les morts.'" *Libération*, Cahier spécial, July 12, 2006: 2–6.
Marin, Louis. *Utopiques: Jeux d'espace*. Paris: Minuit, 1973.
Marquez, Anne. "L'impossible exposé selon JLG : Histoires d'expositions au Centre Pompidou." *May* 1 (Summer 2009): 69–80.
Munt, Alex. "Jean-Luc Godard Exhibition." *Senses of Cinema* 40 (2006). http://www.sensesofcinema.com/2006/40/godard-travels-in-utopia.
Païni, Dominique. "D'après JLG, ou l'histoire de feu l'exposition Collage(s) de France." In *Jean-Luc Godard Documents*, edited by Nicole Brenez, David Faroult, Augustin Gimel, and Michael Witt, 420–26. Paris: Centre Pompidou, 2006.
———. "De *Collage(s) de France* à *Voyage(s) en utopie*: Retour(s) d'expositions." *Cinéma et Cie* 10, no. 12 (Spring 2009): 11–15.

Rancière, Jacques. *La fable cinématographique*. Paris: Seuil, 2001.
Rimbaud, Arthur. *Oeuvres complètes*. Paris: Gallimard, Bibliothèque de la Pléiade, 1972.
Verraes, Jennifer. "L'auto est un avion sans ailes qui rampe sur le sol: L'esprit et la lettre des *Voyage(s) en utopie* de Jean-Luc Godard." *Cinéma et Cie* 10, no. 12 (Spring 2009): 35–42.

Filmography

FILMS DIRECTED BY JEAN-LUC GODARD

Ecce Homo (2006)
Éloge de l'amour (2001)
Film socialisme (2010)
For Ever Mozart (1996)
Grandeur et décadence d'un petit commerce de cinéma (1985)
Histoire(s) du cinéma (1988–1998)
Ici et ailleurs (1974)
Je vous salue, Marie (1985)
Je vous salue Sarajevo (1993)
JLG/JLG—autoportrait de décembre (1994)
King Lear (1987)
Lettre à Freddy Buache (1982)
Le Mépris (1963)
The Old Place (with Anne-Marie Miéville, 1998)
One + One (1969)
One p.m., a.k.a *One Parallel Movie* (with D.A. Pennebaker and Richard Leacock, 1968)
Passion (1983)
Prénom Carmen (1982)
Reportage amateur (2005)
Une bonne à tout faire (2006)
Vent d'Est (with Jean-Pierre Gorin, 1969)
Vrai faux passeport (2006)
Week-end (1967)

OTHER FILMS CITED

Après la réconciliation (Anne Marie Miéville, France, 2000)
Arsenal (Aleksandr Dovjenko, Soviet Union, 1929)
Au hasard Balthazar (Robert Bresson, France, 1966)

Barocco (André Téchiné, France, 1976)

Black Hawk Down (Ridley Scott, United States, 2001)

Bob le flambeur (Jean-Pierre Melville, France, 1956)

The Cat and the Canary (Elliott Nugent, United States, 1939)

The Colour of Pomegranates, a.k.a *Sayat Nova* (Sergei Paradjanov , Soviet Union, 1968)

Les Dernières Vacances (Roger Leenhardt, France, 1948)

Don Quijote (Orson Welles, United States, begun in 1955, unfinished)

Éléna et les hommes (Jean Renoir, France, 1956)

Faisons un rêve (Sacha Guitry, France, 1936)

Johnny Guitar (Nicholas Ray, United States, 1954)

Mai en décembre (Julie Perron, Québec, 1999)

Menschen am Sonntag (Billy Wilder, Curt Siodmak, Robert Siodmak, Edgar G. Ulmer, Germany, 1930)

Il Messia (Roberto Rossellini, Italy, 1975)

La Môme vert-de-gris (Bernard Borderie, France, 1953)

Nous sommes tous encore ici (Anne-Marie Miéville, France, 1997)

On the Town (Stanley Donen, United States, 1949)

Psycho (Gus Van Sant, United States, 1998)

Le Sang d'un poète (Jean Cocteau, France, 1930)

The Searchers (John Ford, United States, 1956)

The Secret Behind the Door (Fritz Lang, United States, 1947)

Das Testament des Dr. Mabuse (Fritz Lang, Germany, 1933)

About the Contributors

Michel Cadé is Professor Emeritus of Contemporary History at the University of Perpignan Via Domitia, and President of the Cinémathèque euro-régionale at the Jean-Vigo Institute in Perpignan, France. In 2010, he edited an anthology entitled *La Retirada en images mouvantes*, which examines the cinematic representations of the largest forced migration in Europe during the 1930s.

John Carnahan has taught English and film at California State University, East Bay, and the University of Wales, Aberystwyth. He has collaborated with Blaengar, Amie Dowling, Sweet Nothing, and The Erika Shuch Project (movement arts), and Social Forum Cymru (arts for The Movement).

Nicole Côté is Associate Professor at Université de Sherbrooke. She has published on Québec as well as Franco- and Anglo-Canadian Literatures. She has also translated several works from Canadian authors and edited or co-edited three books, the last one being *Expressions culturelles des franco-phonies* (2008).

André Habib is Associate Professor of Film Studies in the Department of Art History and Film Studies at the Université de Montréal. He completed his master's thesis in 2001 on Godard's *Histoire(s) du cinema* and his PhD thesis on the "Imaginary of Ruins in Cinema" in 2008. He is the author of *L'atttrait de la ruine* (Yellow Now, 2011). He co-edited with Viva Paci *Chris Marker et l'imprimerie du regard* (L'Harmattan, 2008) and with Michel Marie *L'avenir de la mémoire: Patrimoine, restauration, réemploi cinématographiques* (Presses universitaires du Septentrion, 2013). He is also the co-editor of the Web journal *Hors Champ*. His recent research projects have dealt with the aesthetics of ruins, the archive, experimental cinema, and cinephilia.

Junji Hori is Associate Professor of Film and Media Studies at Kansai University. He is the co-editor of a collection of essays on *Histoire(s) du cinéma* entitled *Godard, Image, History* (2001) and has published articles on Godard (in *For Ever Godard*, 2004) and on Truffaut (in *A Companion to François Truffaut*, 2013). He has translated several books into Japanese, including Colin MacCabe's *Godard: A Portrait of the Artist at Seventy* and Jacques Rancière's *Le Destin des images*.

Russell J.A. Kilbourn is Associate Professor in the Department of English and Film Studies at Wilfrid Laurier University. Russell publishes on film, cultural studies, and comparative literature, as well as on German author W.G. Sebald. His book, *Cinema, Memory, Modernity: The Representation of Memory from the Art Film to Transnational Cinema*, appeared with Routledge in 2010, and he is co-editor, with Eleanor Ty, of a collection of essays titled *The Memory Effect: The Remediation of Memory in Literature and Film* (2013).

Julien Lapointe is a second-year doctoral candidate in Film Studies at Concordia University. He has published in *Film Quarterly*, *CinéAction*, and *The Canadian Journal of Film Studies* and presented a paper at the 2009 Film Studies Association of Canada conference. His research interests include narratology and formalist film theory.

Timothy Long has been Head Curator at the MacKenzie Art Gallery in Regina, Saskatchewan, since 2001. His most recent curatorial project, the *Mirror Series*, is a three-part investigation of mirrors, doublings, and doppelgängers in contemporary art. His other interests include interdisciplinary approaches to ceramics, film, dance, and performance art.

Douglas Morrey is Associate Professor of French at the University of Warwick, England. He is the author of *Jean-Luc Godard* (Manchester University Press, 2005) and the co-author of *Jacques Rivette* (Manchester University Press, 2009). His current research focuses on the legacy of the New Wave in French cinema.

Glen W. Norton teaches in the Department of English and Film Studies at Wilfrid Laurier University. His research interests focus on phenomenological approaches toward the study of the cinematic experience. He has published in numerous journals, including *Studies in French Cinema*, *Post Script*, *Senses of Cinema*, *Film-Philosophy*, and *Cinema Scope*. He is the curator of *Cinema=Godard=Cinema*, an online hub for academic information and discussion about the work of Jean-Luc Godard.

Céline Scemama teaches film aesthetics at the University of Paris I (Panthéon-Sorbonne), and her areas of research include the works of Michelangelo Antonioni, Jean-Luc Godard, and Robert Bresson. She has published *"Histoire(s) du cinéma" de Jean-Luc Godard: La force faible d'un art* (L'Harmattan, 2006) and the website *La Partition des Histoire(s)*.

Jürg Stenzl has studied music in Bern and Paris. Since 1996, he has been Professor of Musicology at the University of Salzburg, Austria. He has also been a guest professor in Switzerland, Germany, Italy, and at Harvard University. His areas of research include medieval and contemporary music (Luigi Nono). His most recent publications are *Jean-Luc Godard—musicien* (2010) and *Dmitrij Kirsanov* (2013).

David Sterritt is Chair of the National Society of Film Critics, Adjunct Professor at Columbia University and the Maryland Institute College of Art, and chief book critic of *Film Quarterly*. His twelve books include two about Godard, and he has written on Godard's cinema for *Journal of French and Francophone Philosophy*, *Cineaste*, *Film-Philosophy*, *The Chronicle of Higher Education*, *Senses of Cinema*, *Cinema Scope*, *The Christian Science Monitor*, and others. He has lectured on Godard at the Museum of Modern of Art and the National Gallery of Art.

Tyson Stewart holds a master's degree in Cinema and Media Studies from York University. His writing has appeared in *Enterprise & Society* and *Historical Journal of Film, Radio and Television*. His current research is concerned with documentary films on academic celebrities, like *Derrida* (2002).

Christina Stojanova is Associate Professor at the University of Regina. She is co-editor with Bela Szabados of the critical anthology *Wittgenstein at the Movies: Cinematic Investigations* (Lexington Books, 2011) and co-author with Dana Duma of *The New Romanian Cinema* (Edinburgh University Press, 2015).

Index